I DON'T CRY, BUT I REMEMBER

I Don't Cry, But I Remember

A Mexican Immigrant's Story of Endurance

JOYCE LACKIE

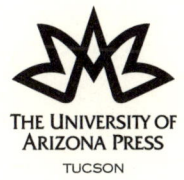

THE UNIVERSITY OF
ARIZONA PRESS

TUCSON

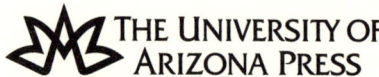

THE UNIVERSITY OF ARIZONA PRESS

www.uapress.arizona.edu

Library of Congress Cataloging-in-Publication Data
Lackie, Joyce, 1942–
    I don't cry, but I remember : a Mexican immigrant's story of endurance /
Joyce Lackie.
        p. cm.
    Includes bibliographical references.
    ISBN 978-0-8165-2996-4 (pbk. : alk. paper)   1. Salguero, Viviana,
1911–2000.   2. Mexican American women—Colorado—Biography.
3. Immigrants—Colorado—Biography.   4. Mexican Americans—Cultural
assimilation—Colorado.   I. Title.
    F785.M5L34 2012
    305.8968'720788—dc23
    [B]

                                                                    2011042123

∞

Manufactured in the United States of America on acid-free, archival-quality
paper containing a minimum of 30% post-consumer waste and processed
chlorine free.

17   16   15   14   13   12   6   5   4   3   2   1

Contents

Maps

Acknowledgments

MANY FRIENDS AND COLLEAGUES contributed support and advice toward the completion of this book. I owe a special debt of thanks to two women: Maria Lopez and Dollie Zamora. Maria, Professor of Spanish and former Assistant Dean of the College of Arts and Sciences at the University of Northern Colorado, recognized the importance of Viviana's story, urged me to put it in book form, and spent many hours helping transcribe the tapes. Dollie, Parent Educator with the Department of Human Services in Weld County and the daughter of immigrants herself, gave unstintingly of her time, bilingual talents, and friendship. Her insights were invaluable, and the book is richer because of them.

I also wish to thank Lucía Gonzales, Lidia Rios, Ines Florez, Cynthia Florez, Patricia Escobar, and Angeles Navarro for their help with translation. Thanks to Sharon Wilson, Chair, and the University of Northern Colorado Faculty Research and Publication Board, who awarded me a grant to carry out my research and purchase the necessary microphones and transcribing machine. In addition, I appreciate the Catholic Community Services of Greeley and their Hispanic Elderly Outreach Program, through which I met Viviana and Jorge Salguero.

I am fortunate to know some fine professional writing consultants, among them my dear friend Barbara Warren-Sams. She read the manuscript through many versions, always offering constructive suggestions and emotional support while refusing adequate remuneration. Her insistence on avoiding assumptions in my interpretation of Viviana's words kept the book honest. Another good friend, Linda Gray, not only sent me relevant books but also tolerated my reading parts of this work aloud to her and followed up with suggestions for major improvements.

While writing the final drafts of the book, I joined a writers group, and I wish to thank Gloria Geiser, Cecilie Scott, Mary Richardson, and Barbara Young for their insights and willingness to read at least twice as many pages each session as their previously established limit. Thanks also to Robert Sanford for relentlessly rearranging my paragraphs so that I had to write new transitions. That and his suggestions for tightening the prose helped immensely. I am grateful to Alfonso Rodriguez for rechecking the accuracy of the Spanish passages and to Mike Corley for generously giving me Spanish lessons. Without the technical skill of Alicia Katz Pollock, the computer and I would never have formatted this work correctly for publication.

Reference librarians are my personal heroes. Colleen Stewart at the University of Northern Colorado's Michener Library and Peggy Ford Waldo of the City of Greeley Museums were especially helpful. I don't know the names of the many others who have helped me; I therefore thank all who help others seek out information as their life's work. I have found them cheerful and curious, willing to pursue each question not as part of a job but as an intriguing puzzle to be solved. Without them, the world of information would be much more difficult to travel.

Viviana and her family are the heart of this work. Her story has been a gift—a journey through the life of another—that turned our relationship from a friendship to a friendship with a purpose. We both enjoyed following a series of reminiscences that would put together her story, not knowing exactly how, when, or if we would reach a finished product, but realizing more fully month by month how important the process was to each of us. Her children and grandchildren were helpful as well, and I cannot thank them enough for welcoming me into their homes, sharing their parents' birthday celebrations, and cooking their wonderful food for me. No one makes enchiladas like Mercedes. Roberto and Beatrice gave me formal interviews, adding fascinating details to their mother's story and answering questions about their parents. Baseball fans Roberto and his wife Leticia took my husband and me to a Denver Rockies game and continue to offer their home as our home. Diego shared his own stories of the Salguero boys growing up, and Memo showed me several photo albums. Granddaughter Pilar has been post and beam in the construction process. Her help with translation, her knowledge of family history, and her genealogical project all contributed beyond measure. I count myself fortunate to know her as a friend.

My own family and friends have been amazing. My sisters Elaine and Helen have never ceased to believe in me, especially when I wasn't so sure I believed in myself. In addition, Helen spent hours photocopying and binding to create packets for Viviana's family. Christi, John, Rene, and Linda not only moved to Oregon to keep our family together, but John and Rene have given us our beautiful grandson, Eli, who is still amazed by the world around him—but would prefer it without vegetables. Our junior partner and surrogate grandchildren, Ryan, Faith, and Andrew, are an ongoing inspiration of courage in the face of challenges, and my singing partner Kay gives me a joyous outlet to balance the quiet isolation of research and writing.

I am fortunate to have a life partner who cherishes not only his own but also my autonomy. For encouraging me in the beginning, attending countless potlucks and parties alone, and never playing the guilt card, I thank my dear husband, John Hendricks. He has kept a semblance of normalcy in the house and yard, with clean dishes put away, broken appliances and pipes fixed, recycling taken out, and plants automatically watered. But most satisfying of all, his accepting attitude has created an agreeable environment in which to work. I think I owe him a nice long trip, but this time, we'll both go.

I DON'T CRY, BUT I REMEMBER

Introduction

THE ROOM SIMMERED QUIETLY with anticipation and not a little fear, a bubbling pot of incompatible tongues, as at least a dozen languages momentarily emerged and receded in the hot room. Viviana and her son sat on folding chairs in the open space between balustrades that lined both long walls. "*¿'Tá seguro que me preguntarán en español?* Are you sure they'll ask me in Spanish?" she queried for the fourth time.

"*Ma, ¡te dije!* I told you! They even let you study in Spanish. Don't worry about it." She was silent again. How had she let her son talk her into this? She had tried to study the naturalization guidelines several times, but someone always had to read them to her, and nothing would stick in her head. When she took the classes with the other women, it seemed to her that she was the only stupid person in the room. Many of those women could actually read and write. What made her think she, a sixty-three-year-old woman, could learn all those facts about branches of government and civic duties when she had less than a first-grade education?

On her right, a pale woman in a sundress was immersed in a pamphlet bearing a US flag over a faint eagle on its cover, plus a lot of words Viviana could not read. She thought she recognized *United States,* but that was all. Beyond the woman, a couple spoke animatedly to each other in what sounded like German.

She looked at the rows of people facing her from behind the balustrades—so many people! Those seats were for onlookers who came either to support friends and relatives or to watch the process as preparation for their own citizenship exam. There must have been as many, if not more, people in the balconies as there were seated around her in folding chairs on the floor, today's hopefuls. Flags from many countries hung along the walls above the side windows.

"*¿Crees que me requerirán nombrar los derechos de ciudadanía?* Do you think they will want me to name the rights of citizenship?"

"I don't know, Ma. Just tell them what you remember and—hush, now. Here they come."

Two uniformed men, one stocky and dark-haired, the other taller and lighter complected, came in and stood behind the table at the front of the room, each holding a clipboard full of papers. Behind the table on either side hung the flags of the United States and Colorado. Silence gradually followed their appearance, and Viviana felt a rush of the long-ago cold dread that had surged over her when she entered her small elementary school with her younger brother, knowing he might be beaten on the ears for not knowing his lesson, while she could only look on helplessly. Well, at least if she failed here, no one would be beaten for it.

The officials conferred a moment before the taller one began to speak loudly in English. Viviana was hearing the words, but even though she understood some English, nothing registered. Before she could try to concentrate harder, she heard her name called. "Guillermo Salguero and Viviana Salguero!" The very first names called! With no time to marvel more at the strangeness of what was happening, she stood with her son and let him guide her to the front of the room, where she was confronted by the tall official. "English or Spanish?" asked the darker man to her son.

"English for me, Spanish for my mother," replied Memo.

Turning to Viviana, the tall official didn't change expression other than the hint of a smile in his blue-grey eyes. "Where were you born?" he asked in her clear, lovely Spanish.

"*En México,*" she answered, pleased to hear her voice actually produce the sounds.

"And do you still love Mexico?" came the second question.

What a silly question! "*¡Claro!*" she said, caught up now in the dialogue. "Of course! I could never forget Mexico. It is the land of my heart, the land that gave me my birth."

"But you want to be come a citizen of the United States of America."

It wasn't a question, but she knew it required a response. "I love the United States, because it gave me my freedom. Mexico gave me life, but the United States gave me freedom."

Smiling openly now, the official glanced briefly at his papers. "OK, who is the current president of the United States?" he asked.

Viviana felt her body stiffen. Who is the president? She had studied all those questions, but nothing would come to her brain. The president. Sometimes her husband, Jorge, talked about the presidents, but the only name she remembered was something like *Rusebel,* and she knew that was from years ago, when the family had first come north. She became aware that Memo, close beside her was speaking softly, his lips not moving. It sounded as though he was saying, "Neesa . . . Neesa."

Afraid to speak and afraid not to, she decided to be bold. *"Nise,"* she pronounced.

Hesitating only slightly, the official followed up. "What does the president do?"

Remembering a conversation from one of her study groups because it had intrigued her, she had a better answer this time. "He leads the country, but he can't do just what he pleases. He has to do what the Congress tells him."

Appearing bemused, the official asked another question. "Even though your heart is in Mexico, do you pledge your loyalty to the United States of America?"

"O, ¡sí! Life in the United States is a great gift."

These must have been the right answers, because the interrogator offered his congratulations. *"Felicitaciones, Viviana Salguero.* You have successfully met the qualifications for citizenship of the United States of America."

Now it was Memo's turn, but she heard little of the exchange between him and the stocky official. She was a citizen! She would later tell me, more than once, that she had become one of the blue eyes, *¡una de los ojos azules! ¡Sí, sí, sí, sí, sí!*[1]

That story, one of the most positive I was to hear from Viviana, marked one of the proudest achievements of her life, ranking only after the rearing of her children and her relationship with the deity, her *Diosito.* I first met señora Viviana Salguero and her husband in 1988, through a program that provided companionship for the elderly. They wanted someone to visit with; I wanted to improve my competence in Spanish. Since our needs complemented each other, the relationship was mutually satisfying from the beginning. The

Salgueros became my teachers, and I their friend. At that time, Viviana was seventy-eight years old, her husband, Jorge, eighty-seven.

My earliest impressions of Viviana were of a small, quiet woman, interested mostly in cooking and foods, her children, and religion. Shorter even than my own 5'3", she looked as though she couldn't weigh more than ninety pounds, dry and fully clothed. An occasional wisp of mottled gray hair escaped from its twist on the back of her head to curve softly over one ear. Always smiling when I arrived, she gave the impression that her day would revolve around my long-awaited visit.

Jorge was a big man, standing at least six feet tall. He had bad knees and could walk only with a cane when I first met him, later switching to a walker. He was politely formal with me but obviously enjoyed my visits. Fascinated by history, he would tell me long stories from the times of Pancho Villa to the Depression years in the United States. He also recounted stories from both the Old and New Testaments. I would come to learn that he was self-taught and had sometimes read to his family in the evenings from one of two books the family owned, a history of Mexico and a Bible.

Viviana seldom spoke, and when she did, Jorge often interrupted her with a story of his own. If I looked directly at her, encouraging her to continue, he curtly ordered her to the kitchen to bring me some juice, which she did. Viviana's eyes would light up when she had the opportunity to speak, however, and she had unfailing patience in trying to teach me new words.

During the time I was coming to know the Salgueros, Jorge's knees became worse, and he became almost housebound. To complicate matters, he fell on the ice in the winter of 1990–91 and required surgery. He never returned home. Frail herself, Viviana realized that she could not care for him—he needed help with the smallest daily tasks, and if he should fall again, she would not be able to lift him. He moved to a local nursing home, where he spent his last year and a half.

While Jorge was in the nursing home, I alternated visits between him, in his drab green institutional room, and his wife, in their modest two-bedroom frame home. With Jorge absent, I now began to hear Viviana's full story and to see her personality emerge. This unassuming woman who had seemed interested in few issues began to tell me stories from the past, to comment on current events and politics, and to espouse her philosophy and moral values. This was a voice I had not heard before.

As her story began to unfold, we revisited fiestas in Mexico, surrounded by pageantry and bright colors; we relived the fear and homesickness of a young bride whose possessive husband would not allow her to visit her family; we trekked into the United States and across south Texas, nursing an eleven-month-old child and cooking frijoles in the battered fragment of an old metal bathtub. We established the merits and demerits of governments, educational systems, and social institutions. She may have had little formal education, but Viviana had amassed a lifetime of opinions and experiences chronicling the transition from culture to culture, from peasant child to woman of wisdom.

I began to wonder how much of her story Viviana's own children knew. Had her grandchildren sat at their *abuela*'s knee and learned of the old country? Did her great-grandchildren have any idea of the fascinating *cuentos* I was hearing? Such stories and the wisdom accumulated with them should be preserved. In 1994, I asked Viviana if I might record her life story, and she liked the idea. It would give our visits more of a focus, it would improve my Spanish, and it would leave a legacy for her descendants. It would also encourage Viviana to reflect on eighty-four years of joys, sorrows, and struggles.

Once every two weeks, I arrived at Viviana's house to the sounds of her barking dog, warm greetings from Viviana herself, the Spanish TV station, and at times the chatter of preadolescent grandchildren. Surrounded by the pictures of children and grandchildren on all available furniture and most of the wall space, we caught up on what had been happening in our lives recently and then settled down to her story. We began casually enough—Viviana reminiscing and I taking notes—but when I showed those notes to a colleague whose Spanish course I had attended, she was so charmed by Viviana's honesty and mix of rustic Mexican/southern US dialect that she encouraged me to tape our sessions and make Viviana's story available to a wider audience. Viviana readily agreed, but although she repeated some of what she had told me in our first sessions, I never did get it all on tape.

My methodology varied between conventional oral history and improvisation. Because our original intent was less ambitious than the construction of an oral history, I inadvertently developed some fortunate procedures and fell short on others. Viviana and I already had a warm rapport, established in part because I was the student and she the teacher. Not only did she have more life experience than I did, but we were working in her native language, a language with which I had requested help. Thus, our experience mitigated somewhat "the distinct imbalances in power and privilege that characterize most women's oral history projects."[2] I usually sat on the floor by Viviana's knee, an arrangement that allowed me to adjust the microphone on her collar if need be and manage the tape recorder as well. After we had established a comfortable routine, I brought enough tape to allow her to speak for as long as an hour and a half if my schedule permitted. I seldom interrupted her unless I couldn't understand what she was saying or I needed clarification. She was free to talk until she was finished with a particular subject.

On the other hand, the project's casual beginnings are the reason I don't have our first three interviews on tape. I also lost one later interview entirely and had to change the playback speed on another because of failed or failing batteries. By the time we were well into the process, I had learned to check my equipment carefully and carry extra tapes and batteries.

Between our visits, I began transcribing the tapes, did background reading, and developed themes and questions for our next meeting. My Spanish-professor colleague was kind enough to spend many hours on the manuscripts with me. When her professional duties made it impossible for her to continue, I obtained a research grant and hired a series of graduate students. The tapes generated about five hundred pages of material, more than I could complete with the grant money.

Fortunately, I had come to know one of Viviana's granddaughters by that time, who graciously consented to help finish checking the translations. Her help was invaluable, because where others of us had struggled to figure out exactly what Viviana had said or what she might have meant by a particular phrase, the granddaughter in most cases knew immediately how to interpret her grandmother's speech. I cannot thank her enough. The process of transcription and translation took almost five years after Viviana and I completed taping. My full-time teaching load and my translators' schedules were part of the reason for the slow pace, but we also spent many hours on each tape, working hard to be true to Viviana's words.

When it came time to edit, I eliminated many of those hard-won words, primarily repetitions. Viviana introduced and separated many phrases with "well" or "so"; I also removed many of those. I rearranged words at times for clarity, identified vague pronoun references, added transitional words, and worked to make tenses consistent. Lisa Krissoff Boehm points out that "transcription is an art form, and a transcription is always an approximation of what was said. Much is attributed to a conversation by body language, voice modulation, nuance, and contextualization."[3] At times, Viviana paused to consider just how she wanted to say something. Those pauses are indicated by three dots, and I used dashes when she used an interrupter or changed topics abruptly. Unless they were necessary for clarity, I eliminated the questions I asked, and I combined stories from different interviews because Viviana often returned to a subject more than once.

I kept all copies of the transcriptions because I first transcribed the language phonetically, keeping the grammar and pronunciation of her dialect (e.g., substitution of "–mos" for "–nos" endings, "-ao" for "–ado" endings, *pos* for *pues,* etc.). At times, I added Viviana's words in Spanish to give the flavor of what she actually said. My reading in oral history, however, convinced me I did not want to create a persona on paper that denied Viviana her dignity or made her sound quaint. For that reason, as I worked the narrations into the text of each chapter, I standardized much of the grammar and pronunciation. To try to capture some of the rhythm of her language, I used ellipses for pauses and dashes for topic changes or asides within a sentence.

Having standardized the dialect in one language, I still had the issue of recreating Viviana's colloquial dialect in English. Languages do not translate word for word, and colloquial language has even less equivalency than standard registers. Does one use "ain't" for "is not"? "He don't" for "He doesn't"? "I didn't see no problem" for "I didn't see a problem"? These phrases would not match the grammatical or pronunciation patterns of Viviana's colloquial Spanish, but they might create a similar register, or level of informality. That issue has no satisfactory resolution. I therefore standardized the English as well.

I have also used pseudonyms for Viviana and her family. Not all of her living children were willing to have their names used, and it is not the aim of oral history to invade anyone's privacy. In choosing the names, I tried to be sensitive to the significance of the individuals' birth names or what I knew of their personalities. It was not difficult to choose the name Viviana. From the root word, *vivir*, to live, I found it a perfect expression of Viviana's strong life force, her perseverance in the face of adversity, her refusal to give in to despair, her commitment to giving her children the most she could, her conviction that life is a lovely gift. Salguero is a topographical name for someone who lived by a weeping willow; it could also refer to a spot where salt was given to cattle. Considering her and Jorge's rural roots and involvement with agriculture, it seemed appropriate.

No one tells her story in neat chronological order. The question of how to organize the material presented some problems because we had discussed so many theoretical issues, but a life story does have a certain progression. To give the story continuity, I decided to tell it chronologically, bringing in Viviana's positions on various social and philosophical issues as they related to the subject at hand. This method worked up to a point, but it became clear as I worked that three aspects of her life were central to her character; they defined the woman she had grown into through a lifetime of struggle, the woman she was proud to be. Chapters 1 through 5 are chronological, but Viviana's love and concern for her children, her religious faith, and her status as a US citizen then claim chapters of their own.

Unfortunately, I was never able to read the narrative to Viviana after I had it on paper. By the time I had the transcriptions finished and was beginning to organize the material, her hearing was failing and her health had become so fragile that she could no longer live alone. She was living with her daughter, and we had no private space in which to work. Had she been capable of it, I am sure she would have enjoyed reworking our discussions and answering many of my questions, enriching the manuscript immeasurably.

Viviana and I began our work in July of 1994 and taped our twenty-seventh interview on June 30, 1995. Neither she nor I would claim that what follows is a complete picture of who she was. Not only can we never know ourselves or another completely, but in any dealing with the past, we inevitably must deal with what Sandy Polishuk calls "the complications of memory and motive."[4] In speaking with Viviana's children, I saw her from different perspectives and heard details she had either forgotten or chosen not to tell me. At times, she may have intentionally cast herself in a good light,[5] rather than admit any moral failing, but at others, even though she might not have lived staunchly by her own advice, I believe she actually put into words wisdom she didn't realize she had, offering the best of what she had learned from a difficult life.

Her narrative was also shaped by her interaction with me as interviewer. In the first place, we began with one intended audience—her descendants—and then broadened it to anyone who might like to read a book about her life. In her earlier stories, she concentrated on the factual events of her childhood, but gradually, after I asked if I could possibly publish her story, she dealt more often with generalizations and guidelines for living. I influenced not only the content but also the style of her narrative. Always aware that I was still learning Spanish, she repeated much more than I believe she would have with a native speaker. She wanted to be sure I understood. A different interviewer would have elicited a different story in several ways.

Alessandro Portelli makes the point that oral history is the result of "what the source and the historian do *together*."[6] This may be Viviana's story, but it is Viviana's story as shaped and interpreted by Joyce Lackie, Anglo daughter of a midwestern US farmer and a teacher, privileged earner of two graduate degrees, survivor of two failed marriages, English professor, and eager Spanish student. Growing up five miles from the nearest town, population nine hundred Caucasian-heritage inhabitants and with a high school of fewer than 150 students, as a child I had no concept of diversity. I am not sure how old I was when I saw first saw a black person, through a high school fence in a larger town, but I do remember that my mother said little at the time. Evidently, it was not a remarkable phenomenon, and since both of my parents encouraged treating all people with the same courtesy and respect (as long as it didn't come to dating or marrying outside your race or religion!), I didn't think much about it until I went to college and became aware of the bias and discrimination directed toward groups because of their ethnicity, gender, sexual orientation, or other characteristics. Only then, in the early 1960s, did civil rights marches and pictures of policemen threatening black students with vicious dogs begin awakening the public and my own consciousness through television. Perhaps it is that absence of diversity in my early background that leads me to enjoy interacting with people from different ethnic and cultural heritages.

If I relate to those who have experienced injustice, it is in large part through their telling, and not my experiencing. Even as a female, I have felt little pain from the discrimination that exists in our society. By the early sixties, when I entered college, women were making inroads into many formerly male-dominated careers. In high school, I briefly considered a career in mathematics, but my love of words and literature won out. Even the discrimination of salary disparity, though unjust, bothered me more for my colleagues than for myself. Very busy with a job I loved, I was focused on teaching. It was primarily through the daily news—the civil rights movement, the women's movement, the labor struggle—and my reading in literature that I was exposed to undeniable suffering. Writers such as Dickens, Kafka, and Steinbeck, among others, revealed the harsh realities of an unfair world, inviting me to put myself in the place of the subjected. (Mary Wollstonecraft's *The Wrongs of Woman* was not yet a part of the undergraduate curriculum.) That empathy helped to promote my social consciousness.

I shared almost nothing of Viviana's background: ethnicity, level of formal education, socioeconomic status, age, language, or the discrimination she had experienced as a result of those circumstances. Gender was our connecting point, and it was a powerful one. It would be hard to imagine her sharing many of the following stories with a male interviewer. Besides the fact that another woman wanted to hear her story, she was also pleased that I had the skills to record it. With her great admiration for education, she respected my role as a professor. We were both aware, however, that she was the expert on the subject at hand—her life as told through her language. Considering our age difference as well, she had the superior position. Boehm found that in researching with older women, "the interviews often took on the format of an older, more experienced person telling a younger one how the world had functioned in the past and offering insights on the struggles of . . . daily life."[7] In these ways, Viviana was the expert, but she trusted me to put her story to paper and communicate it to the outside world. I have done my best to honor that trust, but because I was not able to read back to her any of the analysis, the finished product has less of her than I would like. I have added empathy and what perspective I could gain by reading other oral histories, Mexican history, western women's history, and Chicana studies, creating a story that is both less and more than who she was.

Though unique, Viviana's story must share elements with those of many families who came to the United States just after the Second World War. The Salgueros migrated to the United States in 1946, joining a large number of undocumented workers who were encouraged to come to Texas to fill a labor shortage.[8] They left behind a Mexico that had been struggling for decades to modernize its economy. In an attempt to better proportion the distribution of wealth, President Lazaro Cárdenas had instituted land reforms in the 1930s, the early years of Viviana's marriage. His administration broke private landholdings into *ejidos* to be owned and worked jointly by groups of former peasants. Although some peasants benefited on a local level, by 1937 commercial agricultural production became stagnant, leaving unskilled workers like Jorge to continue the scrabble for survival. The conservative presidents who followed Cárdenas, convinced that industrialization was the way to defeat Mexico's continuing cycles of poverty and dependency, moved away from land reform and toward an industrial, exporting economy. Vast numbers of the rural poor came no closer to breaking out of poverty than they ever had.

In the 1940s a US Department of Labor report concluded that only 32 percent of the Mexican labor force was "gainfully employed."[9] Thousands lived at subsistence levels, doing temporary work as day laborers or farmhands, sometimes finding something to sell, struggling to feed their families. Like the Salgueros, many moved from place to place, vagabonds seeking odd jobs. Wages declined throughout the decade, reaching a low of two to three pesos per day in the central plateau. In 1944, in Michoacan, one of the central states, a *campesino* leaving for the city explained that he was earning one and a half pesos for a day's work. He could not even feed his children, let alone meet other expenses.[10]

People who moved to the cities to take factory jobs faced a life often more harsh and dangerous than that in rural areas. Factories and refineries routinely ignored the health and safety of their workers.[11] Economic and quality-of-life conditions for the majority of the population were grim. One can well imagine that conversations in many homes, like Viviana and Jorge's, were turning to *El Norte,* where agricultural workers were finding employment. Rather than leave his rural lifestyle and seek work in a factory, Jorge wanted to seek his extended family in Texas.

The United States needed farm workers in particular. The industrial buildup of the war years had encouraged much of the rural US labor force to migrate to the cities,[12] while at the same time, the war had left Europe heavily dependent on American imports of food products.[13] In response to calls by growers, the government had developed the Bracero program (from the Spanish word for "arms"— *brazos*) in 1942 to legally import Mexican labor. The situation in Texas, however, where the Salgueros crossed into the country, was unique. Texas had not entered into the Bracero program, partly for reasons of its own and partly because the Mexican government had serious concerns about ongoing abuse of its citizens in that state.[14] Undocumented labor was even cheaper than documented because growers didn't need to worry about contracts, minimum wage, housing, or health care, and US congressional representatives of southwestern agribusiness had deliberately kept the border patrol understaffed, so as not to shut off the undocumented labor supply.[15] No one was informing people like Jorge and Viviana about this reality, of course, since fear of being sent back across the border kept complaints about unfair conditions to a minimum. Viviana and her family arrived in this country incognito, hiding in the woods and not knowing whom to trust.

From that point, Viviana began her journey from frightened and battered immigrant to proud US citizen. She and many others like her would follow the migrant trails of the Southwest, cooking and changing diapers in the out-of-doors or ramshackle houses, and helping in the fields. Most of their stories, unlike those of Mexican American union organizers, community leaders, and career women, will go unrecorded, but the lesser-known elderly women who lived those middle and latter decades of the twentieth century have a wealth of stories that helped shape current generations. Those stories are important not only for the families' progeny, as insights into their identity, but they are part of our national and regional histories as well. Devra Weber points out that Mexicana workers, when present at all in agricultural history, have been represented only as "faceless, powerless, passive, and ultimately outside the flow of history,"[16] particularly those who lacked the skills to leave any written record.

Many of those workers would remain poor while a developing middle class of Mexican Americans went to college, joined professions, and bought homes in the 1950s. The struggling families would send their sons to war in the late 1960s and watch their grandchildren achieve mixed success in school during the 1970s and 1980s. By the 1990s, some of those grandchildren were breaking the cycle of poverty, but others continued the futile struggle in the hamster's wheel. Viviana's story is simply one thread in this vast tapestry, but just as one strand of DNA can open the secrets of many, her experience can tell us much about what not only she but others like her faced during those decades. Her story includes broken car windows and empty piggy banks, a near-death experience because of a doctor's neglect, houses with sand blowing in through the cracks, and the constant fear of a battering husband.

By 1946 Viviana and Jorge had nine children; they would have three more after moving to the United States. They would eventually settle in Colorado, where the sugar-beet industry offered jobs for six months a year, and a family could supplement that work by harvesting onions, potatoes, and other produce. The winter months were slow, but they failed to lighten Viviana's workload. She didn't have to go to the fields, but meals still had to be prepared; dirty clothes were heavier and more abundant, besides harder to dry; cleaning and mending were never finished. She didn't say whether Jorge was less prone to violence during those times, but it would seem likely that his reading to the family occurred on cold winter evenings when no one wanted to venture out. Those must have provided a respite from his all-too-common anger.

I once asked Viviana's eldest son about his parents' personalities. Regarding his quick-tempered father, he expressed only perplexity, but he was clearly in awe of his mother. "Oh, she was nice all the time. She treated us like a mom. To take care of twelve kids takes a lot. I don't know how she used to do it—fed us, washed and ironed, everything. No machines—boil the water, boil the clothes. How she used to do it, I don't know." The woman who reared those twelve children is as much a part of US history as any dignitary or war hero. Hers is part of the multicultural history of a nation, a history that until recently recorded only the lives of those who gained fame or notoriety. Rather than allow the relegation of an entire group of Mexican immigrant women to unexamined stereotyping, her story gives voice to the individual.

I

The Early Years

1910–1926

Amor de padre o madre, que lo demás es aire.
Love of father and mother, the rest is pure air.
—Spanish dicho

VIVIANA'S STORY BEGINS on a ranch called La Hacienda Jiménez in the state of Durango, Mexico, where she was born in 1911. The Mexican Revolution, or as many Mexicans see it, the civil wars of 1910–14,[1] had begun to rage, in part because of the vast inequities between the wealthy and the struggling poor. During the administration of Porfirio Díaz, the rural families had been driven off their small farms, until 90 percent of them were landless.[2] Díaz ruled Mexico as virtual dictator for thirty years, during which time foreign investors and the already wealthy prospered while the majority of the population—primarily Indians and mestizos (mixed-bloods)—lived nearly destitute. An economic depression in the first decade of the twentieth century, affecting the entire population and helping to foment the war, made the situation of the peasants even worse. Although Viviana's father was the foreman on a ranch, earning more than most of the workers, his salary was scarcely adequate to feed the family.

Viviana seemed unaware of the wars that played out during her childhood. Her parents, a loving but serious-minded father and a temperamental mother, had little or no formal education, and only limited access to news outside the nearest village. What they did have was a daily struggle to make ends meet, a struggle shared by the entire community of ranch workers.

> When I was a child, I lived on a ranch with my father, mother, and two brothers. The closest town was a little village called Sacramento in the state of Durango. Two of my four brothers died when they were little. The family lived during the depression, and they were very poor. Everyone, in fact, was very poor. When people came from other ranches or areas, everyone helped everyone else because nobody had anything. Nobody had money.
>
> My father earned very little, a small salary. His regular work was on a ranch, but on weekends, he cut hair and shaved people in exchange for sugar, coffee, beans, corn, lard, and other food. He was a very serious man, and he never joked around. He wanted to maintain others' respect. We called him our *tata*. My mama was more easily amused, but she was practical also.
>
> I remember two stories from when I was a child. When I was no more than two years old, my mama had to take breakfast to papa. She left me in the house and closed the door. It was a half door, and the cat came in through the open part. I was afraid of the cat, and I started to scream. We didn't have stoves in the house in those days, and we had a wood fire. I grabbed a piece of wood. I was wearing a flannel dress, and it caught fire. The flames spread over the left side of my body, and I screamed and screamed. Mama heard me and came back to the rescue. Because there was no hospital or doctor nearby, mama and grandma cared for me. I still have the scar on the side of my abdomen.
>
> I didn't know how they cured me or anything. They cured me with Mexican herbs, because there are no doctors on the ranches there. You have to go a long ways to the town for the doctors. And without money, with what would we pay? There are many good herbs for pain, salves in little boxes, to put on. My mother used to say that you could see my intestines, I don't know. But, well, I got well. God helped me.

That was one of Viviana's earliest experiences with the healing power of Mexican herbs. The second story she recalled, however, revealed a less compassionate side of her mother's nature. It was not uncommon in economically struggling families to assign tasks to children from a very young age,[3] but Viviana remembers her mother as angry and vindictive rather than simply asking for her daughter's help. Her abuse was not only physical; as Gloria Anzaldúa and others point out, abuse can be psychological as well. Often the "mother's allegiance was to male children."[4] Cherríe Moraga describes her mother's stronger devotion to her sons than her daughter as a betrayal,[5] and Maria Elena Lucas even wondered if she was actually her parents' daughter, in part because her mother always favored the boys.[6]

> When I was older, I had to take care of my little brothers. One time when I had only one brother and he was very little—he couldn't walk, but he was crawling—Mama went again to carry breakfast to Tata. She left me locked up in the house and told me to take care of the baby. I think I was about three years old, and I was supposed to watch my brother, but I wasn't being careful. I was playing. The baby chased a *pinacate*—the ones they call stinkbugs in Mexico, a black insect with many legs—across the floor, caught it, and bit it in half. He really chomped down on that critter. He swallowed a part and spit out the rest. Those insects put out—how can I say it?—well, it's a rustic word—one says, they fart. [Esos animalitos echan un—¿cómo le diré?—bueno, es una palabra rústica—que "se peyó."] [She laughs.] These insects don't sting, but they cause blisters. Later, my little brother had blisters all over his mouth and tongue. He was walking around with his little tongue out because it had bitten him. Because of this, my mama spanked me and spanked me and spanked me. She gave me a good one. I was playing and didn't watch him.

Viviana never mentioned any resentment toward her younger brothers, perhaps feeling instead a sense of responsibility toward them. Her mother's disciplinary tactics plus her parents' amicable relationship created a harmonious household, at least when mother was content with daughter. This family dynamic might not have been unusual. In a study by Aída Hurtado, many young Chicanas expressed a strong sense of personal responsibility toward younger brothers, often working to help them succeed.[7] I once met the younger of Viviana's brothers, who had come several hundred miles to visit her and obviously enjoyed her company. If there had ever been any animosity between them, it had not made a lasting impression.

> I got along well with my brothers. Both of them were younger than I. We didn't fight; we got along well … because my mother and my father, I never saw them fight. I liked my brothers equally. We always got along. If we fought, my mother hit us on the head. "You don't understand? Aren't you brothers and sister?" She hit me to see if I understood. It hurt. That's why we didn't fight. And if not, look, she grabbed us so that we wouldn't be fighting.

Even though she was not jealous of her brothers, Viviana still longed for the love and approval of her mother. Instead, she found herself subject to violence.

> My mother didn't love me … just because I was the only girl. I was the oldest. I don't know why she didn't love me. She beat me; she hit me. She wasn't a good mother. She was very temperamental; she had very high blood pressure. She ordered me around as I was growing up, ordered me to do things immediately. She would say, "Viviana, do this!"
>
> "Yes, ma'am. Yes, ma'am." I couldn't tell her, "I'm coming." Sometimes I didn't hear. "Viviana, aren't I calling you?" No, and when she came to me, she grabbed me because I didn't hear right away, because I didn't come right away and see what she wanted.
>
> My father was very respectful, very loving. And my mother was harder with me. She used to hit me for nothing. For nothing she kicked me [she gestures, kicking]. She also put my face between her legs [gestures, slapping her thigh twice] and slapped me. With whatever she could find, with sticks or whatever was handy, she hit me. She was very quick to anger.
>
> One time she hit me in the eye with a poker. It's a wonder she didn't take my eye out.

Viviana's father acted as a kind of counterbalance to her mother; he made her feel adored and special. He couldn't erase her mother's treatment, of course, but he could offer her love and a sense of self-worth. She was his only daughter, his dear *hija*. Her relationship with her father may have provided a great deal of her core strength.

> And my father, no, he was a good father to his three kids. He loved me very much. He was not a beater. Only once he spanked me, but with his hand. He was very loving. My father never called me by my name, Viviana. He called me, "Daughter. Dear daughter."
>
> My father was never drunk. Never. He wasn't a drinker, nor a smoker either. He never set a bad example for us. Therefore, the three of us lived well. And like I told you before, we were very poor. My brothers didn't have much schooling because my father took them working with him. What he was making was not enough. That's the way our life went.

The three children were often on the edge of hunger, living only a little better than the poorest of the ranch workers. A 1914 *National Geographic* article on the Mexican hacienda explains that the workers were responsible to "a *mayordomo,*"[8] or manager, who assigned the men their tasks, supervised the work, and reported to his superior. Wages were low, thirty-seven cents per day for the workers on a hacienda in the state of Zacatecas,[9] Coahuila's neighboring state to the south.

> My father was the foreman on the ranch, but what he made wasn't enough. That's why he had to cut hair. People came to have their hair cut and paid my dad with what they had. With chile. That's how it was.
>
> There in Mexico it's a different life. They don't have the help [social services] that they have here. There the people beg for alms. "Help me, please. A tortilla or help me with something. Give me something to eat. Here are my grandchildren." Here, no. In Mexico, yes. But we never begged for alms.
>
> There where I grew up are nothing but fields. My father used to bring us a watermelon, and if not a watermelon, he brought

some corn on the cob. Sometimes he brought fruit . . . because he was working. But when he came, he would bring whatever he could—like sweets or bread.

We never had much food, but my grandfather gave my father a cow. Often, there were no tortillas, but we had *molinos* [small hand-operated corn mills], and it was possible to make five or six tortillas for the children. The people were very close and humanitarian, and when a neighbor killed a pig, he shared it with the other families.

Not only was the economy unfavorable to the workers, but De Mente relates that "Mexicans had to develop ways of protecting themselves from the corruption and excesses of those in power. This included exercising . . . caution in their behavior toward their superiors, catering to them in a variety of ways and using respect[ful] language and an obsequious form of body language."[10] Viviana remembered not only the image of the men standing in line for their pay—sombreros doffed, heads probably bowed—but even how much money they made.

The workers received fifty-two cents per hour in those times. They went to the pay window on payday, and they took off their hats to show respect for the boss.

The poorest people did not have much. One family could have two or three naked little children without pants or underwear. The little girls had cotton cloth diapers. They lived in the mountains, and when it was cold, the poor people didn't have enough clothes.

Our house had only one room and the kitchen. We would sleep outside. That's the way we slept. In the summer, we would go to bed outside, and they made fences of branches, but they wouldn't make any doors to close. And there a lot of the dogs had rabies. But we slept peacefully. God helps when one is asleep.

Even though Viviana didn't remember her mother ever expressing love for her, as a child she did admire some of her mother's abilities, and she learned a variety of domestic skills from her. Her mother's life could not have been easy, especially considering the difficulty of carrying out even the most basic household tasks without running water or labor-saving machinery. If she was an inspiration to her daughter in any way, it was in teaching her the essential life skills for survival of the family. Much of the day's activity revolved around hauling and using water, a precious commodity on the ranch.

Viviana carefully described the apparatus for delivering and using water, indicating how important it was in the daily life of the workers in their semiarid environment. Just as humans needed water, it was also crucial to their livestock.

> We had to carry water from the faucet a long way away, farther than from here to the church [she points across the street]. We had to bring it in buckets. My mother would carry the bucket of water on her head. She would let go of the bucket—and balance it on her head, and it wouldn't fall. I don't know how she did it. I never could.
>
> She would make a little circle of cloth to put under it and then put the tin on her head. They called the little circle *yagual*. It's a little circle coiled around the hand, and then one puts it here on her head. And that is what one did in former times.
>
> Most of the people used the water like that. And if they didn't, they sold the water. A man with some poles walks by with the cans here [gestures that he is carrying the pole on his shoulders with cans suspended from it]. They go and get the water and then sell it at the houses. That's the way it was.
>
> There was no river close to us. There was a well with a faucet, like that in a sink or a bathtub. There are water wells on the ranches for drinking water—for the animals. They give the water to them in pails, in tubs. If they don't use those, they make a trough from wood, like the feeding channels the ranchers use for the cattle mangers. With an axe they cut out the heart of the wood. There they put the water for the animals, with a pail. Then they put a pulley to hold the bucket in the well.

Water was central to housekeeping and other chores as well. When I asked Viviana to describe a typical day in her household, much of her account involved the tasks of taming the pervasive dust.

On a typical day, we would get up early in the morning— in the dusky light just as the dawn is breaking. You get up to sweep the patio, outside, because there isn't cement as here, just dirt. And then you bring water from the pumps, and first thing, water down the patio so that it looks nice.

In my house, I would bring water, sprinkle it in the kitchen to make it fresh, sprinkle it out on the floor and spread it around, so there wouldn't be any loose dirt. It wasn't like here—the floor—like linoleum or whatever. Just a dirt floor.

You had to go early because the water would run out. They would cut it off. They didn't want you to waste water. If you began to water down the dirt, so that the dust wouldn't fly, they would cut off the water. And if you got it to drink, you got some, and if not, well, you were left without. Everyone is treated the same.

In addition to gathering water and sweeping, Viviana helped with the laundering, sewing, and cooking. The women spent hours each day soaking and grinding the corn for tortillas, a process unchanged for centuries.[11] As the eldest child and only girl, Viviana was responsible for many of the daily chores, while her little brothers, not yet old enough to help their father on the ranch, had fewer duties. Her contribution was an integral part of the family's daily survival, contributing to the strong work habits she would maintain her entire life.

We had to wash by hand in the washtub. I was the one who had to do the housework. If we had time, we had to do needlework—such as embroidery, knitting, or unraveling.

Over there in Mexico the girls in the past were very good cooks. We knew how to do everything—grind corn, make tortillas, everything. The tortillas you had to grind on the *metate* and then put them on the *comal* [griddle]. That was what I did.

The fire was in the kitchen, a little room. We made the fire on the floor. There we cooked on the floor. Very hard, the life.

My brothers did sometimes help. The three of us gave a hand. But almost always my mother would tend to them. She would give each his little meal. What there was, she would give them. And if we had nothing else, she would make some gorditas and put a little butter on them.

Those who could manage had four small meals a day, none of which could be considered overly indulgent.

[When you first get up,] you make your breakfast, well, whatever you have. You drink a glass of milk, your piece of bread. Then, like about ten, you come to have breakfast. You cook your egg, if by chance you have eggs, a few beans, and there is breakfast. Then my father would go back to work again. And in the afternoon about midday, at one or two, is dinner. Many people made their beans, their soup, their chile—chile isn't scarce there in Mexico. At night, supper. If some food is left from the midday meal, it is eaten, so that nothing is left. There they have four meals: an early bite, breakfast, dinner, and supper. Dinner is the biggest. [But] many don't have supper. Many have only one meal a day.

Two previous depressions, one in the early 1890s and the other from 1907 to 1909, had led to the widespread hunger. Remembering how her mother coped with the meager amount of food, Viviana had developed strong feelings about wastefulness and appreciating one's resources. People learned during those times to cook and eat not only tortillas and beans, but also an intriguing variety of uncommon foods.

There were these black beans—they called them "Black or dark"— my mother would put them to boil, but she would boil them twice, the first time and then the second, so they would be a little better. Because the water she threw out was very, very, very black, very dark, black, purple. She gave these beans to my father. And when we didn't have enough, when they had given him just a little bit of beans, we would break them in the metate. My mother would break them in the metate so they would be done fast and ready to eat. We couldn't eat until the beans were done.

There was scarcely enough food in the house. Not like here. Here, there is a lot of food, and many people throw it away. They throw food in the trash. They make a meal, eat it, and what is left over goes in the trash. And there—what would one throw away? I don't like throwing food away.

In these mountains, the land gave fruit and cocoa, and it was also possible to eat armadillos and skunks. The intestines of the armadillos are poisonous, but the meat is similar to pig meat. There are opossums, with hairless tails. Jorge ate burro meat and horsemeat rinds [crackles] in his youth. These meats are a little sweet. His family ate hare meat, rabbits, and turtles. Turtle tastes like chicken.

People also ate the snake that bites, the rattlesnake. The dried meat from the inside of this snake is used to treat leprosy. This meat can heal acne. Also, the rats found in corn heaps were eaten. The white rats were bigger than the ones here, and they had an agreeable flavor. To prepare a soup, it was necessary to boil the rats in water with salt and rice. Rats with rice were good. On Thanksgiving Day, we ate turkeys.

[Like a traveler home from a difficult journey, Viviana was glad to have left the hard work of those days behind.] Now everything is different. Now things are the same in Mexico as here because over there they have mills for making tortillas from corn, or flour. And there the women no longer grind the corn. Everything we have here, they have in Mexico, like cans of fruit, cans of food, such as beans, refried beans. They are delicious.

Although there was little time for play on the ranch, children create and share what diversions they can, sometimes getting into trouble in the process. In one instance, Viviana suffered a painful injury resulting in little sympathy from her mother. In general, however, she remembered the games as infrequent but amusing pastimes. More than simply fun, they also served as means for children to learn social skills and manners.[12] In the Sweet Orange game, found throughout Latin America, children greet, hug, and bid farewell to each other as they move in and out of a circle.[13] In The Little Onion, children form a kind of train and pass through an archway or tunnel formed by the other players.

One time we were playing in the neighbor's house. They had a vicious dog. Where we were playing, we fell, and I fell on top of a little girl. And the dog stretched the rope until it broke and came and grabbed me from above and bit me. It made me walk on my hands and knees afterward, because dog bites hurt, yes, how they hurt! Well, then afterward, I couldn't go and play. I was with my leg like this. [She holds her leg up off the floor and laughs.] "For being over there . . . ," my mother said. "For being a tomboy [por andar de machetona]"—another rustic word— "Who told you to go? What did you go for? Only so the dog could bite you." Well, yes, but one looks for companions to play with. Because we were playing Sweet Orange, that's why it all happened.

The games there in Mexico are very creative. In Sweet Orange, everyone takes hold of each other's hands, forming a wheel. "Sweet honey orange, / a slice of lemon, dear / if I could hug, / if I could have you near." That is the Sweet Orange song, and then they take a spin. And then two of them would plant themselves, and everyone had to pass through the middle of the arch that the two of them made, passing through two at a time to play The Little Onion. We all grabbed each other from behind. They would stand like this [making the arch], and each one would pass through the middle, everybody holding on to each other at the waist—to do The Little Onion.

There weren't any other games—like Carnival or others. Only those invented at home or such like. We would remember everything, and then afterward we would play with the neighbors. We all played together there.

Even though she stressed that such pastimes were few and far between, talk of games sparked Viviana's memories of the community's religious celebrations, definite highlights from her childhood. She recreated scenes of vigorous colors, elaborate costumes, music, and dancing. Behind that color and activity vibrated the religious principles, the foundation for the fiestas. These were Catholic traditions, of course, but having converted to Protestantism in later life, she had her own beliefs about saints, a point she made more than once in our discussions. Although they had undergone some changes, her religious convictions were essential to Viviana's character.

The holidays were very different than they are here. The community worked very hard to teach the children its traditions. Everyone in the town or on the ranch went to the celebration near the little church. During Christmas, there was a program about the shepherds and the angels. They wore costumes with masks and walked from one place to another. My husband, Jorge, had a role in this procession.

There were cowboys with spurs and horses. There were costumes with many colors, crowns in people's hair, paper flowers and ribbons, and straw hats for the shepherds. There were dancers with maracas and musical gourds. Those who represented saints wore blue or red skirts. Some of the costumes had little mirrors and wide paper ribbons. Some carried feathers. Also, there were Indians in white dresses, pants, and shirts.

This Christmas celebration honored many saints, including the Virgin of Guadalupe, the Virgin of San Juan, the Virgin of San Ysidro [the patron saint of farmers], and other child saints and little saints. Also the Virgin of Refuge was honored sometimes. It is important to remember that the photograph is not the saint. They taught the children also that the saints do not work miracles. Only Jesus can work miracles.

On festival days, the community pooled its resources and created tantalizing feasts. Although she was not a drinker, Viviana remembered liquor, a type of whiskey made from cactus, as a part of the festivities. Tortillas were still the staple, but people brought as much dairy, meat, and sweets as possible to make a variety of savory fillings. Viviana would sometimes breathe a sigh of contentment remembering those long-ago meals.

Maguey is a [cactus] plant that grows in the mountains. It is necessary to cut it, and the branch will grow again. The thick part is used for liquor. The people made liquor from the tops of the maguey over a coal fire with warm water.

Two days before Easter was the Friday of Sorrows. On the following Saturday each family prepared a lot of food for a sacrifice. On Sunday, after the sacrifice, all the people ate a large feast. On this day, there was much dancing and merriment.

Each person had his own saint. I had a saint, and I made food for this saint. Then these saints enjoyed the food while the shepherds sang.

There was a big pot of *atole* made of sweet milk, milk milk (*leche leche*), cocoa milk, or cinnamon milk. The thick tortillas were in the oven. There were big spoons for stirring the atole and large ovens for making bread. This bread was made of flour, sugar, cinnamon, milk, and water and was eaten with butter. There was no electricity; back then we used embers of wood to cook the bread.

They also made gorditas of dough. I can still make gorditas. You fill them with beans and egg, or egg only, with a little chile, or beans with sausage, with ground meat. Ah, they are well made. You loosen them, the outside, open them with the knife, and put those fillings inside. You can make them with a comál or put them in shortening in a frying pan. That makes the gordita. Just make them round. They also turn out good for putting in the lunch, and they are really good. They are just wrapped in a cloth, and that's it.

There is another kind of food that they call baked gorditas. They fill them with cheese, butter, and salt. And if you want them sweet, well, also, you grind the sweet and then put it to soften. Then, you put it in the dough for the gorditas. You put in butter, cinnamon, and um-um.

During Holy Week, you can eat food of the vigil, food of Holy Week, like fish. On Good Friday, you don't eat meat. You eat fish. Or other foods, like potatoes. You boil the potato until it's soft, and then take off the skin and then smash it, mashed potatoes. And then you put a little butter on the potato, already mashed, and a little salt, and then make potato cakes. Beat the egg, and then when it is beaten, make the cakes and put them in the egg. Turn them and then put them in the frying pan. And they are very good. Yes, and beans, peas, corn, and those . . . little cactus—You haven't eaten them? Cactus?—they eat them, also. You cook them with onion, chile, and tomato. Or egg.

Cook them with whatever you want, maybe with red chile also. And they come out good, the cacti.

Still there in Mexico every year, even the very poor people have festivals. The people are barely getting by, poor, but that Thursday and Friday of Holy Week, they don't make any food at home. They make do with what they have, and then they go to the fields to see the celebrations and everything. They make bread [there in the fields]; they make some gorditas in the communal ovens. Only that week does the woman rest. And then it's over and the year goes on.

Two customs Viviana did not observe firsthand while growing up were the live dramatization of the crucifixion and the crawling of the penitents to the feet of the Virgin. She heard descriptions, however, from her mother.

The people camp out for several days. I didn't get to see it, but my mother talked about a man they crucified alive on the cross, and they put that crown of thorns on him. It was no longer the custom, by the time I was growing up. The Bible itself says that God made the sacrifice for us. When God could not find anyone to send to die for humanity, Jesus said, "Send me, I will go." That's why he came to die for the more than a thousand sinners. The sacrifice is still used in Mexico; they still crawl on their knees, they still bleed from the knees. They still bleed.

Viviana's fond memories of festivals and saint's days sprang in large part from the sense of community among the workers on the ranch. Religious celebrations and feasts brought them all together, creating colorful and harmonious interludes in an otherwise hardscrabble existence. The community became a large extended family, sharing resources for the enjoyment of all. One theory of peasant culture holds that the need for community cohesion precludes any one family's accruing more wealth than any other; such celebrations neutralize a family's advantages.[14] Although Viviana felt the limitations of her father's income in their daily life, his position as foreman must have allowed him more money than the average ranch worker.

She admired the religious devotion that prompted him to save and sponsor a pageant every year.

She called the program a pastoral, the term for a medieval mystery play of Spanish origin. Such plays are popular renderings of the prophecies preceding the nativity of Christ and reactions of the shepherds to the announcements of his birth. They involve devils, angels, and comical improvisation. Her father's devotion and his willingness to share with others contributed to Viviana's sense of belonging to the human community at large and her strong opinions on sharing, ideas that permeated her entire life story.

> When I was young, my father took on a religious duty—they call it a devotion—to a child, baby Jesus. He sacrificed to put on the celebration. There were shepherds who carried a staff of reeds, and on the top, they put a crown. There they put a lot of papers around the edge of the crown, and little mirrors. He put on this devotion every year, every Christmas, his pastoral. He paid all the expenses, for two or three days—to feed the shepherds.
>
> There are six shepherds, men. And then there are a little girl and two devils. There is a fool; Jorge played a fool. They carried sheepskins and the baby Jesus. Jorge made the baby a little bed-roll, a pillow and blanket, and carried him. They called Jorge's character Bartolo.

Criselda Cassell of Greeley, Colorado, recalls watching the nativity play, *Los Pastores,* in a community center when she was a child. The character of Bartolo is a lazy shepherd whose wife has just been influenced by the devil to run away with another man. Bartolo alerts the other shepherds who recover his wife and continue their journey to Bethlehem.[15]

> The shepherds I was talking about carry little pillows they call sheep. They also carry many beads, little jars, little plates, little pans.
>
> My father had a small baby [doll], and there were others who had bigger babies. That is a pastoral. My father had his book to guide him. And then a separate book for the dancers. There are dances for an offering. Those dancers are also beautiful, only

dancing, dancing, dancing. The dancers and the Indians wore sandals, and the shepherds wore shoes.

The portrayers of Indians act the part, but they are just people—they aren't Indians. Sometimes the Indians carried big dolls—a foot high or more—and others carried quivers of arrows on their backs. The old men carry large dolls. They have their dolls hanging here. [She pats her hip.] And they have their bag to use when they go to the houses where the people give them coffee or food or whatever. They put it in their bag so they can take it to their house for their children. All of it is beautiful, and many people come together for it, but it happens only once a year. They still have them in Mexico, these fiestas.

What is so different here in the United States is that everyone celebrates the holidays with their families in their own homes. They don't have the same spirit of community that we had on the ranch. I miss the celebrations, and I think the elderly, the adults, and especially the children of this country have lost out on a precious experience. When I was a child, these were some of my happiest times.

2

Courtship and Marriage

1926–1930s

Antes que te cases, mira lo que haces.
Before you marry, take a good look.
—*Spanish* dicho

NONE OF VIVIANA'S POSITIVE childhood experiences with her father or the tightly knit community gave her the courage to reject a devastating marriage. At sixteen, she was pursued by Jorge, a widower nine years her senior who was known to have beaten his first wife. As she remembered the situation almost sixty years later, she recalled only anger and threats on his part and fear on hers. In the course of our discussions, we mused more than once about what in her husband's background could have made him so angry, but she found no satisfactory answer. Perhaps the poet César Vallejo provides some insight when he writes of "the poor man's anger,"[1] an anger against the seemingly overwhelming circumstances of poverty. Other negative forces had been at work in Jorge's life as well, but whatever the causes, the results frustrated any expectations the teenage girl might have had of a romantic courtship and a gentle, caring husband.

The concept of *aguantar,* to stand firm against suffering, hard work, pain, or a tragic fate, figures prominently in Viviana's life story. According to Earl Shorris, it is the aspect of character "which the older generation of Mejicanos and Mexican-Americans still say is most important in their world-view." He adds, "In the mestizo [of mixed racial ancestry] character of Mexico, the fatalism of the Indians combined comfortably with the Spanish willingness to endure danger and suffering. Thus, *aguantar* came to mean enduring one's fate bravely and with a certain style."[2] As early as the sixteenth century, Montaigne wrote, "It is the first lesson the Mexicans give their children. When they come out of their mothers' wombs, they thus salute them: My child, thou art come into the world to suffer; therefore suffer and hold thy peace."[3] A certain dignity is implicit in the concept. Another Latino writer, Virgilio Elizando, states, "In our Latino realism, we do not go looking for suffering as if it were something desirable, but neither do we deny it or run away from it. We assume it, transcend it, and dare to celebrate life in spite of it."[4]

Looking back, Viviana often expressed anger at her partner's neglect and abuse, but she also conveyed a certain pride at having stayed the course, living up to the societal expectations of a wife and mother. Perhaps the strongest statement she made in our year of discussions came after her description of Jorge's mistreatment of her and an attempt he made to send her away so that he could invite another woman to live with him. After eight years of marriage, her refusal to leave with her children showed in one sense what Yolanda Nava calls "la fortaleza," or fortitude, "courage and strength of character in the midst of pain, affliction, and hardship."[5] Not only did Viviana resolve to endure her husband's temper and infidelities in order to keep the family together and the children fed, but she also determined that he must continue to carry out his own responsibilities. In her world, if one took on a duty, one endured whatever unpleasantness came along with it.

Perhaps today in another culture and with more resources, the young Viviana might make different choices, but such were her times and circumstances. It may have been that she had neither the courage nor the know-how to refuse an older, aggressive suitor. Her father had previously acted as her protector, reinforcing the patriarchal concept that males make the important decisions. It is possible, also, that as much as she loved her father, she felt some resentment at his control over her social life. Her narrative gives the impression, however, that sixty years later, she still felt she had not acted of her own free will in entering into marriage with Jorge. Only after bearing four

children and struggling to make life tolerable for them did she begin
to find her voice.

> As I got older, my father didn't allow me to go anywhere. I was
> the only girl. He wouldn't allow me to go out except when he
> wished. When we would go, like there was a dance, and the
> young girls would come to invite me—four, five, six girls would
> get together and go around inviting the rest—when he felt like
> it, he let me go, and when he didn't feel like it, he would hide. I
> didn't go out anywhere; I just worked, grinding in the metate,
> and then making tortillas on the griddles. Outside, over the
> wood fire. And washing by hand in washtubs and the like.
>   It never occurred to me to get married young. I had several
> boyfriends, but once I became Jorge's girl, I couldn't escape
> him. I couldn't. He got me and he kept me. I was sixteen when
> I got married. And he was nine years older than I was.
>   He was young when he married the first time. I went to his
> wedding. And when his wife died, I also went to the funeral. He
> had been a widower for three years when he married me. Well,
> he also had several girlfriends. But he ended up marrying me. I
> knew all of his girlfriends, but he didn't know my boyfriends.
> When he spoke to me, I already had a boyfriend. I would say to
> him, "You're a meddler."

Viviana didn't explain why her father gave his permission for the
marriage. It was clear that he did not like Jorge or his reputation.

> I had three more boyfriends before, besides him. They weren't
> anything special, just ordinary. [I ask if they were nice-looking.]
> Yes. They were nice-looking. They were just day workers, work-
> ers on the ranches. But when I got married, Jorge asked for me.
> He asked my father for my hand.
>   At first, my father didn't like Jorge, because he was known to
> be of bad character, to have a hot temper. He beat his first wife.
> He had a bad reputation because he had treated his first wife
> wrong. For that reason, they didn't want me to marry him. But
> by then I couldn't escape. I couldn't do anything that would get
> rid of him as my boyfriend. He threatened that if I wouldn't

marry him, he would kill me. He also said, "If you don't marry me, I will come in and drag you out." That's why I married. From the first, he threatened me. I didn't marry for love. I was married by force. I was afraid of him.

A frightened adolescent, Viviana saw no alternatives to marrying. Looking back, she remembered a grand celebration with its abundance of food, the night-long party, and the unusual conveyance she and her new husband used to make their exit. Some of the neighborhoods and small villages of the central Mexican plateau were crossed by railroad segments, privately owned and built to transport ore and other products produced on the ranches.[6] Viviana wasn't sure what the handcars were called, but she explained clearly enough what she meant.

Weddings in Mexico used to last all night. They would end about ten the next day. There they made a lot of food and a lot of coffee. All the food was made outside, because they didn't have kitchens. They made a kind of bower, a roof, with branches, and under the bower they made the food. If there was coffee left in the morning when the wedding was about to end, they would put out the fire with the coffee. There it was customary to have big pots, with lids. These pots had three legs on the bottom, and they were made of clay.

For the wedding, they killed a pig, a yearling calf, they killed chickens, and more food, a lot of food. With the meat of the pig, they made a dish called *asado,* roast pig.

I made my own wedding dress. I made the dress and the undergarments. Jorge bought only the crown, the gloves, the veil, and the shoes. And there weren't cars, like now. There were those . . . what they called platforms. They were run on a rail. They called them jalopies or platforms [handcars], and that was the car we took when we were married. [We both laugh.]

[I ask if she has any photos of her wedding.] Now there are lots of ways one can get photos, but there weren't any then. There were those who took pictures before in the old days, and they brought those cameras with water. They took pictures of the people and took out the film and put it in water, and later they took out the picture. But also, since there wasn't money,

well, we never even saw anyone to take our pictures. Later, the
children asked us, "Well, why didn't they take pictures when
you were married?" And, "Why didn't you have any money?"
We didn't have any money. With very little, we got married.
[She's laughing.] With almost nothing.

Of Mexico's sixteen million inhabitants in the early 1900s, two-
fifths were of mixed indigenous and foreign ancestry.[7] Viviana and
her husband brought a mix of ethnic heritages to their marriage. I
didn't ask her at the time, but when she used the term "pure Mexican," she seemed to be making the point that her maternal grandparents were Mexicans of Spanish descent, as opposed to the Indian
ancestors on her father's side.

The phrase "pure Mexican" is a misnomer, of course, most likely
based on the *casta* system instituted by Spain in the 1600s. The system awarded the highest prestige to those of full European descent,
less standing to mixed-bloods, or mestizos, and inferior status to the
fully indigenous Indians.[8] After the Spanish conquest, Indians' status
had shifted erratically from conquered peoples to "savages without
souls" to "human . . . not animals," albeit humans who must be controlled and protected.[9] Even after the Spanish Crown and the Catholic Church decided that indigenous peoples should be accorded title
to large areas of communal land, thus enhancing the economic status
of many, their social position rose only slightly. The name *Indian* had
become a deprecatory term.

The issue revolves primarily around color. In *Mexican Voices/
American Dreams,* Marilyn Davis quotes a Mexican American woman
whose family still harbors racist attitudes. "I was brought up with the
notion that it was much better to be white. . . . my grandmother
would have nothing to do with anyone who was dark . . . . my father's
favorites are the two lightest in my family, and the one he picks on
most is the darkest. . . . It has something to do with . . . the light soul
or the dark soul."[10] Noting her Indian ancestry, one might wonder
whether Viviana and even her parents could have believed she would
be "marrying up" if she wed the light-complected Jorge. She was
mestizo, a mix of Indian and Spanish, the largest racial category in
Mexico,[11] while Jorge was of European descent.

My father grew up an orphan. My grandfather, I didn't know him—the father of my father—was an Indian. My grandmother was Mexican, and my grandfather was Indian. He was an Indian but I don't know if he was Tarahumaro or what tribe he was. When I married Jorge, both were dead. Therefore, I didn't know my grandparents on my father's side. On my mother's side, I did know my grandparents. My grandparents on my mother's side were pure Mexicans.

Jorge was white. Only he didn't have blue eyes, because he was partly of another race, but I don't know if it was German or something else. He wasn't of pure race. I'm not either. I have Indian blood.

Jorge said that here there are all races—Japanese, Indians, Negroes, Mexicans, whites—well, we don't know what type of white someone is. Now I remember, Jorge had French blood. That's why he was white, also. His grandma's mother was French. I knew only two sisters-in-law. One was named Lupe, and the other Juana. And all of them were very light, very white. They resembled Jorge's mother and his father, my father-in-law. He was white, he wasn't dark.

The couple began their married life with little in the way of material possessions and perhaps even less in the way of emotional and spiritual bonding. The homesick girl found herself immediately subjugated by a jealous and controlling husband. Since Jorge was a ranch hand, the couple's hut was within walking distance of Viviana's parents' home, but that proximity did her little good. Isolation is an effective instrument of control, and Jorge exercised it immediately. Even though the new Mexican Constitution of 1917 had given women liberation from male domination and economic servitude,[12] most of the poor and uneducated remained unaware. Life for Viviana would remain untouched by such liberal ideas.

Even other women were not helpful. Karen Anderson notes, "As in Anglo culture, women often enforce patriarchal authority . . . even when it subjects other women to physical abuse."[13] She adds that mothers and mothers-in-law in patriarchal cultures at times urge their sons to beat their wives;[14] and Maria Elena Lucas, having watched her mother suffer abuse for years, comments ironically, "That is what a good woman does."[15] Lucas herself experienced a similar fate in her first marriage when her new mother-in-law exhorted her son to straighten Maria Elena out, meaning to beat her.[16]

> The bed we had wasn't a bed like these we have now. It was a bed made of carrizo, of reeds. Jorge made the bed from thick reeds, woven. He tied it with agave, thick reeds. And some quilts—they weren't mattresses, they were quilts. They didn't have mattresses. [She laughs.] Because the people were very poor.
>
> From the beginning, he treated me badly. Right after we were married, he began to beat me. No, well, out of jealousy, and he didn't want me to go to my mother and father's house. But I used to sneak out, and when he came home from work, he went first to the neighbor lady and afterward to my house. And the neighbor would tell him when I went to visit my mother. "Well, Viviana went to see her mother," this señora told him. When he got back from work, he was already mad at me. And immediately he hit me because . . . [I interrupt to ask why the neighbor ratted on her.] Well, it's that, there are . . . there are bad neighbors, who are gossiping about you, so that the husband treats you badly, mistreats you. If he is good, he holds back, and if not, well, you pay for it. I was pretty beaten up by him.
>
> Anyway, when someone gets married in Mexico, she should think carefully whether it is good to marry or not. [De todos modos cuando una se casa allá en Mexico, debe de pensar bien si es bueno casarse o no.] Before long she's going to be disillusioned about that boyfriend . . .

The child of a loving father with a stable job and a strong sense of integrity, Viviana had just married a near-penniless day laborer whom she describes as revealing no love in his heart and having a hair-trigger temper. Besides adapting to his volatile personality, she soon had another radical change of lifestyle, becoming in actuality a kind of nomad, following Jorge's work from season to season.

> His first job after we were married was to care for the boss's pack mules in the mountains. He had already married me. So

I went with him to the mountains, to cook for him. We didn't have anything; he didn't have a house. Nothing. Outside, only outside. There we built the fire outside; we had nothing, nothing.

We didn't stay there very long, two weeks at a time, there in the mountains. Because we would go there and I would take my metate with me to grind *nixtamal* and then make the tortillas.[17] Then after two weeks our provisions would run out, and we would come back to the ranch to get more. In the mountains, we stayed under a little roof, not a hut, just the shade of the trees. When it rained, well, everything got wet because there wasn't anywhere to take shelter, to get into. There you would just curl up into a ball . . . because there wasn't anywhere.

For almost the majority of the year we lived in the mountains with the mules, because the work down on the ranch had stopped . . . and the mules were taken to the mountains to forage for food. The mules went down to the water by themselves. But the caretakers always had to check on them in case they were short a mule or a horse or whatever, so that it didn't get into the water and drown or wander off. They had to be vigilant.

When the time came to go back to work, then, the other workers all went back down to the ranch, to take up their jobs. And from there in the mountains, we would come to get food supplies. We would get, well, enough to eat for fifteen days. Just corn and rice, beans. The corn was for nixtamal. And we had to take lime for the nixtamal.

There were only two of us wives, my baby's godmother and me, there in the mountains, and some old women who were there alone. They were tending cows. Their cows grazed freely on the mountainside. Their only concern was to be ready to herd them together when they went down the mountain so that they weren't missing any cows. Because one could be snared out there in some mesquite by the head or some other part. Even if only one animal was missing, they would go look for it.

Those who round up the cows, the mules, are foremen, *caporales*. The caporales would come check on them there. They would ask the old women, "How are my animals here—those belonging to Sancho?"

"Well, they're fine . . . they're fine, Chaya . . . they're still fine. The others are around here also." The animals would come to the water. There was a very large canyon with water. They came and drank and then went back again, back up the hill.

Those old women were the first ones who had the little huts. We, no, we didn't have anything. They had, each one had her little house.

Once when we came down to the ranch from the mountains, I was already expecting Mercedes. Jorge came on a horse, and I came on another horse, a mare—the male horse's companion. That's how I came to the ranch to get provisions. [I ask if Jorge thought it was necessary to provide a house for a wife who was expecting a baby.] No. No. No.

We suffered a lot in Mexico. A lot. It was his fault. He was very neglectful. We suffered a long time, a long time.

Viviana had her first child without her own home and certainly without the help of a doctor. She credited God with helping her through her birthings, but she didn't seem to remember them as especially traumatic. Perhaps her pride in her children overbalanced any negative memories. With the birth of her daughter Mercedes, seventeen-year-old Viviana was beginning to establish her value as a wife. Karen Anderson argues that within the Mexican heritage, a wife could prove herself through domestic toil and obedience to her husband, but her most effective means of creating viability was pregnancy. "Maternity provided the main source of dignity and self-respect available to Mexican women in a system otherwise predicated on a radical distrust and devaluation of women."[18] Considering that males were often valued more than females,[19] Viviana may well have gained some additional self-esteem from the fact that she bore mostly sons.

I had all of my children without doctors because there in Mexico there weren't many doctors. But God helped me so that I had no problems when I had my children.

Mercedes was born in 1928. In '30, Roberto was born, and in '32 Beatriz was born. Then in '34, César. And in '37, Vicente, the one who is in Texas. From then on, I had six boys in a row—six boys. I have eight boys in all.

After becoming a mother, Viviana did get her own shelter, one perhaps similar to what *National Geographic* described in 1914: "Cheer and comfort are scarcely known to the peons' habitations. They are usually without the luxury of windows, the door serving to admit all the light that enters. . . . The poorer huts have merely a hole in the wall as a means of entrance and exit."[20]

By the time I had two children, we had the little huts, the little houses. It isn't the same as a house. Just one room, and the kitchen, that was all. The kitchen was outside, for cooking.

We made the little huts with *quiotes* [cactus stems], the quiotes that grow in the mountains. They are very large stems. Those quiotes are eaten. But there are some the people don't get a chance to eat, and they get hard. They dry out. Those quiotes serve as the roof and the sides of the house. Anyway, we would get along. We built with dirt, we built with a lot of mud. And then we would plaster them. That's how the quiotes held together. We would gather them and then plaster them . . . so that the room would be warm. We made only one room. What did we need with more?

They built the huts not too straight, because if they made them too straight, whatever they put on top would run off—mud or whatever. And they built them rather low so that the roof wouldn't leak. They would put on the carrizo leaf, and then on top of the carrizo leaf they would put the mud, mud they made with the shovel. They would dig a well, and there they would make the mud, enough, and then mix in the straw—to make it stronger. There the houses don't have a door. Not like here, where all the houses have doors. We hung canvas in the door.

Outside, Jorge would dig me a deep hole, and he would put the wood there. The hole was to put the comal in. The comales are round, and they are of solid iron. They have three legs. You put the comal there, and you put the nixtamal in it. Our life was very hard, very poor.

In the winter, one would need blankets. One would make a fire on the ground. And then we would bring the coals inside to heat us. Because, well, that was all one had. Blankets to keep warm. Well, one got along very well; everything was done in

God's name. God gives us the strength to endure, that's all there
is to it.

As the children kept coming, the family began to move from place
to place in search of better wages, but Jorge could not find work that
paid more. I asked how Viviana managed to clothe her children with
so few resources. She did not say whether she had made clothes for
her younger brothers when she was still living at home, but it seems
likely. Having made her own wedding dress, she was already skilled
with needle and thread.

> Down there in Mexico, you didn't go around buying new
> clothes for the baby. No. With what would you buy them? I
> made the little shirts from Jorge's shirts or from my dresses
> for when they were born. The diapers—there they call them
> *pavigos*, or *mantillas*—I also made those from rags, the diapers.
> With what would you buy them if you didn't have any money?
> You didn't have any. So, well, I made do however. I also made
> for the girls, for Beatriz and Mercedes, dresses from little flour
> sacks. By hand. And without any little underclothes, nothing
> else, nothing more than the simple little dress. That was all.
>   For the boys, from Jorge's pants, I would make their little
> pants. I would open them and then cut them from the back and
> then fold them. From Jorge's shirts, from the back, I would
> make their little shirts, also. [I suggest that also she had to mend
> the clothes by hand when the children tore them.] Yes. But I
> sewed them well. Oh, the thread, I would pull it out and pull it
> out again and fold it. [O el hilo, lo sacaba y lo volvía a sacar y lo
> doblaba.] And then I would put a knot on them to sew them.
> So they wouldn't come apart. And my blankets—I also made
> them by hand.
>   And I would alter, put patches on Jorge's pants. Here the
> only thing left the original color of the pants was the waistband.
> [Acá ya nomás le faltaba pura cintura, pa' que fuera del color del
> pantalón.] They were nothing but patches. No one had three
> or four pairs of pants. There wasn't anything to buy them with.
> And then after the kids, well, with what? There was scarcely
> enough to buy clothes for Jorge.

It was clear from her narrative that if Jorge recognized how resourceful Viviana was, he gave no sign. Her skills stretched the available food, provided clothing, and contributed to cleanliness as much as possible. Fine and Weis argue that to a certain extent, "good mothering" requires resources: money, time, and freedom from violence.[21] With scarcity in all of those areas, Viviana coped.

Her memories of those early hardships led to a discussion of things taken for granted in modern middle-class life. To those who have never lived without refrigerators, sewing machines, and automatic washers, those appliances don't seem miraculous, but to those who have lived without, they are the ultimate in convenience.

As for me, like this dress, if I had only this dress, in the night every three or every four days, I would take it off to wash it. Because I didn't have a change. Now people have the closet full of clothes to wear. Like this dress and other dresses, when I take them off, I don't want them any more. Don't you put yours away in a box and give all the old stuff away, and buy new?

We didn't have iceboxes or stoves. There were only coal and wood heaters. The stoves were the same, of coal and wood. At night when we got ready to go to bed, we would put in a lot of wood or coal. It would run out and we would get up to put more in so the house would be warm. Because we didn't have furnaces.

I told you we washed in bathtubs, in a tub with a washboard. We didn't have built-in bathtubs like now. There were some long bathtubs, and those you bought to bathe in with water from a bucket. We made a fire outside with wood to heat the water to bathe. Well, just so it was warm.

Now women don't have to struggle with anything. They just push [a button on] the machine to wash the clothes. They take the clothes out and put them in the dryer, and there it is. In a little while or longer, it's done. And before, we didn't have those kinds of things. Our cooler for the meat was in the middle of the window, in between the glass and the screen. There we put the meat and closed it because there were so many flies. The milk, we bought it only for today and for tomorrow morning. That was all, because it would spoil—it would go bad. It was harder in those days than now.

The couple's poverty was not a result of indolence on Jorge's part. Expropriation of land during the Díaz administration had created a vast pool of rural labor that depressed wages and kept them low.[22] Earnings of fifty cents a day would scarcely buy a family adequate food, let alone other necessities. Viviana emphasized that her husband was a hard worker, a character trait she admired in him.

> Jorge was born in Texas, but he grew up in Mexico. He became a man there, and he worked at all types of jobs. Nothing was difficult for him, nothing. He was a very good worker. It didn't matter to him whether it was cold or really hot. He worked where it was possible to work. He wasn't a man that one calls useless, that finds it difficult to work, where to work, or how to work. He would do anything. And my sons are the same. It doesn't matter to what job they are put, they do it.

Mining, farming, and stock raising were the main industries of the ranches on the plateau,[23] providing a variety of jobs from cooking to field labor. Hard liquor and its production had also figured in the lives of the country people. *Pulque*, an alcoholic drink made from the agave (maguey) plant, had been popular in the region since Toltec times.[24] By the nineteenth century, the most commonly produced liquor from the maguey was mescal, and the distilling of mescal resulted in tequila.[25] Countrywide, in 1911, the maguey and cereal beverage industry was worth ten million dollars per year.[26] No matter what the industry, though, day workers saw little return for the long hours they put in. Whether Jorge found it difficult to hold a job or he simply kept changing positions to try to make more money, over the years he worked at an assortment of occupations.

> At one time Jorge was a cook; he took care of the kitchen and washed dishes and everything. He was also a coal worker. He worked with the coal, and he worked with the whiskey. Before he got married. Well, they call it whiskey, they call it *sotol* [grain alcohol], they call it *mezcál*.
>
> Are you familiar with peyote? [She probably means maguey here. The two are often confused, but liquor is made from the maguey plant.] They made liquor from those plants. They

would pull the heads off from below. Then they would make a kind of oven with mud, with sludge. They made them big and then covered them with brush, and made the covering pretty thick. They would light [the maguey heads] with a match, and they would stay that way for three or four days, a week, until that stuff was thoroughly burned.

When I was nineteen, my father-in-law showed me how they did it. When they were ready, the cooks would grab a little stick and poke the heads with the stick in the oven. If air came out, they were ready. And when none came out, they were raw and they would put them to cook again. Then they would take them out of there, and they had mills; there they suspended them so the whiskey could strain out. It comes out like honey, like sugar cane. They sell it. It's good. From this same stuff they make a type of food called *cajeta* [caramel]. It's a sweet food. It's good also. All of that comes from the maguey.

Jorge suffered a lot in Mexico. He would go to work in the fields with nothing more than a tortilla with chile—two or four tortillas. And if there wasn't any chile, only with salt and that's it. That was his whole lunch—a very small lunch. Very hard. Very hard.

And he took his bottle of water. There in Mexico they call them "canteens." They are portable clay canteens—little canteens. And if they don't have canteens, there are gourds; those gourds come from plants like watermelons. They grow large, the plants. Some of them you carry tandem and others on a little belt for carrying gourds—with the belt here around the waist. And that was what he carried.

But after we were married, my father had a few cows, and he gave Jorge one. Then after that, he took his bottle of milk to the fields, and his tortilla with chile.

By the early twentieth century, the highlands in this north central plateau, though still well timbered in some areas, were experiencing a high demand for wood, both for export and for domestic energy. The nation was energy poor, struggling with few coal reserves, no dams or reservoirs for hydroelectric power, and ignorance of their natural gas reserves.[27] Dependence on wood, including

charcoal, had denuded much of the timberland near densely popu-
lated areas.[28] Thus, foraging for and hauling wood provided another
means of making a living. Moving the family to a village called Jauja
in the southwestern part of Coahuila, Jorge tried this line of work.

> Later on, Jorge carried the wood in wagons, like those in
> wagon trains. He would gather the wood to sell, and I gathered
> some for the house. Every third day, he would bring a wagon
> of wood and sell it for twenty-five pesos. I went with Jorge out
> in the countryside. I carried my armful of wood for me, and he
> brought his wagon. He would fill it really full of wood. With
> those twenty-five pesos every third day, we supported ourselves.
> Today we went for the wood, then the day after tomorrow. He
> would deliver to a bakery that used wood fires. Today, the bak-
> eries use electricity.
>
> There were two bakeries, so he would sell to one, and the
> next day, he would sell to the other. And if there wasn't a sale for
> him, then he would go to another little ranch to sell the wood.
> Every week twice a week, he would go for the wood.
>
> Twenty-five Mexican dollars. What was that? It wasn't
> money, then. With this money we bought all our food—very
> cheap everything, very cheap. We were eating beans from the
> *jarro* [a ceramic Mexican pot]. We couldn't buy butter. We
> didn't eat bread—how would we have bought any?—only tortil-
> las. Beans from the jarro—with chile, that was all. There wasn't
> any coffee—with what would we have bought coffee? Water.
> We suffered much then.

One reason Jorge may have decided to sell wood independently
was that his jobs on the ranches paid so poorly. Ranch workers often
owed almost as much as they had earned at the end of a harvest.
Because wages, even in the relatively prosperous area of Coahuila,[29]
where the family was living, did not come close to meeting expenses,
having a job did not mean a worker might make enough to feed his
family. Those who had any jobs at all, however, were better off than
the poor who had to resort to begging. Writer William Showalter,
after a trip to Mexico in 1914, related his impression of the large
numbers of supplicants in the streets: "Beggars flourish everywhere.

'*Un centavo, señor,*' rings in your ear day and night."[30] Viviana took pride in her family's having avoided that fate, giving credit to her hardworking husband.

> Yes, we were very poor, but we never, with all of my children, we never went begging, never, never. Jorge was a man of his obligation. [She begins to weep.] There in Mexico and here, he worked very hard to support them. My children never went begging for a lunch, a little taco, never. We ate what he brought us.

Although she admired Jorge's work ethic, Viviana was equally as forthcoming about his infidelities as she had been about his physical abuse. She mentioned his unfaithfulness first when relating his attempt to send her back to her father about eight years into their marriage.

> Once he wanted to send me to my father. He was flirting with another woman. He didn't feel his obligation to support his children. And I didn't go. He wanted to have another woman. He wanted me to go packing to my father and mother.
>
> He tried to run me off. "Get out. There are four roads. Take whichever you want. After all, I wasn't born with a woman. I wasn't born with children . . ."
>
> How would my father have supported four more? No. There they do only day labor, the workers, in the fields. Father was the foreman there, but what he made wasn't enough for them. Because they were four—my father, my mother, and my two brothers. And then yet I arrive with four more? My father had no business raising a family that wasn't his, struggling with a family that wasn't his. I didn't go, I didn't go, I didn't go. I never, never left him. Never. Instead I took it! I took it! I took it!

Viviana's words, *aguanté, aguanté, aguanté,* could be translated several ways. I chose the words, "I took it! I took it! I took it!" in an attempt to capture the passion in her speech and to reinforce the plosive (stop) sounds of the *t*'s in *aguanté*. The sharp consonants indicate the intensity with which she expressed the memories of those difficult times. There was pride in the statement—she was, after all, both subverting Jorge's plans to live with another woman and avoiding the shame of going back to her father—but what I heard more strongly was her determination. The person who is himself injured while rescuing someone else from certain death on a snow-covered mountain may wonder at being asked why he did it. His response is not a matter of pride so much as an assertion of what had to be done.

With motherhood, Viviana was coming into her own as an adult. Her primary responsibility was not to obey her husband before all else; the lives and care of her children had to be weighed. Jorge's demand that she leave must have seemed absurd and frightening. The welfare of four children mattered more than cultural dictates such as that expressed in a working-class newspaper during the age of Porfirio Díaz: "To be a wife is to be a woman preferably selected . . . for her docility."[31] Or as Octavio Paz wrote, "A woman is expected to be a pure, long-suffering wife and mother. . . . The father is the undisputed head of the stereotypical Mexican family. He has a domineering relationship with his wife and children."[32] The contradiction Viviana saw in this logic was that Jorge would be no father at all if he sent his family away.

Not a healthy social structure, the pattern of male domination often contributed to domestic violence, alcoholism, infidelity, and abandonment,[33] taking its toll on the Mexican family. Viviana may have felt caught in a web of violence and lack of respect from which the economy and the culture offered her no way out, but she still expected Jorge to meet his responsibilities as a father. He had not demonstrated the familial contributions she had seen in her own father—love, tenderness, and respect—but until he tried to send her away, he had provided financially. Now he was trying to shirk that role as well. By standing up to him, she asserted her own authority in the only way she could.

> I would think to myself, "Well, why should I leave? Since he's the one with the obligation? No, I'm not going. He must support them by any means." And no . . . we never even separated, we never left each other, nothing. I took it all.
>
> It's very important, the responsibility of marriage. It's a responsibility you are taking on. As much for the woman as

the man. A responsibility also to share the burden with the husband, and the husband with his wife. Not to take advantage of the man because he is good, or for the man to take advantage of the woman because she is good.

[A friend of mine once asked Viviana how she felt when Jorge would leave her at home and chase other women. Was she sad? Did she cry?] Why would I cry? Because he was out there running around? I was only frightened because we almost always lived on ranches outside of town. And us with one of those huts that didn't have a door, only a piece of canvas. And on the side of the road. I was afraid that someone would come in there and whack me, with my kids there and everything. Because he was out with the happy women, he was gone.

Perhaps because she saw marriage as a contract that her husband was breaching, or perhaps because she had not felt loved or cherished from the beginning of the relationship, Viviana wasted no emotion on jealousy or grief at her husband's philandering. As in any marriage, the interplay between Viviana and Jorge was complex. We can only surmise what cultural and psychological factors influenced Jorge's attitudes toward his wife, but Viviana's narrative makes it clear that, although she began her marriage in fear and subsequently became frustrated with her husband's cruelty and faithlessness, she was also able to give credit where credit was due. When one lives day-to-day with another, she sees the whole person, weaknesses, strengths, and ambivalences; and commitment to work was one of Jorge's strengths. As one Mexican American told Marilyn Davis, "For the poor person work is like medicine."[34] When a body has it, it functions optimally. Even when inadequately compensated, work represents an attempt to deal with life constructively.

Inadequate pay, however, drains the worker and the entire family. It seems possible, even likely, that no matter how many hours of drudgery he put in, the stress of not being able to support his family could have contributed to Jorge's attempt to send his wife and children away. In a discussion of how sexist roles oppress men, Irene Blea reports that "the very nature of the socially defined male gender role" contributes to men having more successful suicides, ulcers and heart attacks, "more social alienation . . . and lack of appropriate social skills."[35] Viviana recognized that her husband's life included multiple frustrations.

> The suffering is worse there than here. Because here when you start with a rancher, you ask for a loan until you start working. He gives you the loan, and you go and get your flour, your potatoes. You work and then you pay the rancher. And there, no one loans you money because you don't have work. So the people can't figure out what to do.

Jauja was about a half-hour's bus ride from Torreón, a bustling commercial center just across the state line from Durango. I asked Viviana what the area was like and if they were able to find more comfortable living accommodations there than the huts she had been used to.

> One caught the bus there for Torreón. Or Gómez. Or Lerdo. All of those little towns are there. One little town, sort of a little ranch, they call Luchianas. El Banco. Pompella. All of those are just little ranches. Well, we call them little ranches, but they are tiny little towns. The little ranches are like one, one, two, or three little houses. That is a little ranch.
>
> No, we didn't find a better house. Well, what would we have left? The twenty-five pesos would be gone immediately, just on food. We had to buy, like, for today, we bought food. And then we had to buy food for the next day . . . and then for the day after tomorrow when he would go over there to get more wood.
>
> We lived in a little room that Jorge built. They let him use a little corner by a house. He built a little room there and put a roof on it. With only one wall. It was a room. That was all. It was the kitchen and it was the dining room, and it was for sleeping and everything. That one room was everything. [I ask if she helped to build it.] Me, no, the boys. Just little tots that they were, he would order them to help him. And hurry it up, get a move on. [Así chiquillos como estaban, los mandaba pa' que lo ayudaron. Y ándale, y ándale.] In little canisters with the mud, and a rope to pull them up to the top for the roof. Jorge never let the kids get lazy . . . run around in the streets. He showed

them really well how to work . . . whatever work he gave them, they worked. They didn't go around saying no.

Just as her husband worked hard at various jobs, Viviana put in long, demanding hours as a young mother. When she wasn't making clothes, carrying water, or cleaning, she was cooking over an open fire or watching out for the health and safety of her active children. Although they were full of mischief, Viviana took pleasure in hearing the sounds of children around her.

> Well, I told you that my work was washing by hand, and then, kneading and making tortillas, of flour, because there weren't any ready-made ones. They didn't want bread; they wanted only tortillas. But like now everything is already made. And there are tortillas of dough, flour tortillas. One doesn't have time to knead the dough in order to make tortillas. Now, no. [I ask if the tortillas she made herself were better than the store-bought ones.] Oh, yes. Yah, yes. [We smile at this.] Yes, well, I can still make them.
>
> The children were naughty and always into things. Well, Roberto was very serious. He was growing up very serious; he didn't like to play. The others, yes. They liked to play and everything, but Roberto was a loner, very solitary. He didn't have much schooling, but he's smart about some things now that he is older. The others were mischievous, all of them. . . .
>
> Mercedes was the smartest; she had the quickest mind. Well, all of them were very intelligent, all of them, from the time they were little. And the others, well, intelligent and full of shenanigans. There are babies who are very creative, that is to say who are very ardent, very eager to please, very smart about doing things. And there are other children who are not interested in anything.
>
> Well, I never had any trouble with my kids. Yes, they were naughty, but they weren't bad kids—kids who run in the streets, doing bad things, in gangs, with the other kids. No. But there weren't any bad kids around; we were on a ranch. There the ranches are like little towns where there are only school and games for the kids, ball games for them to play. That's all. All the kids could be heard playing there on the ranches. In the city,

no, in the city are lots of people; the youth are like here, very . . .
"disoriented."

She seemed to enjoy the incident in which a teacher corrected her
husband because he showed no compassion toward today's youth.
Her delight, however, may have had as much to do with seeing her
husband in a position where he had to respect someone's opinion, in
this case, a female's, as it did with the issue at hand.[36] She herself
expressed some disgust with young people who show no respect for
their elders or for tradition.

> One time a teacher corrected Jorge because he said, "Today's
> youth are very bad, troublemakers." Then the teacher said, "No,
> sir, that's not the word. The word is, 'They are disoriented.'
> Because," she said, "they are lost. Today's youth are lost. Now
> they want to do just whatever they please."
>
> Now the youth, you order them to do something and they
> don't do it because they didn't hear—or they just don't want to.
> Today's youth don't want you to order them around. We three
> were obedient to my father and my mother. With our aunts and
> uncles, our relatives, we were obedient and respectful. We lived
> near our relatives. There was no such thing as *tú*. No. We used
> *usted*.

Film producer Moctezuma Esparza writes, "I learned from my
dad that if you weren't familiar with someone you used the formal
address, *usted*. To this day when I talk to my aunts and uncles I
address them using *usted*. This form was used as an indication of
respect, including respect for elders. That was also very much a part
of my everyday life."[37] Many Latinos and Latinas who learned the
traditional values comment about the value of showing respect, not
only for elders, but also "for others whom we do not know or who
are different from us." Nava comments that such social action is
"actually a training ground for self-respect."[38] Some of Viviana's children and grandchildren addressed her formally, but others did not.

> It was different—everything—than today. Well, when Bea-
> triz comes, she shakes my hand. She greets me. My brother,

also, greets me in the old way. It shows respect. And people now, no. Only "Hi." Jorge used to say, "Now they just leave you on 'High.'" [He is scornfully making a play on the word "High," indicating how ludicrous it is to greet someone with a term that means drugged or intoxicated.] Well, César comes and his greetings are only, "What's going on?" That's the way he greets me instead of saying, "Mama, how are you?" Right? [with scorn] "What's going on? What's happening?" This is not greeting each other.

Jorge didn't like any of that because he wanted them to respect him, and he didn't want them to call him "tú." He would say, "Don't call me that. I am not equal with you children. To me you have to show respect because I am not your child." He did not like the kids to call him "tú." And now, no—people call us "tú." César calls me "usted." Memo also calls me "usted." Well, most of them do. The grandkids call me "tú." That is the fault of the parents. . . . Everything is changing. Young people want to go wrong. Everything is changing.

Although there were schools in the region, Jorge believed the children were more valuable helping at home. Neither he nor Viviana had had more than sporadic formal education, a common situation for rural laborers whose first concern was sustenance for the family. One of the most significant achievements of the Mexican government following the revolution was to make education available to the public; by 1940, almost four million children were enrolled in elementary schools, but that still left 41 percent of school-age children unschooled. Nevertheless, the Salguero children did attend school periodically, and Viviana believed they began to develop their talents there. They also managed to get into trouble now and then.

All Jorge did was work. Sometimes he would take one [of the children] out, a day or two from school, so they could help him work. And sometimes they went to school all week. Jorge didn't give them much schooling—because he was taking them to work. He used to go get wood and take Roberto with him so he could help. One time Jorge went to work, and he had to return the wagon full of wood to the baker. So he made Roberto go with him to carry the wood. And I don't know how Roberto fell—it wasn't bad—but he hit himself on the head. Well, here comes Roberto with a little cut on the head. From outside the corral, he was throwing the wood into the corral, and he fell.

My children are all interesting because they know how to do something. All of them. But when they were young, Jorge almost always had them at work. They didn't have time to be curious, to do things out of curiosity—to get a hold of something with their minds. The only thing they would do was, like, with Beatriz and Mercedes, who were the first girls, we didn't have any way to buy them toys. They would make little cars with those sardine cans, with little spools of thread. They would make the little car, and then with some wire, they would put it through here [she demonstrates] and they would fix the wheels so they could turn. [She laughs.] So they could give the dolls a ride. Because there wasn't anything to buy with.

But there in all, they were all very naughty. They would hit each other. When I would hear a scream and I would rush out in a hurry, Jorge would tell me, "You look like a chicken with chicks. As soon as you hear a child scream, there you go." I say, "Well, why not? I don't know what they are doing to each other, or what they are going to do." He would tell me, "Wait on me, wait on me. Leave the children alone." Because there were times when they were playing and there was no end to what they would do. One time I was inside and one of the boys, with those Indian arrows, one of them threw one up in the air, and Memo kept looking and the arrow came and wham! it went into his cheek. So there is Memo with the shaft of this . . . All the kids came. Sancho grabbed it and pulled on it and took it out.

Treating scrapes, cuts, and bruises must have become routine by the time the family was living in Jauja. Two girls and six boys, all of them lively and curious, encountered their share of injuries and illness. One of the most serious incidents happened when Roberto, the oldest boy, was only four, and Viviana had to act as pharmacist, nurse, and doctor.

Well, we struggled with them. The mother struggles more with her children than the father, because the father goes to work and the mother stays home. Roberto got burned, a foot, in Mexico. We were at the ranch, and we didn't have a house. We were living in those shacks that they show on television—here they call them *jacales*—of reed, and it had only one little room. I would make the fire and cook outside. I finished cooking and the fire was almost out, but there was still a fire underneath. And Roberto was riding a reed horse. He would get on it, and there he was, going back and forth and back and forth on the horse. Then he stuck his little foot in the hole with the fire, and he was barefooted. I heard him scream, well, he burned the whole side of his little foot.

But what doctor? There weren't any doctors. . . . [I ask if she knew of herbs or some other healing treatments.] Yes, I cured him with Listerine and Vaseline. I would take the Listerine and then the Vaseline and mix them. Then I would put it on his little foot. He was about four.

As the fire wasn't very alive, he didn't burn himself very much, but his foot is still spotted [scarred]. The top layer of skin never grew back again. You can tell. It is noticeable, but he walks well. He only burned one side.

I made their medicines. They would get sick on me, and I would give them little herbs. I almost never took them to the doctor. No. There is a medicine with a little hose, a tube, to give them an enema. When they had a high fever, I would give them an enema. With the enema they would go to the bathroom, and with the water, it would bring their fever down.

There is a little herb they call *malvas* [cheeseplant]. They grow it here in the US. Cheeseplant. That is boiled, with the water, for the fever. You add it to the medicine, and then you put a little in the tube. And if you don't have the herb, you use warm water with a little soap. There in Mexico there is soap, they call it *pan*. Only a little is added to the water because the soap is strong. With that, the fever is brought down. And if it didn't come down, then I would mix lard with what they call baking soda here. Then I would cover them completely for the fever. Those were my medicines.

Curanderas, or healing women, passed the knowledge of herbs down through the generations, trusting what their grandparents before them had learned. In the words of one such woman from New Mexico, "Mexican herbs. That's all you need—that is the reason God put all those herbs on the earth."[39] In one interview, Viviana spoke with me for nearly an hour about various herbal cures, but to my chagrin, the batteries failed on the tape recorder that day. I could never get her to repeat the information. She did not call herself a *curandera,* but it was clear that as a young mother, she had developed a knowledge of cures.

> They would get sick but, even then, Jorge would not take them to the doctor, never. I would struggle with them. There wasn't any money. And then in Mexico, the doctor wasn't close, he was a long way away. There weren't doctors there like here. And if there were stores near there, with what would I buy anything? [Besides], in the stores, sometimes there were medicines, and sometimes not. People would come in to sell herbs in some baskets, big baskets with handles. They would come in to sell little bunches of herbs—chamomille, rose of castille, and wormwood. All of those herbs are good for the stomach. A little. Because they are very bitter. One would buy that if she had the wherewithal. And if not, she didn't buy it. With what? That's why almost no one there sees doctors. They are cured only with herbs. Only with herbs. And they are better . . . herbs are better than medicines.

3

Crossing the Frontera

1940S

> Really I am suffering doubly. There must be several
> thousand women like me in the fields.
> — *Unidentified migrant worker*[1]

BY 1946, VIVIANA'S NOMADIC MARRIAGE, the bearing of nine
children, and the balancing of her own values and needs against her
husband's unpredictable temper had forged her remarkable strength.
Now she was about to experience another major life change—immi-
grating to a new country. For what she and the family were about to
endure, she would need every bit of that strength. The Salgueros
would make the passage at a time of high demand for agricultural
labor in the United States, but their situation was still precarious.
Jorge had been born in Texas, but after moving to Mexico with his
father in 1916, he had never documented his US citizenship. He had
returned as a laborer without papers in the early forties, crossing and
recrossing the border undetected.

With the war over and the world agricultural market thriving,
many laborers were entering the United States under the legal
auspices of the Bracero program. Texas farmers, however, wanted
to avoid what they considered the bureaucratic controls of the
government-sanctioned program and sought politically powerless
labor over which they could exercise complete control.[2] Even when

Texas governor Coke Stevenson did request some Bracero labor, Mexican authorities refused to send braceros to Texas because of egregious racial prejudice in the state.[3] Workers were often shunted into colonies or camps, inadequately housed, poorly fed, and severely discriminated against.[4] Indeed, such discrimination would become a significant focus of Viviana's concerns as she described the family's lives in the following decades.

Either unaware of or undeterred by these drawbacks, Jorge decided to resettle the family in Texas. By selling what few possessions they owned and sending four children to live with the elder daughter, Mercedes, who had married by this time, the family managed to scrape together enough cash to travel 340 miles northeast to the border. Migrating families often had to separate, leaving all or some of their children behind with relatives or older siblings.[5] Jorge and Viviana brought the three oldest boys and the baby, who was still nursing. Leo Chavez has compared the migrant experience to more conventional rites of passage, with their three phases of separation, transition, and incorporation.[6] The first stage, the actual leaving of one country and moving to another, requires leaving behind not only family but also any sense of security and structure one might have known.

According to Viviana's eldest son, Roberto, the six Salgueros rode the bus from Torreón through the states of Nuevo Leon and Tamaulipas to the crossing point,[7] and then resumed the trip on foot.[8] Viviana never mentioned the bus trip, however. Her memories were of endless walking with a baby at her breast, hiding from immigration authorities, and enduring the harshness of the elements. Some oral historians maintain that "reminiscences can rose-color or soften the past,"[9] but that didn't seem to be the case with Viviana. Perhaps her sorrow and anger were reinforced by the knowledge that things could have been different.

It is possible that Jorge was not aware of his citizenship status, but Viviana clearly believed he just didn't want to bother going through official channels. Basing many of his hopes on finding his siblings in Texas, he made no effort to go to the American consulate in Mexico, either to obtain papers for himself or to register his children as US citizens. He chose instead to bring the family over the border in stealth, a decision for which his wife never forgave him. They crossed

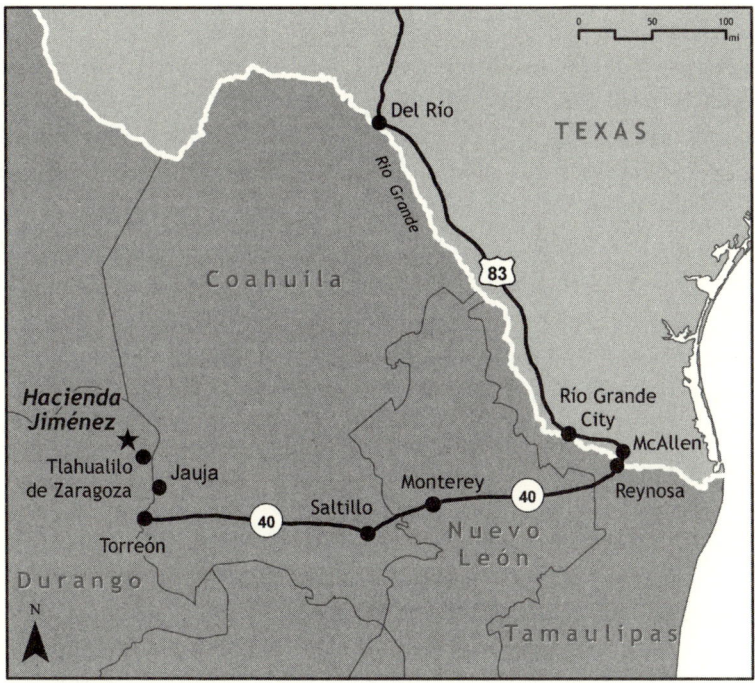

I. Route the Salgueros took from Torreón to Rio Grande City and then later northward through Texas in 1946 (drawn by Colin Kamemoto)

to the new country quietly, shrouded by secrecy, braving the frontier "we dare to cross only at night,"[10] as Carlos Fuentes describes the border between Mexico and the United States. Jorge may have harbored a long-standing distrust for the authority of governmental institutions. He had grown up in a border culture where rules were often flouted,[11] and his father, who did not always stay on the right side of the law, lost most of the family property through failure to go through legal channels. Jorge may also have feared not having evidence enough to prove his citizenship and therefore losing face as well as the opportunity to work.

Viviana did not say what she had expected of life "on the other side" or, indeed, even whether she wanted to leave Mexico and come north. She may have shared Jorge's hope that he and the older children could find steady work and pull the family out of poverty. Marilyn Davis maintains, however, that no one "ever has a realistic view of the United States before arriving, and it can never live up to their expectations, either as a place or in the possibility of fulfilling their dreams."[12] Considering that moving from one country to another may have been one of the pivotal points of her life, it is notable that Viviana did not describe the actual crossing. Her son told me that they found a boatman, one of several available, to ferry them across the river in the middle of the night.[13] They crossed the Rio Grande, or Rio Bravo del Norte, as it is known in Mexico, near Reynosa in Tamaulipas. This brought them into a rural part of Texas in the Rio Grande Valley near the small town of Hidalgo, where the main crops are citrus, primarily grapefruit and oranges. At the time, the river crossing may not have seemed of major significance to a haggard and exhausted wife, since life improved little from one side of the river to the other. In fact, her story reveals that it became decidedly worse for a while.

> When Jorge had first come to the United States, he came as a day laborer, to pick cotton. He came with some companions. I don't remember what year. Once they finished the contract, then they returned. Then after seeing how we were doing, that we didn't have enough for anything, he decided to come back to the United States to look for his family, to see if he could find them.
>
> When he decided, it was 1946. He wasn't making enough there on the ranch. We came on foot, walking . . . from Mexico to the United States. We arrived in Texas. We suffered because it's far. We walked all day—on foot. And with little Memo. We didn't bring a car or anything. I had Jorge, Ruben, and we had César. And I had little Memo. And Roberto. We left the others in Mexico with Mercedes. We're the only ones who came. [After crossing,] we went more than three days walking through open country, and I was nursing Memo. And hiding from immigration—hoping that Memo would not break out crying and then they would get us. But Jorge was very impulsive. He never thought about making things less difficult before we left Mexico, he didn't think.
>
> At night we stayed near the little towns. We slept outside. And there in Texas, there are many mosquitoes. They call them *mollotes*. There were a lot of them. We needed to have a fire outside, a fire lit all night so they wouldn't come near because

of the smoke. Since Memo was little, and I would fall asleep, they bit Memo on the top of his head and made a sore there. He was tiny. Jorge and another man who had come with us, with a hat—that's all they had for the mosquitoes—tried to protect Memo. There was a water canal where we stayed; that's why there were a lot of mosquitoes.

A lot of sores developed—like blisters, when one has been burned—they came out on his little head. Very ugly. We couldn't get them to heal. With what? We didn't have money, nor did we know anyone there. Only a man who was tending the water canal. He found us in the country. So then he went and told his father that there was a family there. The father came and took us to his son's house. By that time, Memo was in very bad shape from his little head. So they bought me a salve which was very good. I bathed him, and then I put it on him. And he got better. With God's help, that medicine cured the bad spots he had. Yes. Well, God, as I say, is everywhere.

Viviana had lived in the open with nothing but the barest essentials when she was first married, but now she found herself in a strange country with four children to care for and no belongings, not so much as a dish. Not only did the family have no money, at this point they had no social capital either,[14] no network of people who could help them. They had not yet found Jorge's relatives, who could introduce them into the system. Because the job market was strong, however, Jorge did make a contact who helped him find work.

In the mornings, Jorge would go and buy lunch in the little town. We would buy only a little, because the men didn't have much money.

Well, Jorge went to work with a man who was the first friend we found in Texas. He went to work with him, and I stayed to make the lunch for noontime, but we didn't have any dishes, none. So I would go to bring water from the canal, in a bottle. And they said that there was an alligator in that canal. So I went down there to fill my bottle to make the lunch. I filled it, but I spent the whole time watching and watching so that the alligator wouldn't come out and eat me.

Fifty years later she could laugh at herself for her fears of such legends as the alligator in the canal, but it seems only natural that she would have felt exposed and vulnerable. With the exception of the irrigation canals, the area was dry and somewhat desolate, dotted with the thorny brushes of mesquite, acadia, mimosa, and prickly pear. The canals and mesquite provided water and a source of wood for cooking fires.

The Salgueros needed to be resourceful just to keep themselves fed. Researchers have found that women's memories are often shaped by the problems of obtaining and preparing food, reflecting an emphasis on survival.[15] Vicki Ruiz tells the story of an immigrant woman whose mother used a steel barrel as an improvised stove,[16] but Jorge had to be even more creative if the family wanted their tortillas cooked.

> We stayed in the outskirts of town. Jorge wandered around there looking, looking, and found a piece of a bathtub with two sides. And then he beat it good with rocks. [Y luego lo machucó bien, bien, con piedras.] One rock on the bottom and the other on top, and he flattened it. There I kneaded the dough. And I used that piece of bathtub for a griddle. I put it on the fire to make the tortillas.
>
> In those cans—like those they sell with food, like corn, peas, green beans—we would buy for ourselves, but afterward, I would cook in those cans. There I made beans, I made soup in those little cans. Ah, yes, we suffered to come here, to the United States. Because of Jorge's negligence. He didn't get his papers early. Because of his just wandering about, carefree.
>
> We carried lunches, just a little food. Tortillas with beans, with potatoes. We came to the little settlements, and I, with Memo, was not giving the bottle. I was nursing him.

Viviana maintained that she and her family were safe camping near the small towns and villages. As far as they knew, there was almost no crime in the area, and besides, no one had much for anyone to steal.

> The people in the towns were not dangerous as they are today. Now you can't stay outside, because someone will come and

give you a—wop! [she gestures]—hit you with a club. And there in Mexico, no. The people were very harmonious. There wasn't so much discrimination among themselves. They took care of each other. There wasn't a lot of vandalism by trouble-making youths like we see today, hoodlums. I didn't fear that somebody would assault us. The people were very poor, but they were very peaceable. There weren't many crimes here in the United States either in this time. It wasn't like now. One could stay outside in the outskirts of town, and nobody would say anything. Nowadays if you go and stay outside the town, well, there they kill you. They kill you—to rob you. Getting around was safer back then.

Making a living was not necessarily any easier in Texas than in Mexico, however. Historically, whenever the need arose from the 1880s through the 1930s, the United States had encouraged Mexican workers to cross the border as an abundant supply of labor that would work for substandard wages. Treated as expendable, the workers were then deported when the economy soured and domestic unemployment rose.[17] Latino historians point out that the Bracero Program simply continued that cycle.[18] The issue was not solely how many workers were available but what money they would work for. Growers fostered a labor surplus to keep wages down.[19] Federal agencies, state employment agencies, and employers consistently colluded to create the overly large labor pool, "the Bracero Program, the 'green carders,' and the use of illegal Mexican aliens" cases in point.[20] As one grower described the system, "We used to own our slaves, now we rent them from the government."[21]

Undocumented laborers were even more vulnerable than braceros. Caught in this web, the Salgueros were not earning much. Roberto, now sixteen, and César, twelve, put in full workdays when they could and scavenged in the citrus orchards to supplement the family's food supply.

When we arrived from Mexico, Jorge began making two dollars a day. They were paid very little and worked all day. That was in '46. And Roberto was making one dollar, and César was making fifty cents. It wasn't enough money to live on. But then everything was very cheap. It wasn't as expensive as now. We got along OK. No, we weren't eating good things like meat or anything. But we got along. Life was very cheap. Well, God gives one life.

Often we went hungry. As Jorge went to work, sometimes we had tortillas and sometimes we didn't. When we had tortillas, we didn't have anything else. I packed the tortilla with only salt on it, his little taco. I packed him two tortillas, two, for the whole day. If I had chile, the food of the Mexican, well, I grabbed it and spread it on the tortilla. God bless! To work the whole day!

We suffered until Jorge got a job in McAllen, Texas, irrigating. He watered—in Spanish, they call it *hortaliza y viña*— orchards and vineyards. Fruit, grapefruits, lemons, there was everything in that field. Jorge watered them. Then the landlords didn't pay attention to the fruit that was on the trees. The kids, César and Roberto, would go and bring sacks of fruit to the house and they would squeeze it into jars and then . . . [she gestures of drinking deeply].

Jorge had to go asking for a ride so they could take him to the food, and sometimes there wasn't a ride. He would go on foot to bring the food. And it was far, it was a long way. By this time, we had a house, not very little, not very big. But yes, we had a good house.

We didn't bring clothes, only what we had on, scarcely any clothes. And then, they started giving us clothes, the neighbors. Jorge had started to work, and we had started to buy a few clothes, also.

This new job not only brought a steady paycheck, adequate housing, and the means to buy a few extras besides food, but it also gave the family time to try to forge some connections with Jorge's past. Born in Texas in 1902 to Mexican American ranchers, he was the first and only boy in a family of six daughters. His mother, who had evidently been a woman of some means, died when he was young, after which his father formed a new union with a Mexican woman. When World War I began, "many Mexicans left the United States . . . for fear of being drafted,"[22] Jorge's stepmother and her son among them.

Jorge's father soon followed, taking fourteen-year-old Jorge with him and leaving his ranch in the care of an acquaintance. His father's headstrong nature and lack of foresight might shed some light on Jorge's own decision making.

In 1916 Jorge had left Texas as an adolescent, very young. He said that my father-in-law didn't talk to him at all. He never said anything about that ranch he had. When Jorge went to Mexico with his father, he was fourteen years old. My father-in-law did not want to serve the government. He repatriated in Mexico because he did not want to be a soldier. So he left.[23]

My father-in-law never talked to Jorge, like we would say, "You know you're from Texas; you have relatives there." And Jorge didn't make the effort until he was older—to find his relatives. He knew that he was from here. And he knew that my father-in-law had left a ranch. He left, I don't know how many cattle he left, and land, he left it all. But he lost it all. Because after he went to Mexico, he never cared about anything. So Jorge had little sense of purpose, he never cared for anything. I don't know that Jorge didn't think, he was just thinking about other things. He didn't think to say, "Well, man, there in the United States my father left this. I'm going to see how it is or what happened to it." Never. Never.

When Jorge arranged the papers for all of us, the immigration officer here said, "If you knew that you were from the United States, you should have gone to the American consul to register your children. You would have made them Mexican Americans. [Los hubieras hecho méjicanos-americanos.]" But that never occurred to him. The consul asked him, "Why? Why didn't you register each child as it was born with the American consul in Mexico?" He said all of them would have been Americans, as if they had been born here. Jorge didn't know that because he just liked to run around—he didn't pay attention to children, he didn't appreciate them. He couldn't bother to register them, to arrange their papers correctly.

If the elder Salguero had not exactly been a model of prudent thinking, neither had he managed to remain completely on the right side of the law. He was not alone in his transgressions, however. In the border culture, smuggling had been a regular and, in some circles, respected way of life since the 1800s. Most of the citizenry condoned the disregard of customs and immigration laws,[24] especially considering that the Lower Río Grande was separating an ethnically related people, many of whom had family on both sides of the river. Contraband included products from clothing to tequila, and smuggling reflected a kind of indifference toward political boundaries,[25] except by border guards, of course.

Not all of the smuggled goods were benign. During the Mexican wars that began in 1910, the time period that Jorge's father would have been involved, revolutionary general Pancho Villa armed his followers with US guns. Smugglers traded the weapons for cattle Villa was raiding from haciendas in the state of Chihuahua.[26] The way the story came down to Viviana, her father-in-law was not running guns, but the fact that he was shot might indicate that the law thought otherwise.

> My father-in-law was a man who didn't talk to anybody—a very rigid temperament—of bad character. He never said anything about the ranch they had. He didn't say much to anyone. When he wanted to say hi, he would say hi, and when he didn't, no. [You might say], "Good morning, sir." [She gestures that he doesn't even acknowledge the greeting.] When he was in a good mood, he would answer, "How are you, kid?" before you even greeted him. But his nature was very hard.
>
> My father-in-law was also a smuggler. He smuggled things from Mexico to here in the United States. He was smuggling clothes, packets of clothing. Afterward, they smuggled liquor. When they wounded him, he and his companions were carrying a load of clothes. There in Texas, the government employees, the sheriffs, shot him in the leg—one shot. And that's where the bullet stayed. They didn't take it out. He couldn't go see the doctor, because he was a smuggler. He always walked crooked after that.

Jorge's father might easily have been a difficult person no matter what the circumstances, but he had faced some limitations brought about by institutionalized racism in Texas. Among the strategies for keeping Mexican Americans in their place was segregation in the schools and public facilities.[27] Jorge's father would likely have been of school age in the 1870s or 1880s, when south Texas school districts were just beginning to develop their public programs, and before there were many facilities at all for Mexican American children.[28]

> My father-in-law didn't know how to read either. Because in those days, then, the government didn't offer school for the Mexicans. School was only for the whites. They had to have a separate school for the blacks and the Mexicans because they were not admitted with the gringos; they didn't permit them to be together.

Viviana said little about Jorge's mother's personality or strength of character. Had she lived, that cattle ranch might not have caused so many problems for their children. Her death seems to have put into motion an unfortunate chain of events.

> On the ranch, they had cows and sheep—they had goats, also. My mother-in-law, Jorge's mother, had more capital than my father-in-law. When my mother-in-law died, my father-in-law got everything. He did not give any inheritance to the kids. He got it all. He had three hundred and seventy-five acres of land. They bought that land for fifty cents an acre. That's why there are many ranches in Texas that have a lot of land, because they bought it cheap.
>
> After Jorge's mother died, he had a woman, Jorge's step-mother, and this woman went to Mexico. And my father-in-law followed her. There in Mexico, in San Pedro, I believe, the woman left my father-in-law. She didn't want anything to do with him. Afterward, my father-in-law wandered around, struggling, both he and Jorge, working, the two of them. But he liked it there in Mexico, so he didn't come back.
>
> When my father-in-law went to Mexico, he left in charge of the ranch a man he used to call "Mr. Italian." Who knows what his name was? My father-in-law never came back to see that man he had left in charge, so the man kept the ranch. He died, but the children of that Italian were left.

One of Jorge's sisters, Juana—her husband was from Mexico—also went to Mexico. Jorge's other sister stayed here. She was called Lupe, the one who stayed in Texas. And she knew everything. She knew all about the land, how it was and everything, because she stayed here.

Lupe sold fifty acres. Later, when Jorge wanted to claim the land, my sister-in-law said, "Well, I don't know, Jorge. Why are you meddling in things you don't know anything about?" She didn't want Jorge to know that she had sold his fifty acres. [softly] Robber. So, he had 325 acres left, because she had sold fifty. Three hundred and twenty-five acres were left, and those 325 were lost. The ranch, the land, it was all lost.

The struggle to reclaim all or part of the ranch was a losing proposition from the start, rendering the family vulnerable to clever solicitations for money. In the heyday of Chicano activism, the 1960s and 1970s, Reies López Tijerina attempted to help Mexican Americans in New Mexico regain lands that had been fraudulently stolen from them after the Mexican American War. The Salgueros' situation was different, however, in that the loss of the land was due to abandonment and neglect. The older sister Lupe must have had title to at least the acreage she had sold, but that was of little help either.

Much later, when Jorge wanted to fight for the ranch, the one who had been left in charge of it had died. The children of this overseer were left in charge. When he came to reclaim those lands, it had already been sixty years. So by then, the man my father-in-law left in charge had already grabbed all that land and enclosed it. So then when Jorge came, he went to Texas and got a lawyer to investigate that. But it was already very late. Many years had passed, many years.

Now, later, Roberto got a paper, like a newspaper, from Texas, looking for many who had left the ranches and forgotten them there in Texas. They were looking for the families who owned that property because of the oil, the mineral rights. Because the man my father-in-law left in charge of the ranch was in charge of only the land, the surface, but the minerals, no. The minerals, those were separate. The officials in Texas wanted a lot of information; they were looking for the rightful heirs.

Roberto cleared up that that land belonged to my father-in-law. Then they sent a letter to all of the kids telling them that they had to send twenty-five dollars a month. They kept sending us letters, and Jorge had to give them a hundred dollars. And the kids twenty-five dollars. They were like that for a while, and then, they didn't want just twenty-five, they wanted fifty, then more. And they kept asking for more and more, and as I told you, the kids didn't want to send any more money. It was better to lose the ranch. And it was lost.

It was all lost. And César told Roberto, "Well, I want them to give me at least enough to go there and build a shack. At least, I should get enough to go build a house there, even if it's just a shack, to live." Well, no, he didn't get anything, and they lost it all.

Viviana didn't say how Jorge established contact with his sisters, but once he had found his aunts and cousins near the city of Rio Grande, the family was able to tap into a social network. Such networks might consist of family, friends, or a combination of both, but they can make all the difference between going it alone and finding help when needed.[29] Jorge's aunt helped him obtain documentation, some legal and some counterfeit. Until September 11, 2001, fraudulent documents were not difficult to come by, particularly in times of worker shortages when officials made it clear they would look the other way.[30] In fact, the call for labor in the postwar years was so intense that, probably unbeknownst to the Salgueros, immigration officials themselves legalized undocumented workers at the border by providing them with photo identification cards complete with fingerprints.[31] Viviana didn't explain why they obtained false identification even though Jorge had found proof of his birth in Texas, but it likely came about because they needed to go to work immediately. Jorge's sister was a work contractor with connections in the Colorado sugar beet industry. As Viviana described the first few months in Texas, they were full of hard work and hiding from authorities, but after finding Jorge's relatives, her tone changed somewhat to hint at a sense of adventure.

We were only there in Texas temporarily, half a year, six months.
That was when Jorge arranged his papers. He got his certifi-
cate of baptism and his registration. His aunt took him to find
his birth records. She knew that he was born there in Texas. In
Rio Grande City. Formerly, there were doctors, but there wasn't
money to pay for them. She helped the woman who saw to my
mother-in-law with Jorge when he was born. We arranged the
passports; they were fake. We used another surname.

Then my sister-in-law there, Lupe, brought us here to Colorado. Lupe was living in Corpus Christi. She would go to Colorado from Texas and would get contracts with ranchers for
work, in the potatoes, and in the topping, in the beets. When
she came, we came with her because she would load one of
those big trucks. And immigration had no idea that we came
to Colorado. They didn't catch us, or anyone; we got through
freely. And that's why, well, now, I tell them that I have
become one of those blue eyes, now I'm an American citizen.
[We laugh.]

Viviana used the term "blue eyes" more than once to indicate her
status as a US citizen. Dark-eyed and dark-complexioned, she always
used the term with a twinkle in her eyes, as if the idea were rather
amusing, indicating the silliness of a power structure that favored
one eye color or complexion over another. She didn't give the impression of being particularly proud of her skin color (mentioning her
husband's coloring, while never specifically referring to her own),
but she was not willing to accept an inferior status because of it.

The notion of the racially superior blue-eyed race gained a foot-
hold early in American colonial history; Antonia Castañeda writes
with notable sarcasm that for both Native American and Mexican
women, "marriage to the blue-eyed strangers saves them from . . .
the savagery of their race, culture, group, and nation."[32] The term
"blue eyes" is used by older Mexican Americans, though disdained
by many who consider themselves Chicanos.[33] For Viviana, it
appeared to indicate freedom from discrimination. Not actually
being of Anglo ancestry would lead her to experience frequent prejudice, but it was more likely her appearance as a poor countrywoman
that led Lupe to "paint her up" for a trip to Colorado.

The Texas/Colorado border crossing had been a trouble spot for undocumented workers since 1936, when Colorado's governor Edwin Johnson called out the National Guard to deny entry to Mexican migrant farm laborers. He softened that position under pressure from federal government and other public officials, but border checks still presented an obstacle to the Salguero family.

> Immigration was always ready there. It was staked out there at the crossings, in Texas. But since they already knew her [Lupe], they didn't even search the truck. She had already come up here several times. She came every year with her kids and brought people. They trusted her. I came with them in the car. My sister-in-law painted me all up, put lipstick on me and everything so I could get through.
>
> Later, she would laugh, because after she stopped, they said to her, "Pass." Well, we came through, just flying. I came through painted and colored. And Jorge came with my brother-in-law, her husband. He was riding inside the truck. They didn't even ask him anything. Once they got me all lipsticked up, you know, well, we came here. We didn't have any difficulty at all; thank God, we made it.

Viviana found that story humorous, I suspect because she had never before worn makeup. Besides the lack of money for such vanities, it was not uncommon for Mexican husbands to restrict their wives from anything that might heighten their sexuality,[34] and based on Viviana's account, Jorge was a jealous man. Now as part of Jorge's extended family, Viviana was interacting with other women, something largely denied her previously. That may have lightened her mood as well.

Conditions in Colorado were marginally better than in Texas. The 1937 Sugar Act had determined that beet growers applying for government benefit payments must at least pay fair and reasonable wages,[35] and subsequent worker shortages during World War II had also stimulated pay increases. Beet-work wages rose by 50 percent during the war.[36] In 1938, workers in northern Colorado were earning on the average $570 a year.[37] Raising that income by 50 percent to $755 by the end of the war, however, still left the farm workers earning less than a third of the national average—$2,900 in 1945—making it difficult for many families to meet expenses.[38]

Not only did the limited income keep the Salgueros' diet sparse and their wardrobes minimal, it also guaranteed Viviana would be busy from dawn to after dark with time-consuming household chores. Even after the family had sent to Mexico for the four children left behind, Jorge insisted that all the children stay in the fields, not allowing any of them to come home early to help with meal preparation or other work. Other women recount similar expectations. Takaki tells the story of another young mother: "Like the men, women worked in the fields, but they also had to raise the children and do the household chores. 'I am an agricultural working woman,' one of them explained. 'I have to go out to work with the men . . . , taking my baby with me. When we finish work at suppertime, I have to do the cooking and wash the dishes.'"[39] Viviana was one of thousands, working hard, getting little sleep, and struggling as breadwinner, housekeeper, laundress, cook, mother.

> In the morning, there was no bread, only tortillas. No, but at night I made lots of tortillas, and we made do with at least beans or vermicelli. There was very little meat. Every now and then, meat, once a week, that's all.
>
> And when we came, there were no washing machines. We washed by hand, with washbasins in the bathroom, and with washboards. Then I washed until nine o'clock at night. There was a lot to wash, and then to iron. The girls didn't help me. I was left alone in the house; they went to work in the fields.
>
> In 1950 was when they came out with washing machines, with refrigerators. Before that there were refrigerators, but with ice [iceboxes]. Well, it was very difficult. We put those blocks of ice in a little box. We did it by hand. And there we put meat, chile, butter.
>
> We didn't buy bread for two or three days or for a week. There wasn't any place to get it. We lived near the little town. There we went to buy tomatoes, chile. We had a lot of sand, and we would wet it down and put the chile in it to keep it fresh. That was another type of refrigerator.

Not only was the work incessant, but the weather was often harsh. By the end of beet season, it was late fall. Ricardo Lopez of Greeley explains that the beet topping took place "from September to the end of October. The weather could be cold and snowy. My father wrapped the boys' shoes with burlap sacks to keep our feet warm."[40]

> Then we didn't have even the clothes to cover ourselves. Because the salaries, the pay, for the people was very low; they paid very little, so that the people didn't have enough to buy a coat, a warm jacket, to wear. I wore shawls to work, shivering. [She imitates the way she would walk in this condition.] I didn't have clothes to put on them, so the children could stand the cold. Roberto's feet were frostbitten during the topping. Here in the United States. It was very hard in those days.

Another practice used by beet and produce farmers added to the suffering of the workers. Beets needed to be thinned during the growing season. The work was difficult enough, but the short-handled hoe contributed more than its share of pain. The instrument, commonly found in lettuce fields in California and called by Ferriss and Sandoval "the most insidious tool ever used,"[41] was the object of a major controversy in the late 1960s and early 1970s. The hoe forced the user to bend and stoop all day long, leading often to debilitating, lifelong back injuries. Growers argued that the hoe offered more precise thinning and weeding, but workers who struggled with it maintained it was simply a way to control workers and "make them live humbled, stooped-over lives."[42] Maria Elena Lucas remembers watching her mother bent over with the tool. "The reason they used a short handle was to make sure that we were doing the job. If they [the overseers] looked out and we were standing straight up, they thought that meant we weren't working."[43] César Chavez and others fought for years to have the tool banished from the fields, finally succeeding in 1975.

> When we came to Colorado, Jorge worked at the sugar factory. We worked in the fields, in the beets. We did all the jobs there were—thinning plants and other jobs. My sister-in-law, the one

who brought us, worked by contract. She would find houses
for everyone, for her children and for us. We didn't have any
problems finding a house here. My sister-in-law found us work
in the potatoes, work in the beets, and they would give her a
house, the farmers. We also had a house, because we were with
her. It was a big house.

Jorge worked on the farms, and the kids worked, too. They
would get contracts for beets, whatever would come up, potatoes or something. Then, there were no machines for the potatoes—just hands. What they didn't like were the cucumbers.
They pricked their hands. Now there are machines to top and
thin the beets. But then if there were a little plant here, let's say
a beet plant, and here another, we would take this one out, and
leave this one so the other beet would grow. We would take it
out, first with a short hoe, and later with a longer one.

We were able to find work in the cucumbers, sugar beets,
green beans, tomatoes—we would pick tomatoes from the
plants and put them in baskets. I would pick tomatoes until one
was full. Well, we worked a long time. We would work also in
the onions. I didn't like the onions. Neither did the kids because
they are nasty, stinky—very smelly. [She laughs.] They didn't
like to go around smelling like onions. They did it for a while,
but not a lot. I would get onion on me, and I would almost
faint with the smell. But I always went to work with them. And
when I came back, I would make tortillas and dinner.

Well, in the past, life was very hard. Now, it's like it says in
the Bible, you suffer now so that later you will earn that which
you suffered for. God will help us later.

Along with her religious faith, Viviana's sense of humor sometimes helped her through those days. In all the time we talked, she
told only one lighthearted story about her relationship with Jorge,
but it indicated they did have a few pleasant moments.

I worked with the kids in the field; I also went and helped them.
I got little sections of the beet field to thin with the hoe. Almost
all the time, Jorge was the irrigator. When they were plow-
ing the land in order to plant, and when the beets were ready

to be thinned, then he was still irrigating with the water from the canals. When he would go by to water or something on the ranch, I would call to him that he should help me with the thinning. And I would yell at him, "Hey, there is a bear over here." I would yell at him so that he would come to help me. [She is laughing.] So then he would come and help me a little while, with the thinning. Then I would thin an acre or an acre and a half.

Few relationships are all negative or all positive. Viviana's narrative makes it clear that Jorge's anger distressed the entire family. On the other hand, she had to live day to day with him; one of her survival strategies must surely have been knowing when it was safe to chat or joke around. Because she admired his work ethic and his intelligence, and also because she understood the obstacles he had to deal with as a Mexican laborer, there may even have been times when she was proud of her tall, light-complected husband. Such moments could not have lasted long.

Among the obstacles Jorge faced was the contract system for agricultural workers. Although Viviana's sister-in-law Lupe, acting as a contractor, had found work and housing for the Salgueros, they still weren't living on easy street. Contractors found work for the migrants in exchange for a percentage of their earnings. The contract system worked to the advantage of migrant workers in some ways and to their disadvantage in others, especially when it was abused. Shorris explains that some took only small amounts of money "and were generally decent small businessmen. Others were thieves who stole from the wages . . . of the families who worked for them, taking half, even two-thirds of their earnings."[44] It would seem that Lupe fell somewhere in between these two ends of the spectrum, taking about 30 percent of their earnings. Because she was family, however, it is easy to see why they would have expected her to take a smaller percentage.

Lupe may not have felt financially secure herself. Although these postwar years saw the beginnings of a strong Mexican American middle class—what some scholars refer to as the Mexican-American Generation—studies in earlier decades had shown that native-born adults who were longtime residents in the Southwest, such as Lupe, had only slightly better living conditions than immigrants.[45] Mexican

American writers have chronicled movements for social justice as early as the 1920s,[46] but the emerging middle class did not always manifest a great deal of compassion or responsibility toward their less fortunate brethren. It would seem that Lupe was less socially aware than focused on making a living.

> My sister-in-law was doing better. Her children worked and she also worked all day. Then she got a contract for Jorge in the potatoes. They would pay her fourteen cents, and my sister-in-law would pay Jorge ten cents. She was making four cents for herself. The second year we came, Jorge got a job with the same rancher that my sister-in-law had worked with, because she didn't come back. Then the rancher told him, "Last year you guys made real good money." Jorge said, "I don't know how much." The rancher told him, "I paid your sister fourteen cents." And my sister-in-law paid Jorge ten cents. So he said, "You can't be comfortable anywhere, even with your own family." You can't see each other and help each other. She should have told him, "Look, brother, they are going to pay me so much. I'm also going to pay you the same." But no. She was making four cents.

Dependent on seasonal work and managing to buy a series of battered cars, the family would move back to Texas after the harvests were over in Colorado, sometimes traveling through Nebraska to harvest potatoes on the way. The cotton crop matured in the higher, cooler regions of Texas in October or November and offered work in other regions often as late as the end of December.[47] Cotton work did not pay well; in fact, wages were little more than half those for beets. In Texas, the housing situation changed as well. Menefee describes migrant homes as "ramshackle . . . unpainted one- or two-room shacks with single walls, the cracks being covered on the outside with narrow strips of lumber,"[48] a description much like Viviana's, with the exception that the cracks weren't covered in her house. To make matters worse, Shorris describes Texas winds as carrying grit that "strips the paint off cars."[49]

> The first time we went from here to the picking [in Texas], they gave us some very, very simple houses. You could see the light

through the walls, and they were very cold. The sand came in
through the cracks in the walls. The wind blew the sand inside.
And we were all like the sepulchers of the dead, the dead bodies.
[She giggles.] We were all covered with dirt.

Jorge wasn't there. He was with another man, looking for a
new job. We were alone there in that house. And then the wind
came in. We were without a fire, without a furnace. It was cold.
In Texas, it's very windy, there's a lot of wind. Almost every
day, it's windy. All the cars there are pitted, rotted out, the bodies of the cars. They have a lot of tiny holes from the sand that
beats them.

As Viviana described the early years in the United States, her comments indicated a growing political consciousness. She especially
began remarking on issues of social justice. Still ascribing much of
her fate to the will of God, she began to address human social responsibility also. She could not have known all the history leading up to
the discrimination she witnessed, but she and her family had migrated
into a society securely grounded in bigoted attitudes toward Latinos,
as well as blacks. Few agribusiness owners worried about cold or
sand in the houses of people they considered inferior. As early in
American history as 1815, John Quincy Adams described Latin Americans as "the most ignorant, the most bigoted, and the most supersti-
tious of all Roman Catholics," and thirty-three years later in 1848,
Senator John Clarke of Rhode Island stated, "There is a moral pesti-
lence attached to such a people which is contagious—a leprosy that
will destroy."[50] At the turn of the twentieth century, the now infa-
mous Texas Rangers, a law enforcement group begun by Stephen F.
Austin in 1823, lynched Mexican Americans "virtually at will."[51] In
1925, an editor of the Greeley *Tribune* in Colorado encouraged "a
caste system," even though he maintained that such a practice would
be "worse upon us, the aristocracy, than upon the Mexicans in their
serfdom."[52] Signs in restaurants, barbershops, and movie theaters
proclaiming "White Trade Only" or "No Mexicans or Dogs Allowed"
were displayed regularly in Texas and Colorado through 1945,[53] and
in some cases even later.

During and after World War II, the Ku Klux Klan intentionally
maimed and killed Mexican immigrants and Mexican Americans in

several parts of the country. It is no wonder Viviana saw value in
those blue eyes; the light skin accompanying them was well worth
coveting in such an environment. "To avoid deportation, discrimination, or the Klan, several Mexican aliens attempted to 'whiten their
skin' with the chemical hydroquinone. The San Diego lawyer, Alfredo
Montoya, hated by the Klan . . . for helping Mexicans, tried to stop
these dangerous skin treatments."[54] The Klan often worked in remote
farm areas, preying on defenseless farm workers and murdering them
with relative impunity, since local law enforcement refused to act
against them.[55]

Discrimination was rampant in south Texas, where until the 1960s
towns had "two of everything . . . two elementary schools, two parks,
two public swimming pools,"[56] one for whites and one for Mexican
Americans. As Juan Gonzalez describes the earlier years of the century, "By the 1920s, the Rio Grande Valley was as segregated as apart-
heid South Africa."[57] Also by the 1920s and 1930s, districts had
formalized the tripartite system, begun before Jorge's father was a
child, to segregate Anglo, black, and Mexican American children.[58]
School segregation reflected the divisions within the society at large,
those created and reinforced by segregation in housing, wage differ-
entials, socioeconomic imbalances, and racial oppression.[59] Subjected to second-class treatment through humiliation in "restaurants,
barbershops, stores, parks, swimming pools, churches, courthouses,
[and] public hospitals,"[60] most Mexican Americans found many
impediments to improving their social status, not only color barriers
but cultural, linguistic, and educational ones as well.[61]

> Before, in Texas, when Jorge was young, they didn't admit him
> to the white school because he was Mexican. That's why Jorge
> hardly knew how to write, nor did he know much English—
> because they didn't admit him. He only went, I believe, three
> months to the Mexican school there in Texas, in Spanish.

Viviana knew enough Texas history to be aware that slavery had
been outlawed by the Mexican government while Texas was still part
of the Mexican state of Coahuila. The issue touched an emotional
chord with her. In 1830, a year after President Vicente Guerrero had
issued Mexico's Emancipation Proclamation, that government, under

President Anastasio Bustamante, ordered a noncompliant Texas to comply with the new law "or expect federal military intervention."[62] Martha Menchaca argues, in fact, that the Texas War for Independence was primarily a battle over slavery.[63] Although other issues, including property taxes and tariffs, angered the citizenry as well, landowners in the region were flaunting their abuse of the antislavery law; by 1836, there were approximately five thousand slaves in Texas.[64]

> As far as the blacks, they had the blacks working; they were using them with a plow. With that, they cultivated the land to seed it. They had the blacks in the harness that they put on oxen. The blacks were the mules. Only a president of Mexico—I don't remember which president, it seems it was Benito Juárez—he told someone from here, "Give the Negroes freedom, or I'll go to war against you." And that was how they gave the Negroes their freedom.

Viviana had her president wrong, and she oversimplified the historical sequence of events, but her premise was correct. Texas was no stranger to oppression, first through slavery and, after that practice was outlawed in the United States, through blatant discrimination.

> Look, when we first got to Texas, Mexicans couldn't go into a restaurant to eat or drink coffee. You entered and sat down, but there you were seated until finally you would rather leave, because there was no service for Mexicans. Even less for blacks. One time when we were coming from Texas here to Colorado, Jorge said, "Here's where we are going to eat supper." I already knew that there wasn't service in all restaurants for Mexicans. So I told him, "Well, you go in first, and then I will." He got out of the car and went in, sat down, and there he sat. Then the waitress came—in Spanish they're called *meseras*—and then Jorge said, "Well, I want coffee and supper." She said, "No." She said, "There is no service for Mexicans here." Well, Jorge came out very angry. Well, yes, why not?
>
> The Bible says to love your neighbor as yourself. Like, let's see, you and I, we should see eye-to-eye because we are neighbors. And many don't like each other. I say that discrimination

toward the Mexicans is still not over. How much did the blacks fight to be able to mix with the whites and everyone? They fought because the whites didn't like them either. Until finally, now they mix, and they are together.

Several writers have observed that World War II was a turning point for many Mexican Americans.[65] They fought with distinction in that war, nearly half a million strong, lost a disproportionate number of their young men,[66] and became highly decorated, winning twelve of the prestigious Congressional Medals of Honor.[67] "A people that had won more Medals of Honor than any other racial or ethnic group during the war could not feel quite so humble at home."[68] Having in many cases earned the respect and friendship of their fellow soldiers and increased their sense of self-worth through official recognition, returning Mexican Americans took advantage of veterans' benefits such as the GI Bill, enrolled in colleges and universities and bought homes.[69] They could no longer be expected to assume "a deferential body posture and respectful voice tone" when dealing with Anglos, as had their ancestors.[70] Viviana recounted one of several stories about Mexican American soldiers returning to Texas after the war. In Brownsville, for example, when Congressional Medal of Honor winner Sergeant José Mendoza López was denied service in a local restaurant, "it touched off a furor among *mexicanos*."[71] According to a 1996 article in a Greeley, Colorado, newspaper, a similar incident occurred in Greeley. Resident Tito "Butter" Garcia recalls:

> There was a highly decorated army officer by the name of Jess Ugalde, who went to a barbershop here in town and told the man who owned it: "Why don't you hang that sign [White Trade Only] up on the front lines?" . . . It came out in the paper the next day, and that's when the signs started coming down.[72]

Still, Greeley residents recall seeing signs, *No Dogs or Mexicans,* in some downtown businesses as recently as the 1960s.[73]

Viviana continues:

> Discrimination never stops, still. In Texas, it's harder than here in Colorado. In Texas, a former soldier went, like us, into a café

to eat. They told him they didn't serve Mexicans. So then, when he left, he broke the windows of the restaurant. Right away, they got the cops after him, the owners. He said, "Yes, I did it." He said, "Because here, there is discrimination. And when we go to fight, there is no discrimination. Over there, everybody is going to fight. And here, no. They didn't want to serve me here because I was a Mexican." He said, "Over there everyone fights, Japanese and Mexicans, and all. Over there we all are brothers. And here, no." He said it well, right? Well, they didn't do anything to the kid, they didn't do anything for what he had done.

Yah, well, do you believe that people are not embarrassed, saddened? Yes, they are humiliated. If you go into a restaurant and they tell you, "No, we don't serve your kind," you get up in shame — that the people heard what went on — and you leave. Why? Why does all this go on? Let's see. For example, here in Colorado there are more Mexicans than in Texas. Here, if it weren't for the Mexicans, the harvests wouldn't be brought in. Like corn and everything, beets. When we were working, we all went out gathering potatoes, throwing them into containers, chopping them. And if it weren't for the Mexicans, the Americans wouldn't get in their harvests. Because you don't see a white man working in the fields, you don't see a white man working.

During the war, American blacks made the point that the fight was not about saving democracy but about defeating racism here at home. A black-owned newspaper, the Chicago *Defender*, asked, "Why die for democracy for some foreign country when we don't even have it here?" and went on to urge that Americans "bomb the color line."[74] While Mexican Americans were dying at Bataan, they were facing so much racial violence and discrimination at home that the Mexican foreign minister and a Mexican weekly newspaper, in separate instances, protested their treatment. In 1943, hundreds of Anglo servicemen attacked young Mexican American men in Los Angeles who dressed in zoot suits — extravagant ensembles with high-waisted, pegged trousers, long coats, French-style shoes, and prominent watch chains — carrying on a week-long rampage that finally led to intervention by President Roosevelt.[75]

Possibly a backlash against Mexican Americans' growing visibility, the racist attitudes were nothing new. From the late nineteenth century, state governments had been resisting federal laws regarding citizenship eligibility for "Asians, American Indians, Mexicans, and 'half-breeds,'"[76] and in 1909, physician C. S. Babbitt had condemned missionaries for "wasting their energies" among Mexican and African Americans in El Paso, because these "beings . . . are not in reality the objects of Christ's sacrifice."[77] A few years later, in 1927, Harvard president A. Lawrence Lowell was one of the signatories to a petition demanding "the preservation of the nation's genetic purity by including Mexico in the national origins quota system."[78]

Many scholars today affirm that the concept of race is socially constructed, that as Martin Bulmer and John Solomos maintain, it has no "semantic respectability, biological basis, or philosophical legitimacy."[79] They explain that race and ethnicity are not considered "natural" categories; "their boundaries are not fixed, nor is their membership uncontested. Racial and ethnic groups, like nations, are imagined communities."[80] That is not to say, however, that such perceived categories have no sociological or political import. They remain a key factor in the power relations within societies,[81] often serving as the basis for inclusion or exclusion, citizenship or outsider status, recognition or disregard. Viviana had lived in a society still affected by the vestiges of a racial order, Mexico's *la casta* system,[82] but the prejudice she encountered in the United States nevertheless surprised her. A woman of strong religious faith and a sense of history, she didn't need scholarly theories to tell her that discrimination has no physical or philosophical justification.

> This is my idea, my faith . . . that it doesn't matter to the Creator how bad one is, or where one is going, or whatever, in him there is no discrimination. He loves us all the same. Because we're all people of one blood, all of us. Not you because you have white blood, and me because I have dark blood. But here, most people discriminate against others. Why? It's because they don't understand. That's the way life is. Right? Such is life that what we have to do is not meddle with anyone else.

Discrimination often reveals itself through the names people call each other or what groups defiantly call themselves to express ethnic pride. At first, I was surprised at the vehemence with which Viviana objected to the word *Chicano,* a term that had become "an outcry of pride"[83] to followers of César Chávez in the 1960s. By way of background, Elena Aragón de McKissack explains that some controversy exists over the origin of the term, but it is generally accepted to have come from the name of the Mexica, or Aztec, tribe that settled in the central basin of Mexico. According to McKissack, the first recorded usages of *Chicano* in the United States were neutral, referring simply to working-class Mexicans, but after militant and educated youth took up the name in the social protest era, it developed derogatory connotations for many older residents, who dissociated themselves from it.[84] Shorris adds, "In Chihuahua, a chicano was a *marrano* or small pig. . . . The very poor and people who labored at the lowest level were known as chicanos. Although the word was derogatory, it was the mildest of insults. Nevertheless, many older people continue to be appalled at the use of the term to describe people of Mexican descent."[85] Viviana did not seem to be aware of its political implications but saw it simply as a pejorative.

People of Mexican heritage have such diverse ancestral lines and political inclinations that they defy categorization. The US Census Bureau used the inappropriate and unpopular phrase "people of Spanish origin" until the 1970s, when it convened an advisory committee of Chicano, Mexican, Puerto Rican, and Cuban representatives who devised the term *Hispanic*[86] for the 1980 census. The term was a catchall, and although widely used in the 1980s, it was displaced by what Gutmann calls the more trendy term *Latino* in the 2000 census,[87] even though "an extensive study of Latino attitudes, the 1992 Latino National Political Survey, found that most people who might call themselves 'Latino' or 'Hispanic' reject such panethnic, or umbrella, terms."[88] They favor such designations as Cuban, Mexican American, or other terms based on national origins.

Bulmer and Solomos suggest that researchers need to be responsive to the self-definitions of their subjects.[89] Thus, even though Ruiz and others maintain that the term *Mexican American* signifies US birth,[90] Buss uses the term "to refer to people of Mexican heritage who are strongly identified with the United States, either through birth, upbringing, or specified choice."[91] I have identified Viviana in this book as Mexican American to honor her self-identification.[92] She chose the term. She also made me aware of a few pejorative terms

I had never heard before and intrigued me by her interesting take on the term "wetback."

> My brother-in-law from Del Rio calls European Americans gringos, and he calls them *bolillos* [a type of breakfast roll—a term used to refer to whites]. He calls them bolillos and gringos.
>
> [I ask about the term *Chicano*.] I told you there isn't a word among the Mexicans; they don't call each other Chicanos. Chicanos is an animal. [I ask what type of animal the chicano is.] Well, I don't know, but they say it is an animal that is in the water, in the sea. I think it is like, I think, I don't know, like a big fish, like a whale. I think, more or less. The people from Mexico are Mexican Americans. They are not Chicanos. Nor wetbacks either. Those who came [across oceans] from England, from there, from other places, those are the wetbacks. [Los mojados son los que vienen de por allá de Inglaterra, por allá de otras partes, esos son mojados.] They are not those who come from Mexico. The Mexicans cross over in life to earn a cent to support themselves and their families.
>
> There are times they cross when the river is very low. They cross with all their clothes. Wetbacks are those who get all wet in crossing. But others who get wet, to here [she gestures to her hip], when they cross to this side, those aren't wetbacks. Because Mexico and the US border each other. So that was what Jorge was also fighting, that all those words are badly made, badly spoken, because they shouldn't talk that way. They should call them nationals or Mexicans from Mexico. That name is better, Mexicans from Mexico.

Among the several ways I was to see Viviana's confidence in her own judgment, her definite opinions on labeling were among the most striking. I asked again if she had any idea why some Mexican Americans like the term *Chicano*.

> Well, they don't like it, but they get used to being called that. It is like, now we are going to say—forgiving me the word, God and you—they call you white people *sanjones* [not in dictionaries but a pejorative term for whites]. White people, sanjones. It's a

word for the [US] Americans. It's vulgar—but they call whites that. For example, let's see, I'm this Mexican woman, like I am, and you are a white woman, and if I were to call you 'Sanjona,' that's not good for the gringos, yes? [She's teasing me.]

There are many who are of distinct races, but they come here. Japanese, Vietnamese, well, different races come here to the United States from other places. And Mexico is closer to the United States than other lands like England or Spain or others, other faraway states. But [those who come from other lands] are not spoken of like the Mexicans. [I say our government uses the term *Hispanic* for anyone with a certain surname.] Yes, well, *Hispanic* is the same word that one can call the Mexicans, because they are Hispanics, Spanish.

[I ask what she thinks of the term *Latino* as a term for people from Mexico, South America, etc.] Latino? For Latino, me? Well, I don't know what it could mean. I don't know, they say that the Latinos are the Mexicans themselves. [I reaffirm that she prefers Mexican American.] Mexican American, um-hm [for "yes"].

4

A New Country but No New Refuge

1940s and Early 1950s

> All my life, I've seen men treat women with violence, sometimes
> with hits and sometimes by hurting their feelings.
> —*María Elena Lucas*[1]

ONCE THE FAMILY BECAME FAMILIAR with the migrant cycles
and began to follow the harvest from Texas to Colorado and back,
they sent for the four younger children who had remained in Mexico.
Viviana then had three more children and more than one miscarriage, giving her twelve children in all, eleven living with her and
Jorge. Her memories of those early years in the United States revolve
around the challenges of raising her children and dealing with her
difficult husband. Facing inadequacy in everything from food to
medical care was burden enough, but even more troubling for Viviana were Jorge's reactions to the children's mischief. In our conversations, she returned repeatedly to the topic of Jorge's neglect and
abuse, his maltreatment having left deep psychological scars on her
and the children.

A study of Mexican American migrant families in the 1940s found
that men's authority was reinforced because of their function as pro-
viders, their control over economic assets, and their ability to mediate

with the Anglo world.[2] From the beginning of their marriage, Jorge had worked to keep his wife secluded, and once they were no longer working with Jorge's relatives, the migrant life only intensified her isolation. Karen Anderson points out that for married migrant women, "especially those in the rural economy, their insecurity and marital dependence had been increased" by coming north.[3] Even as the family established a way of life in the United States, Viviana's options narrowed.

Although she admired some of her husband's capabilities, Viviana never tried to excuse his violent temper. Much has been written about the cult of masculinity, and it is tempting to speculate that Jorge was acting out what he saw as acceptable masculine behavior. Although the term *machismo* calls up a broad range of stereotypes, De Mente's definition would seem to fit Jorge: "Machismo meant that a man could not let anything detract from his image of himself as a man's man, regardless of the suffering it brought on himself and the [family] around him."[4] For many Mexican men, the public posturing of male dominance served to reinforce masculine identity and self-esteem, contributing to a sense of power.[5] Whatever Jorge's self-image may have been or how he justified his actions, they had devastating results for his wife and children and possibly for himself as well. Saldívar describes the subjugation of women by men as catastrophic for both.[6] Jorge's quick temper combined with the inability to admit a mistake could have led to a revolving door of anger and frustration on his part.

From Viviana's and her children's accounts, Jorge spent almost all of his free time in bars, but he didn't need to be intoxicated to lose his temper. Neither was his abuse all physical. Viviana lived with intimidation and fear, not only of beatings but also of threats on her life. She had to defend her innocence as well as the children against unreasoning jealousy and anger. The husband who had taught himself to read also disparaged his wife's intelligence, reinforcing her own preconceived notion that she was incapable of learning. She saw herself as powerless in some respects, but her tenacity in putting her children first and standing up to Jorge when she could reveals a woman of purpose. Still bearing children, each one to her mind a blessing, she might have found those early years in the new country unbearable had it not been for her strong sense of responsibility to family.

My three youngest kids were born on the farms here in the United States. Isabel was born on a farm outside of Fort Lupton, [Colorado]. Diego was born on a ranch near Santana, Texas, and Constanza was also born in Colorado on a farm—outside of Pierce. But they are registered here in Greeley. Even though they were born on the farm, we registered them in town.

Here there were women like doctors, and they had the responsibility for the woman who was going to have her baby. They call them *parteras*. There are knowledgeable midwives, and there are midwives who are not knowledgeable. But God helped me. We came in '46, and it was the same in Mexico as here. There weren't many doctors.

I never went to the hospital to have a baby, never. Not with any of those that God gave me. One time, no more, I went to the hospital—for a miscarriage. The miscarriages are worse than live births. I lost a lot of blood. I was dying, but the doctor didn't want to come to the farm, because he had already been there. As soon as I got up, I fainted again. So then the farmer's wife called the doctor again, and he didn't want to come. He said, "Well, I've been there already." The woman told him, "If she dies, it is your responsibility. [Si se muere, es responsabilidad tuya.]" So he came back. That was when they sent me here to the hospital. I discharged a great deal of blood until I passed the fetus. Later I had another one, but it happened at home. I had four miscarriages. Little unborn babies.

I had sixteen pregnancies. But twelve lived. Enough. Twelve. There are women who have more than I did. There are families who have twenty. Twenty children! A lot, especially for the mother, because the mother is always worn out the most by the family. Because one loses a lot of blood having a baby. Well, there are many people that God cares for and gives them the strength for so many children. God gave me sixteen, but only twelve lived. Twelve is enough.

Viviana's story about traveling in a car with a rag in the place of a broken window is not unique,[7] nor is the resulting struggle with the sick baby. With wages for cotton pickers low, any emergency could wipe out an entire paycheck.

Once, when she was a baby, Isabel got sick on us. Right after we left here. And then, well, there wasn't any place to put her in the hospital. Well, with what money? We still weren't working very much. Finally, he got the money to put her in the hospital in Levelland, there in Texas. Well, there she stayed about two weeks. She was sick because when we left, the back window of the car had no glass. I was in the back with her, so all the air came in on her, and she got pneumonia. Well, he put her in the hospital, and in two weeks they called and told him she was ready to get out again. He went for her. She got out, and the following day he took her back again to the hospital because she had gotten sick again. She was just tiny.

So then a friend, who was her godfather from her baptism, helped. She stayed another week in the hospital. And they continued picking, but there, since there's a lot of wind, they weren't picking every day. So my friend took Jorge, because they had already advised him that the child was ready. He had only picked about three days. Well, the check for the picking remained there when he took her out of the hospital, because that was what they charged, only exactly that much. And, well, again things went back to the same old way, having to look for something to eat.

We went to pick again so we could pay what he had borrowed to buy food. The girls helped him pick. When we went [to Texas], they almost never went to school because they had to help him work. Eventually, some graduated and others didn't. Some had schooling and others very little. What they know, they know now that they have learned it on their own.

Viviana considered her children a gift, one she should cherish and care for by certain rules, such as who eats first at the table. Stuart Chase, in his 1931 travelogue and analysis of life in Mexico,[8] called Mexican children "the best behaved on earth."[9] One reason the children made such an impression could have been that, as Viviana stated earlier, the entire community worked hard to help educate them. The phrase *bien educado,* or well educated, in Spanish relates more to a child's behavior than to academic knowledge. A well-educated child has learned the mores of polite adult society—good manners, respect for others and oneself, a sense of reverence, and loyalty to family and one's fellow humans. With such attention focused on their development, more often than not, children feel valued. In functional families, they are often told that they are gifts from God and that a large family is a source of strength.[10] In the words of Lea Ybarra, "The very soul of the Latino experience is rooted in the family,"[11] and Viviana felt blessed by hers. None of her youngsters was ever "bad"—"naughty" was the worst they could do. Jorge, on the other hand, was much less tolerant of their antics.

> Family is very necessary. They say, "God gives family to those who deserve it. [Que Dios le da la familia al que lo merece.]" How many families are there that God gives many or two or three? And then they leave their wives. And there the little ones are suffering without a father or mother. Family is very necessary because the blessing comes from God, and it comes through the family. That's why when the babies are little, you should feed them first. God gives our daily bread to us for the children. We should not leave them until last. Feed them and then they will go play; they won't still be there on top of the table, "Give me, and give me." Some people, no, the children are waiting to be called to eat. If the adults eat first, the children are desperate because they want their nourishment, their food. Well, no. The kids first!
>
> One time we went to the movies, to the show, in Nebraska. In Nebraska we would go to the jobs in the potatoes. We went into the show, and Diego and Memo went outside. Sancho was about seven; Diego was about five, or four. Well, near the movie house was a filling station. There are machines where you put in a cloth to clean your windows. Sancho said, or Ruben said, I don't remember who said it, "Put your hand in there where the roller goes around." Well, Diego put his hand in, and the machine tore this finger. How naughty! Ruben took off to come inside the movie theater, "Hurry, Ma . . . Diego cut a finger." Well, there we go, and of the rest of those movies, we didn't see anything. We went out. He comes out with his finger all covered with blood.
>
> Well, Jorge gave them a good reprimand, because he was very strict. One time also we went to a store, after Christmas.

Ruben had a firecracker, one of those small ones, in his pocket. Then he told Memo, "Here, hold this." Memo took it, and then Ruben took out the box of matches he was carrying and lit the firecracker. Well, it went off in Memo's hand. It tore here, the palm of the hand. Here comes Jorge, Memo with his hand coloring with blood.

When it snowed, they would make snowballs and throw them at each other. One time there was snow, so Vicente got a snowball, and they were throwing them at the cars going by. Well, one of the drivers stopped and went and called Jorge. He said, "Look at your kid, what he did to my car. He could have broken my windshield." Listen, he got him and gave him a good spanking so they wouldn't be naughty. But they would do things and laugh. Everything seemed easy to them, everything seemed very funny. [She laughs.]

But he didn't spare the hand. He always gave them his hand, always. One time Memo was standing, and it had rained. There was a puddle. Memo was standing there, and Chente came and pushed him, and he fell in the puddle. Yes, there goes Memo all wet and crying. "Well, what's the matter?" "Chente pushed me." Jorge went out and spanked him. They were very naughty.

In highly patriarchal rural societies, children have few rights,[12] a perspective Jorge appeared to share. As Viviana described them, his consequences were excessive, his role as guide or teacher almost nil. Such behaviors are consistent with Michael Maccoby's description of the Mexican villager parents who "often punish but hardly ever reward."[13] Octavio Paz writes, "The phrase 'I am your father' has no paternal flavor and is not said in order to protect or guide another, but rather to impose one's superiority, that is, to humiliate."[14] These descriptions vary in relation to such factors as socioeconomic status, education level, and degree of assimilation into Anglo culture,[15] but they may help to characterize the attitudes of a man who had little but the strength of his back and arms to get him through life. Other scholars reinforce the theory that male supremacy is the refuge of powerless men,[16] those dealing with the frustration of trying to fill the patriarchal good-provider role through low-wage, physically arduous jobs with no opportunity for advancement.[17]

Another factor might have played into Jorge's rigid parenting. In the migrant labor environment, growers insisted the father have strict and total control of children's labor. Such control could include physical violence. According to Fran Leeper Buss, the "widespread use of this system ensured that grower profit was based on various types of violence against children."[18] That attitude could have reinforced Jorge's already unsparing nature.

> Jorge wasn't a father who would sit down and read to them. "Well, look, sit down so I can read this story. This and this other happened or is going to happen." No. He wasn't interested in the kids' learning. Almost all the time he took them to work in the fields; they didn't have time.
>
> Roberto, Mercedes, Beatriz, and César, those were the ones Jorge hit the most. The younger children weren't beaten as much as the older ones; the older ones were beaten regularly [she changes her tone and laughs], and I right along with them. Because I would break in to defend them, and I would get it also. And yes, not because of anger, well, he beat me and without reason. He had no reason to beat me, but he was also very hard on me.

Viviana didn't believe that Jorge's father had beaten him, thus turning him into a batterer. She drew a possible connection between his behavior and the interaction he might have seen between his father and mother, but in the end, she concluded that his motivations were unfathomable. Armitage and Jameson cite studies purporting that "violence against women is the result of patriarchal definitions of gender and marriage rather than of individual pathology" and that society's sanctioning of male authority is an underlying cause for domestic brutality.[19] Conversely, Buss points out that acceptance of male dominance in families varies according to socioeconomic factors, ethnic identity, and extent of urbanization;[20] and María Elena Lucas ascribes her father's violence to both societal and individual roots. Recognizing that men who don't play the dominant role are often scorned, she also interprets her father's cruelty as indicative of emotional disorder and a pathological need to control.[21] She concludes, "I think my father must have been a sick person."[22] Whatever the roots of such behavior, it receives added authenticity when other members of society choose not to intervene.

> Jorge said that the only way his father hit him was to thump him on the head. It hurt him a lot, because my father-in-law would call him *inmundo*. He said it hurt that he would call him that word. I think that word means something like "useless." He didn't like that, but he was never beaten much. I don't know why Jorge came out so bad.
>
> One of Jorge's aunts, my mother-in-law's sister, told me that my father-in-law had treated my mother-in-law very badly. There in Texas they use the word *ereje*. It's a word meaning bad. My aunt Toña—I also called her "aunt"—told me one time, "No, my brother"—she didn't say "brother-in-law," she said "brother—" "was very *ereje* with my sister." She said, "But I never meddled in their affairs."

Having stood up to Jorge only to receive beatings herself, Viviana did not always intercede when he meted out punishment, but at times his actions were so severe that she found the courage to resist. Not only was his abuse extreme, but it also often seemed motivated by trivial or unconscionable reasons, from children's innocent dawdling to his desire to clear the house for a sexual dalliance. Samuel Ramos and Octavio Paz discuss what they call the "psychology of the oppressed" in relation to the Mexican people,[23] arguing that dominated people accept inferiority. Other scholars have associated such a lowered self-concept with irresponsibility,[24] the belief that one is absolved from responsibility for his actions. Alternate theoretical arguments question the latter assertion,[25] leaving no easy answers as to what makes humans behave viciously to their own family members.

The answers have no more to do with ethnicity than with socio-economic, psychological, or geographical factors. Rosa Linda Fregoso, citing multiple sources, points out that Chicano and Mexican men are no more violent in their treatment of women than those from other nationalities or ethnic groups. "Domestic violence is a leading cause of female injuries in nearly every country, cutting across the axes of race, class, religion, nationality, and ethnicity."[26] In an ethnographic account of one Mexican American family by Reyes

Ramos, the husband explains that people who take their difficulties out on their families do not represent Mexican culture. "Culture of sickness, maybe, not Mexican culture. If it were Mexican, then, we'd all be abusing our families all the time. There is a gringo on the other street who's always drunk and it's said that he beats his wife whenever he's drunk. . . . Now, is he a *macho*? No, he's a drunk."[27]

Jorge did not seem to be drunk in the story Viviana told about his getting angry with the eldest daughter. Although it had to have happened before the family left Mexico because it involved Mercedes, Viviana told it in connection with other stories of abuse.

> Jorge was very violent. He ordered something, and quick. No going around with "I'm doing it." No. "Do it, and do it now." Immediately. One time we were going to work, and Jorge said to Mercedes, "Bring some water! Bring me some water to drink!" Well, Mercedes went to bring the water, and she dallied in coming. Jorge went after her. I was behind Jorge, because I well knew how he was. He got to Mercedes first and grabbed her and gave her a good one. He was hitting her but good.
>
> Earlier there were those cranks for the cars, rods. Jorge had one of those that he was going to hit Mercedes with. When I got there, I was rushing. He had already beaten her and thrown her down on the ground. He had the rod to hit her, to give her another when I got there, and I said to him, "Listen, no, don't hit Mercedes! If you hit her, I'm calling the police. Hit her, but I'm calling the police!" I told him, "You aren't going to let Mercedes have it. Don't you see that if you hit her with that, you'll kill her? And I'm going to call the cops." He didn't hit her any more. That's when he stopped hitting her.
>
> Once he got mad at Beatriz. We had just arrived in Texas from here in Colorado. It was because a friend invited her to go to the movies, and Beatriz didn't have her clothes ironed. [Beatriz, who was present the day of this interview, explained that her friend was the daughter of the woman Jorge was going out with. The woman's husband was going to another town for the day, and Jorge wanted to be alone with her.]
>
> Beatriz had a boil on her buttock. They are called *buttocks*. And many call them, God forgive me the word, *butt*. But they

are *buttocks,* because it sounds more correct, nicer, more appropriate. Anyway, that sore was swelling. If you don't treat it, it ripens there in the flesh, and it becomes very ugly. And Jorge got mad so that he hit her, Beatriz. [Beatriz explains that he grabbed a bicycle tire and cut it in half to beat her with.] Well, he broke it open, he burst her sore.

Beatriz related also that at least one time, when the older boys were in their teens, Roberto urinated blood as a result of a beating.[28] A few days later, accompanying his father as they drove to a work site, Roberto asked straight out if Jorge could explain why he had been so brutal. The angry answer was either a defensive lie or, more likely, the epitome of denial. Emphasizing the "never," he exclaimed that he had *never* beaten Roberto, an answer so flagrantly untrue that it recalls Lucas's description of her father's condition as pathological. Not only did it indicate denial, but ironically, Jorge's excessive punishments of the older children were often for behaviors much like his own. In the following incident with César, the dicho *Hijo de tigre sale pintado,* or "The son of the tiger comes out painted," might be appropriate. It is a Spanish equivalent of "The apple doesn't fall far from the tree."

Roberto was about seventeen; still he was getting those last beatings. Roberto and Mercedes and Beatriz and I—I'm going to count myself—were beaten a lot by him. Us, from César on up.

He hit César after he was already married. When he had already married the first woman, Jorge hit him. Because she came to tell Jorge that César was running around with a woman, there in Eaton—in that bar with the bad reputation that they used to talk about. It's no longer a bar; now it's closed. Do you remember when they caught some people with drugs, there in Eaton? It came out in the newspaper. . . . A couple was jailed. Well, that was the end of it. Now there's no bar. Because that was the end of all that fuss.

César was dancing with another woman. So then César's woman, the first one, instead of going there to the bar, she came to talk to Jorge. And Jorge was eating supper, and then, well, we went to the bar. Roberto was living with us, and the three of us went. Roberto went [in first], and he talked to César. "Pa is calling you," he said. César came. Jorge was really mad, and he said, "Kneel, right there." He made him kneel on his knees. "Kneel." With his arms crossed. And there he was hitting him— so old, and he was hitting him. Because of the daughter-in-law's tattling. He was very hard on all of them.

Jorge would say that still, even after they are married, the rights of the parents don't stop. The rights of the parents don't stop until they die. They always want respect. It was a contradiction. He wanted only that they respect him, that's all. He didn't want to respect anyone. He wanted to give orders so that they were below him, they were crushed. [She laughs sardonically.]

Jorge didn't have any love for them. What he showed them was beatings. He would say in order to make men out of them, that's why he hit them, to make them men, so they would stand up, so they would grow up straight. So they wouldn't be ne'er-do-wells.

Respect for elders and people in authority is an integral part of Spanish-speaking cultures.[29] As Yolanda Nava so aptly observes, however, "respect is a two-way street. One cannot demand respect without giving it."[30] Nava's *It's All in the Frijoles* includes many examples of fathers who modeled the respect they expected from their families.

The advice on machismo I find most compelling is Juan Carlos Heredia's poem about a grandfather's explanation:

> I asked my grandfather what *macho* meant
> he laughed and sat me down next to him
>   It means being strong enough to be kind and gentle
> I don't understand grandfather
> what about those guys who treat people mean?
>   Oh Juanito
>   they're just not strong enough yet.[31]

Gloria Anzaldúa reinforces that concept when she explains that her father's machismo meant "being strong enough to protect and support my mother and us, yet being able to show love."[32]

We can't know what thoughts motivated or helped Jorge rational-
ize his behavior, but Mexican Americans do speak of "straightening
out" their children,[33] so they will "grow upright and healthy,"[34] of
teaching them *fortaleza* (fortitude), so they will be strong in life.[35]
One underprivileged young man in Mexico City, interviewed by
Oscar Lewis, went so far as to explain that parents can harm children
by giving them food and having the table spread for them all the
time.[36] Perhaps being unable to provide gives some parents the idea
that they can protect children by teaching them to withstand misery.

Such a rationalization would hardly seem to apply to Jorge's treatment of his wife, however. If he felt love or even mild affection for
her or for anyone in the family, she saw little evidence of it. Seeing his
attitude from her perspective only, it appeared cold and unfeeling.
Even pregnancy didn't check his hand.

> Another time he hit me. I was pregnant with Diego. When he
> got home from work in the evening, I was standing by the mat-
> tress on the floor, and he gave me a slap. I don't remember why.
> I fell on top of the mattress. Then Beatriz said to him, "Don't
> hit Mom." Well, he hit her too, he doubled the two of us there
> on top of the mattress.
>
> He didn't have any affection for me either, and he never had
> any. Right away [as soon as they were married] he treated me
> badly, right away. I didn't go out anywhere, well, I endured.
> He used to say that he was the man of the house, that he wore
> the pants. And that I had to do what he said. And the girls,
> too. Because he was the man of house, and he gave the orders.
> I endured it all, beatings from him and everything. And from
> there, well, it was my whole life.
>
> He didn't want anyone's opinion. He wanted to run things
> himself. He didn't want to ask an opinion of anyone else, nor of
> his children. What he wanted to do, he did it on his own. [She
> jumps ahead to when the children were grown.] He didn't want
> anyone to tell him, "Well, no, look," like the kids who would
> say, "Well, no, Dad, that's not good. It's not good for you to
> do that." He thought about a thing, and he did it. He didn't go
> around asking Roberto or César, saying, "Look, son . . ."—he
> never called them "sons"—saying "Look, son, I'm going to do

that. Is it a good idea? What do you think? Is that a good idea?"
No, never.

After the children were grown, Viviana once accompanied her husband to Arizona, where Diego and his wife lived. She overheard him talking with Jorge about terms of endearment, a conversation that recalled the young Viviana's pleasure when her father called her "mi hija," or "dear daughter."[37] It also provided the one instance in which she indicated that her husband might have had some affection for his children, even though he seemed determined to conceal it. He may have been recalling another dicho in his response to Diego: *Caras vemos, corazones no sabemos*. Faces we can see; hearts we cannot know.

> Diego reproached him one time, he confronted him. "Listen, Dad, I never heard you call me 'son.' Why have you never called me 'son'?" So then Jorge said, "Well," he said, "You don't know my heart." He said, "In my heart I know that you are my son." But Diego said, "Yes, but I want to hear you call me 'son.'" This is what Jorge answered: "You don't know my heart. I know that you are my son, and I love you like a son." Diego said, "Yes, but I want to hear you call me 'son,' from your own mouth. [Sí, pero yo quiero oir que usted me diga 'hijo,' por su boca suya.]" Nevertheless, he never called them "my sons." Never. Hm-um. He was a father very hard in character.
>
> He was never a loving father. He had his moments only, his moments. But almost never. At times he would talk with them, but not all the time. He had no love for any of them. Even though Constanza was the baby, nevertheless, he treated her badly also.

Among the reasons women stay in abusive relationships, as enumerated by the National Women's Health Resource Center, traditional ideology and lack of resources apply to Viviana's situation.[38] She accepted the traditional thinking of her culture and religion—the belief that marriage is forever. She frequently expressed pride in the duration of her marriage and once disdained those who give up more easily. She also held to the traditional outlook that made her husband responsible for the family's support, possibly agreeing with María Elena Lucas's hesitant conclusion that a bad father is better than no father at all.[39] Even if she had decided to break with conventional ideology, she had few means of achieving a fulfilling independent life. A woman with several children to support, no English-language skills, lack of transportation, shabby clothing, and inexperience of the surrounding culture was not likely to work her way out of her situation,[40] difficult though it was. She told me once that Roberto had tried to convince her to leave Jorge but that she had refused.

> I never hated him because of what he did to me. We were living on the ranch when Roberto entreated me to leave. That I would leave him? No. Never. Never. Never. So many years, sixty-six years, yes. That's a lot. Many years. And I never left him.
>
> Nowadays nobody stays married as many years as we did—sixty-six years—nowadays, they do not last twenty, or even one year. Jorge used to say that it's not the same here or in Texas as it is in Mexico. In Mexico, there are not that many divorced women, because they do not have the help that they have here. Here, they go to the welfare office, and they get food. Here, after one slap, they leave their husbands.

Jorge's abuse went far beyond an occasional slap, however, and that tone of pride disappeared when Viviana spoke of not only extreme physical but also psychological abuse, involving intimidation and threats. She told two stories about his attempts to instill fear in her. When we remember her fear of the alligator in the water, the first takes on added poignancy.

> Let me tell you that one time he made me get into the water where there were snakes. He made me get in to take a bath, in a lake. And there were snakes, vipers up on a mesquite, and I would just watch them as they fell. Here they come, here they come. And I had to get in there.

The second incident must have taken place while the family was still in Texas. Possibly projecting because of his own infidelity, Jorge became suspicious of Viviana's faithfulness. Bernice Rincon describes the role of the traditional rural Mexican woman, explaining that for the "good wife . . . it is impossible . . . to have a personal, private life."[41] Jorge seems to have fit the stereotype of Mexican men, particularly those on the lower rungs of the socioeconomic ladder, who obsessed about the possible unfaithfulness of their wives and sweethearts,[42] constantly harboring fears of betrayal by women.[43] Speaking of participation in the labor movement, Cesar Chávez once said, "We can't be free ourselves if we can't free our women,"[44] a concept that applies equally well to jealousy. Knowing the accusations her husband was making against her were baseless, Viviana pointed out their irony, especially since Jorge was seeing the wife of the very man he suspected of pursuing her.

She obviously did feel some fear of her husband, but as she described her reactions, her lack of guilt and sense of how ridiculous his charges were must have triggered some release in her. She had been living with his threats since before her engagement. Any number of motivations could explain her coolness under duress, but one wonders whether some deep inner strength held her together or whether she simply believed she had nothing left to lose. She steadfastly maintained her innocence, recognizing, of course, that to do otherwise would invite dire consequences.

> Once, he became jealous. He took me out to kill me . . . I hadn't made the tortillas. I went with him. I was not afraid of him, because I didn't owe him anything. He said to me, "If you don't tell me the truth, that you have another man—if you had another man, would you tell me?"
>
> "Yes, why not?"
>
> But what he was accusing me of with another man was not true. Then he said, "Tell me the truth. If you don't tell me the truth, it would suit me just to kill you and leave you covered with rocks and cactus. . . . Who would see you? Who would claim you?"
>
> Well, he was going to force me to tell the truth that wasn't the truth . . . he had already told me what he was going to do to me. "If you don't tell me the truth, I'll kill you." Can you figure that? No, well, why would I tell lies? So that he would kill me and leave me there outside the town in the countryside? No. I

kept telling him, "No, that's not the truth, and that's not the truth, that's not the truth." [Said more softly each time.]

I said, "Why not? Well, yes, why couldn't I tell you?" But no, I didn't—never, never—Beatriz was the one the man was interested in. And Jorge thought it was me. He got jealous. He was going out with that man's wife. And then he would get jealous of that man? I had nothing to do with him.

[She was inconsistent about whether she feared Jorge.] Always there was the fear. But I wasn't afraid of him. I never was afraid. He treated me very badly. And still our marriage lasted only three days less than sixty-six years. Sixty-six years of marriage . . . many years. Always I was a slave. He didn't let me go anywhere, not anywhere. And he didn't take me out, either.

Viviana's description of herself as a slave recalls Kathleen Barry's book entitled *Female Sexual Slavery,* in which she discusses battered wives. While not attending to ethnic or class issues, Barry considers women who remain in unhealthy relationships and refuses to pathologize or stigmatize them.[45] Still, when describing herself as a slave, I find Viviana comes the closest to feeling victimized, as opposed to a woman who believed she had choices. Were it not for her children and an occasional encounter with other farm workers, Viviana's isolation might have been complete. Keeping his wife at home was another form of psychological abuse,[46] reaching its pinnacle with Jorge's not letting her attend even her children's baptisms. She mentioned her exclusion from those events several times, sometimes with a hint of anger, and others in a more wistful tone.

He wasn't a loving husband who was disposed to talk or who would say to me, "Well, let's go out, or let's go do that, or let's go." He never took me out. I never went out with him. Never. So I got so that I didn't miss anything. Anyway, I was already used to it—that he didn't take me anywhere. Not even to the market or like that, to whatever. Or to see my relatives, there in Mexico. He would get angry with his relatives—because we went first to see his relatives—and he didn't need a reason to get angry, and well, he scolded me and mistreated me.

When we were living in the United States, he didn't have the money to send me to see them. He didn't. And my mother died and I didn't see her. My father died and I didn't see him. My brother died and I didn't see him either. Now I have only a brother left.

Now that's why I'm so in the habit of . . . I don't go out. I'm embarrassed . . . going out . . . because I'm not in the habit of it. When I was at home with my father, he didn't let me go out either. I got married, and I continued in the same manner, worse, because he didn't let me go out anywhere. He didn't even go out with me. What he did was beat me. That was what he did.

He would go to the dances, and he came home when he wanted and everything. I would stay at home. That's why I got in the habit of not going out. Even when the children were born, only he went to baptize them, with the godparents. I stayed at home. So . . . I got very used to it all, to not going out.

Viviana's story is not unprecedented. María Elena Lucas tells of not being allowed to name her children. "My mother-in-law and [my husband] decided what to name [my girls]. They didn't tell me they were naming [them] after Andres's old girlfriend[s] . . . but I knew. Only Johnny I got to name. . . . It's nice to name your own kids."[47] Such denial of autonomy is the heavy price women have paid to patriarchy.

[I suggest that one reason she stayed was her decision when she married that she would be a good wife, no matter what.] I intended to be a good wife. Um-hm. But it wasn't his same intention . . . to be a good husband. I was afraid of him, that he would beat me. We would begin to argue, and he would hit me. Well, then I wouldn't say anything. But not even for that reason would I try to leave him, never. He treated us very badly. He told me to get out.

One time he even told me to go to the bar, in Eaton where the prostitutes worked. He said, "Well, if you want money, get out and go to the bar." Do you believe that?

I don't know. He never, never changed his ways, he never changed so that he would be a loving father, amiable with his children, amiable with his wife—to love her like a wife, because she is the companion God gave him. Just as he gave Eve to Adam. It was as a companion that he gave Eve to Adam, so that he wouldn't be alone, not so that he could beat her.

Refusing to leave and tolerating a bad situation should not necessarily be confused with total acquiescence. Many women resist by simply refusing to be destroyed.[48] Physical abuse is not only painful and demeaning but can also be a kind of spiritual death.[49] For many battered women, refusing to be broken, continuing to live by some code of responsibility, and nurturing their children are all acts of defiance.

Viviana's living by her concept of a "good wife," cooking meals, clothing children, keeping a home, all with minimal resources and in the face of uncertainty, fit Buss's definition of resistance as "active or passive opposition to some oppressive situation."[50] Implied in the concepts of *padeciendo* [long-suffering] and *la mujer abnegada* [the self-denying woman] is the idea that the suffering woman quietly accepts her lot, never questioning her spouse's decisions, just carrying out his wishes. De Mente reinforces the idea, maintaining that the bad woman is not necessarily one who has become a prostitute or "fallen" in a sexual sense, but one who acts independently, who comes and goes as she pleases.[51] Although Viviana didn't come and go as she pleased, the resigned woman is not the one whose voice I heard most often in her. Instead, I came to know a woman with a fierce sense of her own identity.

One decision she made without deferring to her husband's wishes was how she would address him. He was not happy with her use of the formal *usted,* but she never said that he punished her because of it. My supposition is that not only their age difference but also their lack of genuine intimacy influenced her decision. It represented a refusal to be dominated.

With me, he used *tú,* and I addressed him as *usted,* because he was an older man, and I just got used to calling him *usted*. And he didn't want me to call him *usted*. He wanted me to call him *tú*. But since he was a widower, an older man, I told him, "I've become accustomed to calling you *usted*. [Me enseñé a decirle de *usted*.]" I decided to call him *usted*. [I ask if she continued this through their entire marriage.] Yes.

Well, we almost never talked. He didn't spend much time in the house. I saw him only when he came to eat, when he took a bath, but he would leave right away again . . . I never used *tú*. Even at the end. He would say to me, "Well, why do you call me *usted*? Call me *tú*." But I was already used to calling him *usted*.

These days, the kids, people in general use *tú*, and the correct word is *usted*. It's an indication of respect. That's why I got accustomed to calling Jorge *usted*, because he was already a widower, already an experienced man and everything. My mother and father used *usted*. That's why I also got into the habit when I got married. Because in former times the people used *usted*, not *tú*. Very few people used *tú*. One reason to use *usted* is to indicate a good—well, I don't say that because I don't have it—a good education.

It seemed those conversations about what Viviana would call her husband took place in an occasionally calm atmosphere. At other times, Jorge's anger did not lead to violence but took the form of petulance.

Jorge would get angry with me. And he didn't even want to eat the food I had made. And I would always go and entreat him. I would talk to him. He would be sitting there outside. I would go, "Come eat. Come eat. . . . I've made dinner, come eat."

"I don't want to."

"Well, don't eat." Like that. Until he couldn't stand the hunger, then he would come and peel potatoes and cut them up and cook them. [With a little laugh] He would burn them—he couldn't see well either—he would burn them all, but that's the way he ate them. He would go two or three days without talking to me. I would always go look for him and entreat him and try to resolve the issue . . . but no. He would be angry. Worse when I didn't want to serve him . . . he would get even more angry. So many years. Sixty-six years.

Rosario Castellanos, Chiapan prizewinning writer, feminist, and advocate of social justice, addressed themes of solitude and despair, explaining in one poem why she had become a writer: "someone . . . said that people like me don't exist . . . I looked into a mirror and no one was there."[52] Viviana never said that she felt invisible, but she told me more than once that her husband had told her she was insignificant. He never gave her a household allowance and seldom if ever spent money on her. Whether he truly did believe that women should have no desires of their own or whether he was just stingy, Viviana indicated that she received not the slightest indication of appreciation. Instead, she heard how unimportant she was, even though she was expected to answer his every whim. Smith and Smith point out that life with a batterer is demoralizing in many ways, not the least of which is constant subservience to one's tormentor. "Maybe the battered woman [is] not beaten every day, but she has to wait on her husband every day."[53] Those middle years provided no respite from lack, not just of money and resources, but also of recognition that she was a human being with needs.

> He told me that I was nothing to him, that I was expendable.
>
> He was very selfish. I never got his check from work. Never. He worked and he claimed the check. He bought the food and the clothes. He bought my clothes . . . until I got my own check from the government. Then I bought them, but he almost never bought me clothes. I never got so much as a pair of stockings from him.

Jorge also informed his wife that she was not intelligent, an opinion she was willing to accept, because he had developed skills that had eluded her. At times she remembered an intellectually curious man who had taught himself to read. The Jorge I met enjoyed talking about history, politics, and social issues. Among the good moments for the family had been times when he would read aloud from one or the other of the two books the family owned. It was from these occasions that Viviana gained her knowledge of Mexican history.

> He had a good memory even if he was a lunatic. Yes, he had a good memory for everything. Before, when he was young,

he would read a lot of stories. But only until we came here to the United States. That was when he changed his lifestyle and changed his way of thinking, acquiring other perspectives [she actually says "acquiring other words." I am interpreting here]. Then he began, in time, to get involved in the Bible . . . to go to church.

Jorge really liked to read the histories. All of these stories are very interesting. For example, Pancho Villa was a great man. They killed him treacherously. They killed him from the back. And he didn't know how to read, Pancho Villa. He was like me. [She smiles.] They would send him a letter, and he would give it to one and then the other, and then the other, so they could read it to him. So he could see if the one who read it first, and then the one who read it second, used the same words. To be sure, he would give it to somebody else—three—to be sure that the words were the same—that they weren't telling him lies. He was an intelligent man.

Well, there are many histories. In Mexico there was a president, Porfirio Díaz. Jorge was saying that one time he went to get a haircut there in Mexico, in San Sancho. Some men who were there, who had been in the war in Mexico, were saying that the president hadn't given them anything. There was a man there who also was getting a haircut. He was only listening, and then he said, "Yes. If Porfirio Díaz had lived longer, we would all be braying like donkeys." Everybody would be braying—Ooooh, ooooh, ooooh [she brays like a donkey]—like donkeys, with Porfirio Díaz, because he didn't give them education. He kept them like prisoners, only working and working. That man lifted his shirt. He said, "I went to the war and look at all I got." He was all shot up, where they had shot him in the war. "The president didn't even give me a ration." He didn't give him anything, like here they get their social security. There, no. There, there isn't any. They give the help to whoever they want, a little help, and the others, no.

The first Bible that Jorge got, I have it here with the history book. The Bible is very old. It doesn't have its top cover. It's very dilapidated. And the history of Mexico, I have it. Not all of it, but a part, almost the whole thing. It has all the pictures of all the ancient people. And there it explains the history of everyone.

Even though she remembered the details of those histories, Viviana was convinced she was incapable of academic learning. Her early experience in Mexican schools plus Jorge's disparagement likely contributed to her attitude. She was far from unusual in her time and place. Until the 1910 Revolution in Mexico, indigenous tribes and the working poor had almost no access to education.[54] A 1914 *National Geographic* article related, "A little teaching of the merest rudiments by instructors whose own education is exceedingly meager, with a dearth of books and a dark hovel for a schoolroom, is a fair representation of their educational opportunity."[55] Though Viviana ascribed her lack of academic success to her own shortcomings, those poor schools must have played a part as well. On the other hand, she thought Jorge was a good learner, giving him credit for learning English in the workplace. That she herself had more limited resources from which to learn did not seem to influence her thinking.

In the distant past [in Mexico], there was almost no school for the young folks. So a lot of the adults couldn't read, they didn't know how, because there was no schooling for them.

When Jorge came back to the United States, the English he learned was self-taught. What he knew, he learned after he came here. Jorge learned English on his own. Listening to the ranchers, he caught on by listening. He didn't know a lot, but yes, he knew.

When he first read to the family, he read a lot of history. Toward the end, he didn't read history, he read the Bible, but he remembered everything. You have to read the Bible a lot so you can inform yourself little by little; you need to go page by page. Before, when both of his eyes were good, he read. Afterward, with one eye, he read his Bible. He read it well. He had no schooling. At night when he couldn't sleep, he would get up and read.

I was in school, but I didn't learn anything. Because there are some of us who have a hard head. Jorge would tell me, "You have a head of rock, and one needs to hit you with the hammer."

Imagine that! He would tell me, "You, it's necessary to whack you on the head with a hammer."

Viviana's early educational experiences reveal a stubborn streak in her personality that may partially explain both her small acts of rebellion against Jorge and her refusal to leave him. When she set her mind to something, she stuck to her course. When she didn't see any way to change reality, she made her own way through that reality, coming to terms with what was.

I don't know how to read. I don't remember the words. I went to school in Mexico, and there were times that in the classes the teacher told my brothers to repeat what they had learned in the class, and because they didn't know it, she would pull their ears. In the past that was what they did, pulled their ears. Well, if they didn't slap them with the ruler, also. And then, I would get angry, I would get sad because she was hitting them, and I would also get stubborn. I didn't really try to read. I used to say, "Those are lies that the letters say. [Son mentiras lo que las letras dicen.]"

My head didn't help me grasp reading. I didn't believe that the letters talk. That's why I didn't learn because the letters don't talk.

I don't know how to read, like they say, not even the "o" for its roundness. [We laugh.] Not even the "o" for its roundness, is how the saying goes. But no, now for what? What do I want with an education now?

5

Transitions and the Road toward Cultural Adaptation

The 1950s

Latinos in the United States do not suffer from total assimilation,
nor from cultural amnesia.
—*David Hayes-Bautista*[1]

WAGES FOR BEET WORKERS were good in northern Colorado, but the beet season averaged only forty to sixty days a year.[2] By 1949, the Salguero family owned a small car for traveling between jobs. Each trip brought its own struggles, from carrying all their gear to keeping the vehicle running. They sometimes traveled with one of the children's godparents, but Viviana found to her surprise that the cultural values of sharing she had experienced on the ranch in Mexico were not as prevalent in the United States. Life north of the border was proving to be a study in adaptation. In addition to the discrimination she condemned in chapter 3, Viviana was taken aback by the emphasis on the individual over the group, a more every-man-for-himself attitude than she was accustomed to. That emphasis plus the family's semiannual migrant journeys contributed to difficulty in developing long-term communal bonds and support systems, leaving them to figure out how to navigate this new culture on their own.

At the same time, a strong trend toward homogenization was developing throughout the country, leading to the devaluing of minority customs and ideas. Mary Margaret Navar, great-granddaughter of a rancher who fled Mexico about the same time Viviana was born, describes the early 1950s in the United States as heavy assimilation years. "Children were punished for speaking Spanish in school. You were sent home, or you were sent to the principal. It was like cultural obliteration."[3] Through Viviana's younger children, who attended school whenever the family stayed in one place long enough and seasonal work was finished, she glimpsed more of the non-Latino world. English words and phrases would have edged their way into the house, and the children would have become familiar with Anglo approaches to holidays, birthdays, and the like. Finally, getting off the road and into a more settled lifestyle would also allow her to broaden her perception of the culture around her.

The family settled in Colorado just before the Eisenhower years, a time of general prosperity but not necessarily of inclusion. The GI Bill was helping many Latino veterans go to college, but it did not reach nonveterans or many agricultural workers, who often found their children unwelcome even in elementary schools. With the advantage of a more permanent home, Viviana could concentrate more on her children and their education. She was pleased to send them to school but puzzled as to why they didn't develop more intellectual curiosity from the experience. In later years, she would take issue with the school system for discrimination against Mexican-origin children, but she didn't comment on that inequity when discussing 1950s Colorado.

When sharing stories of these years, she also began to muse more about the supernatural. The subject first came up as a possible explanation for her husband's violent personality. She had heard accounts of witches and the devil while in Texas, and she was sure *brujas* were active in Colorado also. These stories could help explain the mysteries of human behavior. She was certain, on the other hand, that some of the legends she had grown up with were fabrications.

Viviana charted her own course when it came to cultural adaptation. She had little choice but to accept the less communal society of the United States, but she was so certain she couldn't learn English that she left that task to her husband and children. She actually knew more English than she let on—I think because she took her role as

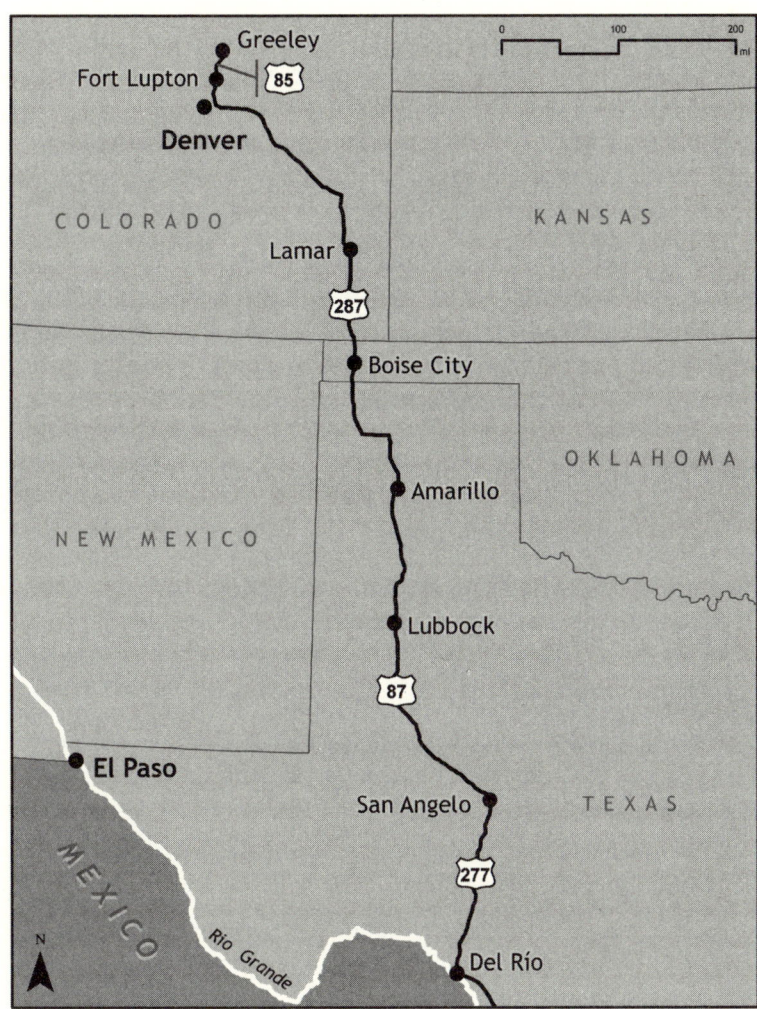

2. Migrant route from the Texas orchards to the cotton fields and then on to Colorado and sugar beet work (drawn by Colin Kamemoto)

my Spanish teacher seriously—but she had little fluency in speaking or listening. She remained dedicated to her native language. Her acceptance of witchcraft would also appear to be a rejection of US culture, but the belief was actually well ingrained in the indigenous peoples of both Mexico and the Southwest. Ironically, it had not assumed much importance for her in Mexico, but she began to consider the existence of witches after coming to her new country.

Viviana changed some of her perspectives willingly and adapted less happily to others when she had no choice. She would later recognize several trade-offs: the benefit of a permanent home and steady income against the loss of the communal society; her children's learning basic academic skills against their second-class treatment in schools; the recognition that established legends were not literally true against the loss of their guidelines as moral standards.

As serious as she was about such issues, Viviana's delightful sense of humor often topped off her narratives. The following description of the family's woefully little car amused her immensely, and she often saw a sardonic humor in human foibles.

> On one trip from the farm near Greeley to town, the inside of the car was full of kids, and all the rest were hanging on the outside of the car. That's why I'm telling you that we looked like *The Three Stooges* [she said the phrase in English]. That's how we came from the farm to here.

Viviana's daughter Beatriz, visiting during the interview, described the vehicle loaded with people and belongings: "Behind the car were the bicycles. Here on one side, a mattress, and on this side was a bathtub and some sacks of clothes. And right on top were more suitcases. We were like hippies. It was just a little car."

> Well, we got here. We had to cross a bridge. We stayed there by that bridge, because the car didn't want to work any longer. So then Jorge said, "We don't have any alternative but to buy a little trailer." So Jorge started looking for a trailer because we couldn't walk. It was morning. He went looking where they sold trailers and bought a mid-sized trailer. From there we took off. He took all our things off the outside of the car. It had been completely covered before.
>
> [The family was on the way to Texas.] Roberto's girlfriend wanted him to take her to Texas with us. Jorge said, "No." He said, "Where would we put her?"
>
> It was tiny, the car. Well, somehow it lasted a little while. Oh, finally, Roberto wrecked it. He and another kid were racing. They turned over, both of them. One ended up on one side, and

the other on the other side. That was the end of the little car. [Se acabó el carrito.] We had to look for another one.

When Jorge concluded that the family was returning from Texas each year with no more money than when they started, he found seasonal work with a Swedish American farmer near Greeley in northeastern Colorado and supplemented that income with work in the sugar factories during beet harvests. For several decades farmers in the northern Colorado area had been encouraging stability among their work force by hiring entire families,[4] and Jorge decided the family could make it through the winters on the money they made during the other seasons. Viviana did not mention any input into that decision. Research has shown that men made the decision to find permanent residence, at least through the 1960s, possibly because they earned the family income; but women were unlikely to object, because they and the children benefited from the decision.[5] Conditions on the road were onerous; thus, a common theme among migrant families was the desire to settle in one place, to live in a home.[6] Settling can also be an opportunity for upward mobility, often increasing the pace of adaptation to a new culture.

The family's last trip to Colorado from Texas may have helped cement the decision to stay put. Viviana didn't say whether Jorge felt as she did, but she felt let down by her baby's godparents. Within *compadrazgo*—the godparent system "whereby good friends are symbolically initiated into the family"[7]—they might have expected some financial help. Usually, among Mexican Americans, "in time of need one can count on family and *compadres* as well,"[8] even to the point that, as María Elena Lucas says, "some of the time, none of us have nothing";[9] but the Salgueros had already learned that, for the most part, Jorge's extended family was interested in helping only if they could benefit as well. The godparents probably had limited means, and with the Salguero family struggling to eat and put gas in the car, it is unlikely that the godparents, even if more financially well off, could significantly assist with the expenses of a large family.

Every year we would go to Texas from here, to pick the cotton. Well, one time, we left here and afterward Jorge said, "But, look, what were we thinking?" We went and he had only

enough money to buy the sacks to pick the cotton. There the
money ran out. We had to struggle to eat, to get money to eat.
[She didn't remember exactly what year they stopped going to
Texas.]

That same year we came back to Colorado again. Without
money. We came only by God's goodwill. We came with Isabel's
godparents, but they were traveling in style and had money and
all; well, they went to eat separately and just left us there. I was
carrying a little piggy bank of dimes. In former years there were
some little piggy banks that held only five dollars when you
filled them. That's all I had. Once in the middle of the road, the
car ran out of gas. It was cheap, all of it. It was really cheap. So
Jorge put gas in it, and we still had some left, money from the
little bank, still.

Viviana spoke often of the compassion that united the peasants in
rural Mexico when she was growing up. Although some outside
observers have argued that the idyllic village life of rural peasants was
a myth, that peasant people were both "nasty" and "nice,"[10] the
majority of Latino writers with rural origins, both men and women,
recall a strong sense of community, cooperation rather than competition, the sharing of resources, and an emphasis on "corazon," or
heart, rather than materialism, as part of their culture.[11] That collective spirit was not limited to rural areas. After the 1985 earthquake in
Mexico City that killed more than ten thousand people, the government was slow to react, but the citizens came together as family, rescuing survivors and offering food, clothing, and shelter to those who
had lost everything. The day after the earthquake, Mexican Americans in Los Angeles filled the coliseum, ready to give blood, clothes,
money, medicine, whatever was needed.[12]

What the people rediscovered through that experience was that
they could depend, more than anything else, on each other.[13] Other
cultures have experienced outpourings of compassion and material
help after disasters, but the ongoing nature of the communal support
has led many writers of color to use the term "culture of collectivity"
for the Mexican and other formerly colonized regions.[14] Mary
Margaret Navar enjoyed visiting her extended family in Mexico,
where still in the 1980s, "every time a cow or some kind of steer is

slaughtered, they distribute the meat amongst the family, the semi-
nary, and convents." She describes the culture she encountered there
as "a study of collectivism versus individuation."[15] Every principle
has its opposite, and she maintains as well that such a worldview can
stifle individual initiative,[16] but it can also create a network, sometimes essential for both individual and cultural survival.[17] Immigrants, leaving that culture behind, can find themselves cut off not
only from their country but also from their traditional way of interacting with others.

> Formerly, people were poor, very poor. But they didn't have, in
> Spanish they say "thievery." Going around just taking things.
> Like rats. That didn't exist. Because all the neighbors helped
> each other. If you had one, two, three, or four tortillas, you
> would give your neighbor two. And you would keep two. And
> if you had some other little bit of food, you would make the
> food and take a dish of it to your neighbor. You would share
> with your neighbor. That's the way the people were in the past.
> They would help each other.
>
> For example, before if you had a male calf, and you raised
> it and then killed it, you would give all of the neighbors their
> piece of meat. You were unified, friends. "Take this, take it," you
> said to the neighbor. And you were done only when you had
> shared it over there and over here. The people were poorer, but
> they had community. In everything. Now, no. There is a saying,
> "Each one scratches himself with his nails." [Everyone for him-
> self.] These days no one wants to give anything to the neighbor;
> one eats everything he has [she laughs].
>
> Everyone on the little ranches, even though they were very
> poor, had their cow for milk, their chickens for eggs, and their
> pigs also. When they were fat, they killed them. And they ate
> the meat and saved the lard for cooking. Like I told you already,
> they gave some to all the neighbors. But nowadays, if I have
> two tortillas and you don't have any, I eat them; and you, well,
> you don't eat. Everyone in former times was very united; now,
> in these times, no. They don't want to share. If you have, you
> eat. And if I don't have anything, well, I don't eat. But, well,
> everything changes.

Not only did Viviana maintain that people were less willing to share, but according to her, they were also less compassionate than they had been in the past.

> It's said that when someone did something criminal or some such thing, they sent that person to jail. There they call jail the *pinta*. They would send them there for four or five years or more. And the people would cry because they sent them to prison. Now, no. Now they send a person for twenty or more years, and the people say, "Well, they should give them more time. The crime was no small thing." And now, people say, now there is no longer compassion. In earlier times, the people cried for that person they sent to jail.

Among the ways to adapt to a different culture is formal education, an option Viviana did not believe she had. She did want it for her children, however, trusting that the school system would treat her children more fairly than it had Jorge when he was young and living in Texas. The system had not changed much from when Jorge's father was of school age.

> He [Jorge] used to say, before, they didn't want the Mexicans in the American schools. They didn't want them mixed in with the whites. They had to hire a teacher for the Mexican children, and another for the blacks, and another for the whites. They didn't want the Mexicans, even less the Negroes. There was much discrimination. That's why he didn't have any American schooling, because they didn't admit him into the American school.

For migrant children, educational opportunities in the United States were not that different from those of their parents. Through the 1940s, when the Salgueros arrived, Texas law allowed separate schools, and according to Fran Leeper Buss, "it was public policy in South Texas to make sure that so-called Mexican children did not attend school past the age of ten or twelve. In fact, school systems exchanged suggestions for circumventing attendance laws . . . [and] worked out techniques to ensure they received tax credits for the Mexican children in their districts while guaranteeing that none of those children would achieve a sufficient education" to become more than a laborer.[18] Not only were facilities separate, but the Mexican schools also suffered from shoddy construction, poor equipment, inadequate resources, and poorly paid teachers.[19] Even after a 1948 federal suit by Mexican American civil rights organizations resulted in the prohibition of separate campuses based on race, most school districts ignored the decree.[20] As late as 1976, the Fifth Circuit district court had to issue another decree ordering complete desegregation.[21]

From 1946 to 1949, the Salguero family was on the migrant circuit, spending their winters in Texas. When they settled in Colorado, the five youngest children would have been in or entering primary school. The six older ones were in their teens and twenties by then and, even though the situation was changing, they might not have found school very welcoming. A 1949 report on intergroup relations found that some communities in Colorado had raised the percentage of Mexican American youth graduating from high school through programs dedicated to intergroup understandings and cooperation, but Greeley was not one of those communities.[22] On the contrary, as Sarah Deutsch reports from just a few years earlier, "teachers who said, 'Oh, why don't you go back to the god-damned beet fields,' did not instill confidence."[23]

Even had they been welcomed with open arms, it is unlikely that the older children had the capabilities or the motivation to succeed in school. They had not developed good attendance habits or many literacy skills in Texas, and Diego once told me that in Colorado he and his brothers made a name for themselves in the bar crowd as ferocious and close-knit fighters. According to him, they spent their time either working or squabbling with other belligerent young men. Their school years were behind them.

Their younger siblings would have a better chance, although they were at some disadvantage compared to their Anglo peers. They attended various schools in the small towns near Greeley as the family moved to farms near Gilcrest, Eaton, and Ault. The 1949 report pointed out that many farm laborers' children lacked money for adequate clothing and extracurricular activities, contributing to a sense of rejection.[24] Earlier research by George Sanchez cited additional factors that would have worked against them, including the language handicap of educators (rather than of children), and poor preparation for school.[25]

By 1955 when the Salguero middle children were ready to enter junior high school, it was still not the norm for Mexican American children to attend any secondary school. A few families had begun to defy that pattern decades before, however. Gilbert Carbajal of Greeley recalls,

> When I attended school in 1942, my parents never took us out of school to work the beet fields. My dad always made us go to school. One day I was really sick and had just vomited on the floor. I told my dad I was really sick (*No me siento bien*) and couldn't go to school. My dad said, "Get going, get going to school, and if you die, I will come get you (*Vamos, vamos a la escuela, y si te mueres, yo voy por ti*)." He wanted all of us to get all the education we could.[26]

These children were part of some positive changes. The principal of one school saw evidence as early as 1946, through repeater records and a social acceptance scale, that Mexican American children were becoming better adjusted year by year.[27] Some of Viviana's younger children did graduate from high school in the 1960s, quite possibly a tribute to her emphasis on education and to the stability afforded by having settled in one location.

> In Mexico our children were in school, and here [in Texas], no, they weren't in school. There wasn't much of a requirement. Almost all the people [migrant workers] had their children at work, working. There wasn't much emphasis on their graduating or learning to read.
>
> [I ask if it was difficult to enroll the children in the schools in Texas.] Well, they were in Texas only a short time. But then afterward, my sister-in-law brought us here to Colorado. Here was where they got almost all their studies. They liked school. They brought a little schooling from Mexico. Because when we first came, they stayed in Torreón with Mercedes, and they stayed in school. So Sancho, Vicente, and Beatriz got more school. And

Mario. Mario was just little, but he also had schooling in Mexico. And the younger ones got more school here in Colorado.

Roberto didn't go to school in Mexico or here in the United States. Nor Mercedes. Because they were the oldest, and Jorge had them working. The little ones were the ones who got the schooling.

Even the children who did finish school were not as intellectually curious as Viviana would have liked—an ironic criticism from the woman who didn't think she could learn—but they achieved a milestone denied the older children.

Now, my kids don't want to know about the stories they can read. They are very, like the president of Mexico says, they are complete donkeys. They don't want to know the stories, which are very interesting. They don't read them because they just want to fool around, that's all. They don't want to sit down for a while to read them so they will know. No, they don't care, they're not interested in anything. Well, the little bit that I know has stuck to me—I don't know much, but yes, I always have in my mind what Jorge read.

When the family first settled, Jorge found a job that provided them with an unusual perquisite—housing more than spacious enough for all of them. It was here, in an old schoolhouse, that Viviana unintentionally turned the tables on her husband, not beating him up but causing a serious accident. She expressed no glee or sense of revenge; neither did she mention any later retribution against her on Jorge's part. It was clear that she intended no harm and remembered the incident as unfortunate.

Once in Colorado, we were living in a very large house. It had been a school before. We were the only ones living there. Well, it was very big, the house. It had an enormous boiler. The kids would cut pieces of wood with the saw. They would put them on a *caballito*, those stools that they use to cut wood [a sawhorse]. The kids would cut the pieces to put in the boiler in the basement. And we would make the food in the wooden stoves.

One time I knocked Jorge down below. He got home from work, and I was making tortillas, because the family always had to have tortillas. He was washing and he soaped up his hands. He grabbed my face and rubbed soap all over it. I got mad and I had opened the door to the basement. I grabbed him and started to push him, and he didn't know that the door was open. When he leaned on the door, he fell to the bottom. He went rolling to the bottom. He ended up very angry. He hurt his ribs and everything when he fell. He was very tall. He had to go to the doctor, and all the doctor did was wrap the ribs with a bandage.

That incident evoked Viviana's sympathy, but more often, she pondered what might have made Jorge so quick to anger. The question led to the supernatural, and although she never directly ascribed her husband's motivations to the devil, she was a believer in Satan's influence on people. She had no doubts about his villainous intrusions into human affairs.

You don't know what's in a man's mind when he is angry, the husband. Isn't it true that you don't know what things he might have in his mind? [¿Verdad que no sabe qué opiniones tendrá él en su mente?] That's why they do what they do. It's easy for them to overpower the wife, and they overpower her completely, just like that. And strangle her, or kill her. But it's like we say, it's the living Satan, the devil who runs around loose. He runs around looking for someone to lead astray, because that's what the devil is for.

And that's why there are so many things happening these days. Before, I wasn't hearing that. Not until now. Before now it happened only a little that one heard of people killing their wives, killing their children, and the babies—did you see that one who pushed the children into the water with the whole car?[28] She pushed it into the water with both of the children. Let's see, did her children hurt her? To throw away such innocent children, so that they drowned? Think of it, poor little ones, right? Yes. Innocents. But that's the way it is. How many infants are being stolen? Also, young girls leaving school are being taken. Young girls. Little girls. They take them and, out there somewhere, they kill them, they abandon them and everything. In former times, the people were very poor. But they didn't do that.

In addition to Satan's evil influence, Viviana was willing to consider other beliefs about the spirit world. Stories about suspicious events surrounding the death of her father had reached her from family and friends in Mexico. Among many Mexicans, particularly rural people of Indian descent, a variety of hexes and spells were thought to be common. If a man suddenly lost his sex drive, his wife or sweetheart often assumed some other woman had bewitched him.[29] Rituals known in Mexico as *toloache* could be used by wives in an effort to control their husbands.[30] When an illness refused to abate, many decided it was the result of someone's casting the evil eye on them.[31]

When my father died, I was already here. He died very young. He was forty-two. They said that someone put a spell on him. It's called a spell. Witchcraft. Well, they said it—I don't know— that a woman who wanted him put that spell on him, that she wanted him.

My father was very respectful, very serious. I don't know any more, if it was she or I don't know who, but he died of a spell, they said. One time they said that it was not a spell, but that he had burst a lung or who knows what. But yes, I knew that he died because of the spell, the witchcraft. She had her spouse, her husband, but she, I believe, wanted my father.

Then my mother was left. She also was very young. She found another husband. But the other husband also died, and she was left again. She buried both of them. And she was left. At the end she was almost my age when she died, eighty-three.

As a child, Viviana did not hear stories of supernatural or strange occurrences other than those sanctioned by the Catholic Church. Her father, a leader in the village and a practical man, shielded his family from what he considered gossip and idle socializing. His perspective aside, however, belief in witchcraft has coexisted with Christianity for centuries in Mexico, including the area that became the

American Southwest. Deutsch writes that "*brujas* were taken for granted" in the village society of New Mexico,[32] and in researching for his 1974 *Witchcraft in the Southwest,* Marc Simmons found that some New Mexicans still refused to visit Sandía, a village just north of Albuquerque, because it was considered a witches' haven. He also heard tales about witch assemblies repeated as truth from the San Luis Valley in Colorado to the Texas border. Viviana affirmed the existence of witches in Texas and Colorado, adding a twist I have not found elsewhere. Very clever, they sometimes outwit even God.

Well, none of us went out much. My mother, almost never. And we lived many years in the same place. We didn't hear any conversation, or anything, because my father was a loner. He didn't like to go to social gatherings or just talking. That's why I didn't find out about things pertaining to witchcraft until later. They said things about witches, but I don't know. When you are just a kid, you don't pay much attention to those things. But yes, there are witches. In the Bible, they're called *hadas*. Um-hm. They say that you shouldn't believe in them, but yes, they exist. Because they are in the Bible.

[I ask her if it is possible that the woman who was interested in her father could have enlisted the help of a witch.] They say that she didn't know how to do witchcraft, but people go to another place, like here you might go to LaSalle or Eaton or Fort Lupton or someplace like that—they go to another place looking for someone who does evil, who makes people sick through witchcraft. They'll do it for whatever reason. You don't realize what is happening to your body. There is no evil or anything she can't do, and you can become more and more debilitated until you die. If you know you are bewitched and there is no cure for you, well, you begin drying up little by little. Your life begins to dwindle because of your obsession with that. If you can't find anyone to cure you, well, you die.

God effects cures, yes, also, but they say that those women can do more than even God. [Dios hace curaciones, sí, también, pero dicen que esas mujeres hacen más que ni Dios.] Because there are people who will kill others for nothing. For all practical purposes, they kill them with these sicknesses. Right now you and I are here talking, but by tonight, I could have died, or you could have died. Because they're very fast. And God would not even realize that. That's why they do more than God.

Marc Simmons cites the passage from Exodus 22:18, "Thou shalt not suffer a witch to live," as the basis for the belief in the biblical authentication of witches.[33] Later in life Viviana became a Pentecostal, a denomination acknowledging Satan, evil spirits, and witches. She might also have talked with other women on the migrant paths and in the fields, including her in-laws, and by the time I knew her, Spanish-language television was usually on in the house. She could have heard tales of sorcery from any number of sources.

Viviana thought it possible that witches had exercised some malevolent influence on her husband's family. It could be dangerous to make a witch, or even a healer, angry. For example, Juanita Sedillo, an elderly *curandera* from near Albuquerque, New Mexico, told of casting a spell on her nephew without even realizing it, because he had antagonized her.[34] Most witchcraft was assumed to be intentional, however. Desire for revenge often provided the motive for hexing a victim.

Consider this, Jorge's step-mother, who was my mother-in-law, fought with a woman who was living with her brother. That woman told her, "Well," she said, "in the end, you'll pay." That's what they tell you, "You'll pay me." When they tell you, "You'll pay me," they are going to do something evil to you. My mother-in-law developed a pain. The following day she died. My father-in-law went to get some medicine, because he thought this was just any kind of pain. But by the time he returned and opened the door, there was a black cat on her chest. When he opened the door, the cat fled. With that pain, my mother-in-law died. It was caused by the woman with whom she fought. Immediately she killed her.

Where they were fighting, the woman [had fallen] on top of my mother-in-law—so my father-in-law went and turned her around so my mother-in-law could hit her. And then, she told him, too, "You are going to pay, also." So she put a curse on his legs. He couldn't walk. He had always walked crooked because, when he was smuggling, the sheriffs shot him. But it got worse when that woman put the curse on his legs.

Well, witches are into vengeance. If I were to do something bad to you, to get revenge on you, so that you didn't provoke me more, I could kill you—put you under a spell so that you would die. That's vengeance.

A lot of people—primarily here in the United States—do not believe. They say these are lies. But yes, there are witches here in the state of Colorado. You don't even know where they are. In Texas, also, they exist. There are more witches in Texas than here in Colorado. I don't know why.

It is actually not surprising that Viviana believed there were more witches in Texas than Colorado. Most of the Colorado stories come from the southern part of the state, limiting the geographical area in which witches are supposed to live, but perhaps more significant are the changing beliefs, particularly in New Mexico on Colorado's southern border. Simmons cites those who still believe making such comments as, "We already have been breaking up the witches. Maybe we caught most of them," whereas a concerted campaign in the press, the schools, and the religious institutions has helped to challenge the credibility of witchcraft. Many believers, in order to avoid scorn or ridicule, now preface their narratives with the paradoxical, "Of course, I don't believe this story, but it happened just as I'm going to describe it."[35] Texas has experienced changes in beliefs as well, but on the Lower Rio Grande, much interchange still goes on with Mexico, continuing customs related to the black arts. Belief in hexes, spells, and charms is still strong, and those who can't get powerful enough magic from the local witches travel as far south as the Valley of Mexico or Guadalajara to obtain what they want.[36]

Viviana told me that her own son César may not have been immune to sorcery. Having married a woman Viviana described as domineering, he had just lost everything to her in divorce court. In the Mexican cult of masculinity, the mild-mannered man who doesn't dominate his wife or girlfriend, especially if he previously cultivated the stereotypical masculine image, is frequently assumed to be bewitched.[37] María Elena Lucas thought her partner may have considered her a witch: "Sometimes I think that Pablo's afraid of me, that he thinks I'm some kind of witch or that I have some kind of powers, and that helps control him. . . . I overheard him say to one of my grandkids, 'Your grandma's got powers.'"[38] Not a believer in witchcraft, César undoubtedly saw the situation in a different light, but his mother harbored her suspicions.

> Consider this, César doesn't believe in witches. But they say that one shouldn't doubt; one shouldn't say that there aren't any. Yes, there are. It's always in the back of my mind that César is under a spell. He still has the spell that woman gave him, Consuelo. Suelo was his wife—until she ran off with another man. She already had family; she had four by her first husband. But they divorced. So then in time, she found César. We had known Suelo since she was a young girl, like about nine or ten years old. After she and that man separated, she ran around here and there. In time she found César, or César found her. She well knows where those women who cure are. She knows. And César, well, he lost everything. When Suelo left him, she had no right to take the trailer. Well, she took the trailer; she took everything. Yes, she left with another man and left him the children.

Witches might walk among us, but about other superstitions, Viviana was more dismissive. One of the best-known legends of both rural and urban Mexico, dating back to pre-Columbian times, is that of La Llorona, the ghostlike woman who roams the countryside in search of her dead children, children she herself killed. Stories vary as to the circumstances leading to her dreadful act, but all include betrayal and abandonment by a man. A kind of Mexican bogeywoman, she is used to keep children from straying too far or misbehaving.

Although the rare woman empathizes with her, focusing on her grief and maintaining that she does not mean any harm,[39] she is almost always a threatening figure, specifically a threat to men.[40] La Llorona does provide a warning to women about how they must behave, lest they suffer societal retribution, but she is seldom if ever referred to as endangering a woman. Some see her as a vehicle for the female desire for revenge, particularly toward *parranderos,* or drunkards.[41] She appears to them as a beautiful woman who, when neared, suddenly turns to expose the face of a hideous horse. She is said to have cured a number of alcoholics.[42] Her cries can also foretell poverty or death.[43] By insisting that the legend no longer had the power to frighten anyone, even children, Viviana may herself have been mourning the absence of any societal restrictions on a man like her husband.

Even if he had no reason to fear La Llorona, Jorge's treatment of his wife did seem to indicate a fear of women in some sense. What if he had allowed Viviana to go out to the market or to visit neighbors? Would he have been seen as less of a man in his or his companions' eyes? Would his structured world have fallen apart if he could not control every aspect of family life? Among the theories psychologists and anthropologists have entertained to explain men's fear of women is the idea that males often project their fears of what they themselves are capable of onto women. Thus, the only way women can be kept from misbehaving the same way their men do is to keep them isolated from the competition.[44] Whatever the theory—and explanations for men's fear of women abound in psychology—La Llorona seems the consummate representation of those feminine powers that men cannot control. She can give birth, she can kill, and she can tempt men to wanton sexuality. What she cannot seem to do is help men and women cross the gender barrier by overcoming fear and learning to trust each other.

> La Llorona there in Mexico—they are all frightened of that Llorona, but that Llorona they were able to capture. She used to scare the people, but one day they set out to spy on her and grabbed her. She was a woman who covered herself with a sheet. She put it on and then carried a stick inside the sheet. She hid herself under the sheet, and she screamed at those hours of the night around midnight or twelve thirty. Everybody was terrified of La Llorona, until one day a drunken man said, "I'm going to spy on her to see who or what she is. Yes. If she has money, well, she can give it to me." Well, he spied on her. He grabbed her, and she was a woman. I think the man almost killed her, that Llorona. The legend wasn't true.
>
> La Llorona was scaring the children so they wouldn't go out in the street, like a policeman, but of the spirit [Viviana is smiling].

The kids around ten or eleven or eight years old didn't go out because they were afraid of La Llorona. All they had to say to the kid was "Well, go out and see how things go with La Llorona," and they didn't go. There they were better off in the house.

Now when they tell them not to go, but to stay, the kids say those are lies about La Llorona, and they go. Now they don't fear even the devil. They don't even fear Satan. Even though you tell them the devil is coming, and, well, he comes. You know they don't listen. "Whatever." ["Ya ve ya no."] [She is laughing while she tries to explain. The children are using an off-hand response, dismissing the adult's warning.] Now they're not afraid of anyone, anyone. In the past, that's what La Llorona was for, to scare the people [adults], too. All those are only superstitions of the people.

Another story Viviana dismissed was that of the Virgin of Guadalupe, a central pillar of Mexican Catholicism. The legend, fostered by the church in the early days of colonialism, provided a vehicle for bringing Indian groups into the fold.[45] The brown-skinned Virgin's appearance to the Indian Juan Diego gave the native peoples a sacred feminine, Catholicism's version of female perfection. As opposed to La Llorona, the hag or the witch who motivates through fear, the virgin represents the opposite stereotype, the asexual woman who inspires veneration because she is not a threat to men in any way. She does not tempt but, on the contrary, exudes only mercy and understanding. Ironically, her image may have done more harm to relationships between men and women than did images of hags and witches. Real women must "fall," becoming sexual beings in order to fulfill their roles as wives and mothers. They also speak their minds, disagree with their husbands at times, and even become angry. Unlike the virgins who appear miraculously throughout Mexico—as Ilan Stavans says of his homeland, "We are awash with virgins"[46]—they do not produce flowers in the middle of winter or magically cure illnesses. No longer Catholic, Viviana and Jorge neither believed in nor worshiped the Virgin, but such archetypal symbols permeate Mexican culture. If the Virgin was meant to give men a reason to cherish women, she, like La Llorona, appears to have fallen down on the job in Jorge's case.

[I ask her if she knows the story of the Virgin of Guadalupe.]
There isn't much to the story. I don't believe it. The Virgin
appeared to a man, in the mountains. She appeared there to
Juan Diego. So then he came and told the priest a young girl
had appeared there, and this girl wanted him to build her tem-
ple. So the priest said, "Well, tell this girl to give you signs,
some flowers." And in this season there weren't any flowers. It
was winter. So then Juan Diego went back to the Virgin. He
told her that the priest wanted some fresh flowers in order to
believe that she would work miracles. So then, well, I don't
believe, but to each his own belief. So she said, "Yes, take them
to him." She put a garden there. He was wearing a carpenter's
apron—she told him that he should go out and cut all the flowers and put them in the apron that he was wearing. So he went
and cut all the flowers and carried them to the priest. He said to
the priest, "Here I bring, my lord, what you asked of the girl."
So the priest said, "Empty them." He dumped them out, and
the image of the Virgin remained painted on his apron.

In Mexico they have the authentic celebration. It's not very
long, the story of this Virgin. It's the same with the Virgin of
San Juan, also. [I ask if her story is different.] Yes, the Virgin of
Guadalupe wears a cape; they paint it with many colors. The
Virgin of San Juan has a blue cape or a white one. One time
she also appeared to a young girl. The girl was going to the
countryside to care for the animals that they had, burros, goats,
and all. Then this girl found a little spring. She began to make
mud there. She began to play in the dirt. Then this young girl
[the Virgin] appeared to the girl, and the girl told her mother.
So the mother took the girl to tell the priest what she had seen.
The girl and the Virgin had talked with each other. And they
had started to make little soaps—little soaps, very skinny, little
wheels and everything—from the mud. The Virgin, through
her power, made them white. Everything they made, like the
toys, she made them white through her power because she was
a Virgin.

So those little breads they sell in Mexico, they are of the
earth. They sell them, for example, for diarrhea, and for vomit-
ing. One tears off a piece of the bread, dunks it in water and

moves it around right away and when it dissolves, drinks it all. It gets rid of the diarrhea. Well, all those miracles the saints do in Mexico. [She is laughing, because all the miracles happen only in Mexico.]

All sorts of Virgins appear there in Mexico. San Ysidro is one. For that one, they have festivals of dance, Indian dances or feather dances for that saint. And other saints—the Virgin of Lourdes and the Virgin of who knows what. They have appeared here also, but they're not declared. [Aquí también se han aparecido, pero no se declaran.] People have only seen her [here in the United States] but it isn't true. In Mexico, yes. It's all very interesting. Well, it depends on one's beliefs.

Another bit of Mexican folklore existed also in the American Southwest, but Viviana attributed it only to Mexico. Tales of hidden treasure intrigued her, although she wasn't convinced they were true. One Mexican saying advises that if you hear voices coming from inside a wall, there is money buried in it. Such stories could have grown out of the 1910 Mexican wars when well-to-do families found themselves forced to flee their homes. With rebel troups approaching and travel unsafe, one can imagine delicious tales of people sequestering away great wealth for some lucky peasant to stumble upon years later. Mexican peasants also frequently used a shovel and the cover of night as a banking system. Carrol Norquest tells of his surprise when he found out that the Mexican laborers on his Texas cotton ranch buried their pay. When he asked them why they didn't put it in the bank, "they looked scornful. 'There is only one in town. They just rob a poor cristiano there. Only *un sonso* [a fool] would carry his money to the bank. *Son bandidos!* [The banks are robbers!]'"[47]

Nasario García, who collected tales of buried treasure in New Mexico and California, describes an incident in his own family. Rumors had circulated that his grandfather, nearly a hundred years old, had hidden his wealth in the crawl space beneath his home northwest of Albuquerque. Upon his death, treasure seekers ransacked his ranch home, ripping up the floors and digging holes throughout the kitchen, finding nothing, but leaving a badly damaged house.[48] Other tales told of chimneys that did hold gold coins,

people finding money that brought with it a curse, and treasure seekers whose dreams were never fulfilled.[49]

The border regions of Mexico and the United States share many
such legends and attitudes, making the question of adaptation a slip-
pery one. Nondominant cultures broaden the arts, the foods, and the
language, among other elements, of the dominant groups, while
changing and adapting in those same areas. Thus, Viviana encountered some familiar cultural beliefs and behaviors in the United
States, but she did not unquestioningly accept those, any more than
she adopted Anglo ways. She would choose her own identity.

> They say that, like before, there weren't any banks to deposit
> your money there in Mexico, and the people who were very rich
> took their money and buried it. They made some holes, and
> they put their money in there. In time, they were getting old
> and then they didn't remember where they had left their money.
> Well, they moved somewhere else and that money stayed there,
> buried. That's why they say that, before, many of their spirits
> came out because of the money that was buried. And a lot of
> people began to find it, that money, because a lot of it wasn't
> buried very deep. Just enough that it was covered.
>
> They say that when there is a white spirit, it means [good
> or untainted] money. And when a dark spirit comes out, a
> black one, it is a bad thing. Satan, the devil, is the agent of that
> money; he is in charge of it. No one can take it out. Only if you
> have the courage to talk with the devil. If not, the devil keeps
> that money. The people say that. Well, I don't know because I
> never saw anything. I only heard that spirits used to come out
> very often.

6

Motherhood in
the Labyrinth

Children need parents to be wise.
—*Yolanda Nava*[1]

CRUCIAL TO VIVIANA'S IDENTITY was her role as mother, the central hub around which her active bunch had grown up, learned to work, left home young, married well or badly, experienced joy or catastrophe, and, in many cases, now returned frequently for a good meal or a chat. In their photographic essay *Americanos: Latino Life in the United States/La Vida Latina en los Estados Unidos,* Olmos, Ybarra, and Monterrey point out, "Despite the stereotypical portrayal of Latinas as passive women, they have always been a source of strength for family members."[2]

I seldom visited with Viviana that she did not see or talk on the phone with at least one of her children. They came to see their father as well, first at home and later in the assisted-living center where he died, but as Limón observes, the sense of family, of "ultimate wholeness of the total community, is often assigned to female, especially to maternal, symbols."[3] Although as the center of the family, part of Viviana's role would have been to convey the traditional values of the culture, I never heard her deliver lengthy admonishments or advice. I can't speak to how she related to her children when they were younger, but from my perspective, she seemed to provide a kind of counterbalance to Jorge's volatility—a steadier, quieter force, not without opinions but less harsh in judgment than her husband.

That is not to say she was a completely reliable narrator. I once asked her if she was a better parent than her husband, and she laughed as she pointed out that of course she would answer in the affirmative. Considering her mother's treatment of her, I would not have been surprised to hear she had been hard on her children at times. I don't know if she ever punished the boys, but indeed, her granddaughter related to me that Viviana had once taken a switch to Beatriz, suspecting her of having been intimate with a boy. Mercedes also hinted in one of our conversations that her mother could be severe. From talking with her children and grandchildren, my impression is that Viviana was honest in what she did tell me; she just omitted details that she had either forgotten or that might make her uncomfortable. From the boys, I have never heard a negative word about their mother, possibly an indication that she too fell into the stereotypical attitude of allegiance to male children.

Her narrative revealed that she did, however, learn from her daughters and their experiences as they adapted to life in the United States. Mother to a family that had crossed cultural as well as physical borders, she could in no way be considered part of a single, traditional culture; rather, she had become part of what Américo Paredes explained as an evolving Mexican American identity, influenced by change, adaptation, and innovation.[4] As her children married and left home, she coped with cultural as well as generational transitions, adapting, for example, to a more lenient attitude toward divorce in her children's generation. Although she would never consider such a course for herself, she expressed admiration for the daughters who divorced rather than continue to be mistreated.

I came to know the elder daughters moderately well, because they came by at times while Viviana and I were talking. Though short, both were larger than their mother, attractive and ample in dress sizes, but the similarities between the sisters stopped there. Mercedes, dark curly hair framing her face, would arrive with her soft-spoken husband, Alonso, greet me warmly and chat. Now in her mid-sixties, she loved to talk and dominated all conversations with discussions about her latest pain medication, her daughter's separation from her husband, another daughter's studies to be an attorney.

Alonso would nod quietly in agreement. Mercedes said little about her younger sister Beatriz during those visits, but after I got to know her a little better, she told me that Beatriz was crazy and wanted to kill her.

Beatriz, who was single, came more often. Whereas Mercedes often wore a dress or slacks, Beatriz dressed casually, wearing shorts and an untucked blouse or sweatpants. The hard life she had led seemed a little closer to the surface. Beatriz was more impassioned, and as we saw in her account of her relationship with her father, more willing to talk about her emotions. Of all the things she felt strongly about, her sister evoked the most vehement response: "Mercedes is nothing more than a snake! An absolute viper!" I asked Viviana once what started the war between the two, but she didn't seem to know. It was obviously long-running, however, with little chance for détente. On the other hand, Beatriz was very close to her mother.

Though Viviana had her quarrels with Mercedes and identified more with Beatriz, she cared for both daughters and valued their happiness over tradition—taking a step away from her conventional values and into the ambiguous world of mixed traditions and loyalties. Surprisingly, few of the disagreements Viviana described with her children resulted directly from clashes in cultural norms. Chicana literature is filled with discussions of mother–daughter conflict, usually reflecting a daughter's conflicting identification with and rebellion against her mother's life and values.[5] Scholars have described a love/hate relationship that can become most confrontational when daughters assert their sexuality: mothers accusing their daughters of assimilation, daughters in turn accusing their mothers of accommodation.[6] Viviana did not mention ever punishing Beatriz. On the contrary, she praised all of her children, taking pride primarily in their work ethic, a principle that, as we have seen, went to her very core. What she professed to value in her children helped explain how she saw herself as a mother.

If Viviana defined herself through her relationships with her children, it made for a complex definition. Her twelve children embodied a series of successes, crises, conundrums, and tragedies. A recurring image of Ilan Stavans's *The Hispanic Condition* is the labyrinth. Stavans refers to Simón Bolívar's deathbed question, "How will I ever get out of this labyrinth?" applying those words to the "complex, curved, distorted, wandering, winding . . . map of the Latino psyche,"[7] and noting how many Latino writers have used that same central image. As our discussions moved through disagreements, ill fortune, and other vicissitudes of her family's life, Viviana looked at the maze of human existence with a mix of sadness, detachment, and humor, finally employing the labyrinth metaphor herself.

Mercedes married at seventeen and left home before the family emigrated from Mexico. Her first marriage did not work out, but she later came to the United States and married well, rearing her children in a stable environment. Although analyses of Mexican family roles have established that the mother–daughter bond is without a doubt the closest of the parent–child relationships,[8] it is not necessarily always harmonious. Judging from their relationship when I knew them, Viviana and her eldest had developed a pattern of alternating between warmth and distance. Viviana was sympathetic at times because of her daughter's various illnesses and injuries but maintained that Mercedes was something of a hypochondriac. She was also indignant because of Mercedes's control of Jorge's social security checks, which he either gave her or had sent to her after he moved to the assisted-living center.

> When God sends an illness, well, they say God doesn't cause illnesses. They say that Satan causes them, the devil. Because God made man perfect . . . like Adam and Eve. He didn't make them sick. And like Jorge told her, God wasn't causing the illnesses, but the devil was causing them. That's why Mercedes has gotten sick, and she says she can't stand the pain she has. She says that she would scream to the devil, "Devil, Devil, take this sickness away from me, this pain!"
>
> Alonso would say to her, "Be quiet!" He said, "I hope the devil doesn't come here because you are screaming." She's better now. After Jorge died, she had no shortage of illnesses. When it wasn't one thing, it was another. Right now she's a little better.
>
> Beatriz and Mercedes can't stand each other. They don't like each other. [Beatriz y Mercedes no se pueden ver. No se quieren.] Beatriz [unlike Jorge and Alonso] says Mercedes's illnesses are punishments from God, "because," she says, "of what she did to you." She said, "What she did to you, taking the money

that Pa left." The four hundred dollars, Mercedes said she had taken it because she bought a television for Jorge. I said to her, "Well, where is it, the television?" She said, "Well, I took it back because Pa didn't want it." But she didn't give me the money.

Jorge told her one time, "Look, when I die, the money that is left, you take half and give half to your Mama." And she didn't give me anything. Instead, she said that I came out owing her twenty dollars . . . from the check Jorge got. Do you believe that I was going to pay that? They gave him six hundred fifty-five a month. She would get the check. The kids are still—how do I want to say it?—well, in Spanish you say "with the little thorn" [they're provoked with her].

Several of Viviana's family members had sustained job-related injuries, her eldest daughter suffering one of the most common, injury to the hands.[9] Studies have found that "Hispanic" workers suffer more work-related deaths and injuries than any other ethnic group, a circumstance due to two main factors: first, this group is over-represented in dangerous jobs; and second, the language barrier often precludes their understanding the safety procedures involved.[10]

Even though sympathetic to her daughter's pain, Viviana couldn't quite let go of the spat about the television. She finally talked herself around to a more generous perspective and decided that considering all the anger and provocations people put one another through, judgment is best left to God.

Well, may God help her. Because Mercedes hurt her hands at work. She was working with the turkeys in Longmont. And she says she put the turkey in the press, and it got her hands, too . . . when it cut the turkey. She says that when she pulled them out, the nerves detached. She stayed like that a long time, like nine months. They just gave her pills there where she was working. Finally she went to see a doctor, and the doctor told her that her hands weren't right. So she got a lawyer. She got a settlement from the company. They had to operate on her hands.

I hope when Mercedes gets older, she will become more loving. Mercedes didn't need to take the money from me. But, well, they say, "It's best to leave it in God's hands." They say that

God waits, but he does not forget. You did this, and you did it here and you did it there, and he forgets nothing. You forget, but he, no.

Beatriz had not been as fortunate as her sister in love or marriage. She, as her mother before her, had married an abusive husband. A National Violence Against Women survey in July of 2000 reported that a third of women who are physically abused by a male partner grew up in a home where their mothers were subjected to violence.[11] Trying to break the pattern, she left him only to find another and then another batterer, all the while dealing with the poverty that comes from little education and single parenthood. Poverty itself has been described as a kind of batterer, relentless and fearsome, keeping one worrying and scraping,[12] always on the edge of homelessness and hunger.

The outcome of that struggle with poverty is crucial for the children. According to Shorris, "Children of first generation parents have the greatest chance of defeating the odds" of failure in school and the continuing cycle of poverty. "If they fail . . . a pattern will have been set, and the fate of the parents will almost inevitably be visited upon the children."[13] The battle is uphill; statistics suggest that the socioeconomic position of a child's family, as opposed to hard work, determination, or intelligence, is probably the single most significant factor in determining future success.[14] Whether she realized it or not, Beatriz was locked in a battle not just for basic sustenance and personal happiness, but ultimately for the success or failure of her children and grandchildren.

Beatriz's first husband didn't appreciate kids. No, it seemed that he didn't have any love for his children. He was a musician, for dances, for parties they had. He would beat her a lot. He just had her working all the time, and he almost never worked. She was the only one who worked, and still he beat her.

He would bring her to see us only once a year. It was almost time for the fieldwork to begin, and he brought her to see us. We were living on a ranch outside LaSalle, and he came to buy a car here in Greeley. And her whole eye was purple where he had hit her.

They were accustomed to greeting and shaking hands, in the old way; when Jorge came to eat breakfast, Beatriz came out and greeted him and took his hand. Beatriz only cowered. Jorge asked, "What did you do there on your face?

She said, "I fell." Um, no. Her husband had told her not to tell Jorge, that she should say she had fallen.

"Well," said Jorge, "we're not going to leave it at that. I have to know how you fell." When Jorge got back from work in the afternoon—he was working on the ranch—Reinaldo was already sitting in the house with us. And Jorge already knew about Beatriz's black eye. Well, he arrived and they greeted each other. Then Jorge asked Reinaldo, "What did you do to Beatriz's face? I don't believe she fell and hit herself on a chair. You hit her." Because by then Beatriz had told him that he had hit her. But he wanted her to get him out of it by saying that she had fallen. Jorge said, "That's it. Today, she is going with you, you are going to take her, but be careful if you lay a hand on her again." Well, they left.

Shortly, Jorge said to me, "Get ready, because we're going to Naldo's parents"—Beatriz's in-laws—so that Reinaldo's father could see Beatriz's face. Well, we went and took them. Beatriz had told us that Reinaldo wanted to kill Jorge. So Jorge had a rifle, a twenty-two—he loaded it and took it with him. And we went to the parents. Well, Jorge bawled out that man good, the father, because Reinaldo's father well knew that he was hitting Beatriz. But he had never said anything. Beatriz had a very bad life with her first husband.

[I ask if the second husband was any better.] No, well, the second, no. No, none of her husbands turned out well. But she put up with them. Later, she was with the second one, and she had a boy. He is the one studying to be a lawyer. That husband got drunk and broke the windows and tore up the curtains and everything. He's from Mexico, but he has his residence card. That lasted only a short time, because he turned out to be a real drunk. She left him, and she was left with that little boy.

Later, she got together with another one, and she had the girl who is in California, Cecilia. Well, that was all; they didn't last. Then, later, she got another, well, from Mexico, Juan. He also had his residence card. She had two children, a little girl and a little boy, with Juan. She had nine in all. But five are siblings of the same father and mother. The others are only related through the mother. They are half-siblings.

One time she and the third husband were going in the truck, I think, in the pickup, and he threw her out on the ground. It's a wonder he didn't kill her. She left him also. She's had other husbands, also. So she had many children. I outdid her, I had sixteen pregnancies.

The only time I ever heard Viviana express envy was in relation to this daughter, Beatriz, and her role as a single mother. She had mentioned before that one reason for abject poverty in Mexico is the lack of governmental assistance, noting that in the United States, those who need help can get it through social services. When Beatriz turned to her own resources and applied for assistance rather than depending on the men she was meeting, her mother felt she managed well. Sociologist Irene Blea discusses the Chicana single-parent family, suggesting that rather than dysfunctional or deviant, it can be seen as "a healthy adaptation to oppression."[15] From a patriarchal perspective, the female single-parent family is not a functional structure, but as an alternative to an abusive or dysfunctional two-parent family, it may provide a more stable environment for children. Even the fact that Beatriz was a harsh disciplinarian impressed Viviana, although that tactic seemed to have produced mixed results with regard to how the children behaved.

The family today. I envy a lot of people I know here where the fathers left the families and the mother raised them quite well. [A mí me da envidia con muchas gentes que yo conozco aquí que también que los padres los dejaron y la madre también que los crió tan bién.] So well that they obeyed them. Look at Beatriz, she is one of them. She raised her children so well, if they got, like the saying goes, bad habits, bad ideas, it was because they got them themselves. Beatriz gave them a taste of her hand like Jorge.

Beatriz's kids went out. A lot of them went out running around, vagrants, when they were young. They even got mixed up with marijuana and everything. Benjamin was imprisoned in Canyon City because he even fought with a policeman. He was there in Canyon City for two years.

Beatriz worked a lot in the fields with her first husband. He would go play for dances, and he wouldn't come home. He would just go and leave her in the field. Then Jorge took her from that man. She kept all the five children she had when she left her first husband. Well, Pilar is the oldest. And then Reinaldo. And then the rest of them. But look, she raised them, struggling, keeping them afloat. The welfare gave her the means to raise them.

Several of those nine children went on to careers from government service to education. One son made a good life for his family working for the post office, and a daughter was working in the communications department of the local school district, thus breaking the cycle of hardship and giving their own children more educational and economic opportunities. In the meantime, while Beatriz was struggling to find a stable partner and rear her family, even more tragic incidents occurred in the lives of some of the younger Salgueros. Viviana recounted with poignant sadness the story of a son's first marriage, an incident that brought heartbreak to two families.

Ruben killed his first wife, but it was an accident. They were newly married. They had been married three months and ten days. He was cleaning a gun, one of those that has two barrels. He was cleaning it, and he broke it down. Then he put it together again. She had bought some new clothes for herself and some for him, for Ruben. So then Ruben put his on first, and well, they fit him. And then she put hers on afterward. So she said to Ruben, "Look, how do my pants and sweater fit?" Ruben said, "Oh, they fit well."

He said, "Move. Move so that a bullet doesn't fire and hit you."

She told him, she said, "It doesn't matter. It isn't loaded." But yes, it was. So then he . . . he wanted to scare her, and he probably pulled the . . . [she gestures] . . . and the gun went off. It hit her here in the pit of the stomach. And she was expecting a baby. He had been getting ready to go to bed, so he already had his socks and shoes off. When he saw her fall, he jumped up and grabbed her in his arms, [put her in the car], and [rushed] for the hospital.

He was near the hospital when the car ran out of gas. A gringo saw that the car was stopped there, he saw what had happened, that Ruben had taken her out of the car in his arms to carry her to the hospital. So the gringo gave him a ride to the hospital. But by the time he arrived, she was already dead.

So there in the hospital, they arrested him. The police got him in the hospital. They took his statement, and then they took him and put him in jail. About one or two in the morning, they told Jorge that Ruben was arrested; they told him the whole story. Well, what were we to do? Only wait. They had already taken her and arranged things.

The subject of the daughter-in-law's death led to a discussion about curses, in which Viviana related a comment by one of the girl's relatives. Viviana didn't seem to be commenting on the irony of the words so much as wondering whether such curses do actually carry power.

Our kids got together and sent her body to Texas, because she was from Texas. Ruben's in-laws, the girl's parents, didn't like him. Before they were married, they didn't like him because the girl was well educated, and Ruben wasn't. The girl's parents wanted her to have a career instead of marrying. But she defied them and married Ruben. Then her mother, they say, I don't know, a relative of theirs, her aunt might have been the one who said, "I would rather have seen her dead than married to Ruben." And that's how it happened.

They say that the mother's curse, and the wife's curse on the husband, comes to pass. In one way or another the person is punished, because the curse is already carried out, the curse of the mother or wife. Well, that's how it happened.

But they didn't punish him. They imprisoned him for two weeks because they were investigating. They went to Ault to investigate. Because it happened on a ranch. So they went to investigate where the store was, where they got food, where they bought clothes, in the bar, to see if he had been drinking. Well, everything, everything . . . how he treated her, if they fought or didn't fight, if he hit her or didn't hit her, and all of that they investigated, all of it. And it all came out well. She had some uncles here, but her parents and brothers and sisters had gone to Texas. They only came for the seasonal work, and they went back. The uncle and his family, the uncle's sons, stayed here, and his wife. So the investigators went and questioned the uncle. He said a lot of good things about Ruben.

Ruben had been working on the ranch. Like Jorge, he was working. So it all came out well. When they let him out of jail here, they took him to Boulder, to use the lie detector, to determine whether everything he was saying was true or he had done it on purpose. When they were taking him to Boulder, the two officers went into a cafe and left him alone in the car to see if he would run, to see if he felt guilty, to see if he had done it on purpose. And no, he waited there in the car. When they came back, they said, "Oh." One of them said, "You're still here."

He said, "Yes."

"Oh," said one of the officers. "We thought that you had gone."

Ruben said to them, "No." He said, "Where?" And all of that helped him. That crime gets one to five years. Since we had recently converted to the Pentecostal Church, Jorge pleaded for him that God would save him. And they didn't give him any jail time; they gave him only five years' probation.

At this point, the Salgueros faced a different concern, their son's psychological torments.

After that, Ruben was very easily frightened. Suddenly, he would jump up in the bed frightened. Always, a lot of the time, he would sleep with the light on. He couldn't sleep with the light off. I don't know what he saw or heard. He would get up at all hours of the night. Until finally the fear went away.

He kept working on the ranch. He stayed with us only the first days. After he began to get back in control, he went back to work.

As she considered the crises and tragedies in her children's lives, Viviana commented frequently on the common denominator that made her proud of all of them and may have kept those crises from turning out even worse. All were hard workers, defying any stereotypes of Mexican Americans as lazy or afraid of work. Throughout the twentieth century, Mexicans in the United States were commonly described as lazy and interested more in taking siestas than in working.[16] Shorris has pointed out that such stereotyping benefited employers in several ways, and many Mexicans and Mexican Americans still work long hours in a variety of jobs. Waldinger and Lichter cite manager after manager in "immigrant-dense regions" who praise the Latino work ethic.[17]

> Originally, he had gotten a job on a ranch because they gave him a [traffic] ticket. So, to avoid telling Jorge, so he wouldn't snarl at him, he chose instead to look for a job on a ranch. On this ranch, he had some friends, and those friends got him a job so he could pay the fine, so he could pay the ticket. That's how he got a job on a ranch. For that very reason, because he was afraid Jorge would reprimand him.
>
> Well, all of my children know how to work at very hard work. No matter where they put them, they worked. [No le hace dónde los pongan, ellos le trabajan.] They didn't go around saying, "No, well, I can't. . . . No, well, that's too hard." No. Wherever you put them, they know how to work. They knew and they still know. Now they all have good jobs.

Another son struggled with his own demons in the form of alcohol before he was able to put his life in order. Only after many serious problems, including a divorce, did he find a more stable lifestyle.

> I have a son in California, Mario. That one his whole life almost . . . he lived it drunk. They would put him in jail—they would pick him up for driving too fast. Only he ended up with a good woman. She is from Mexico, the woman he has, the second. And now he understands that he was living badly, but his first life, his youth, he lived badly. Now that he is getting older—he is more than fifty—now he realizes that everything he was doing

was not good. And now he has quit it all. He finally thought it
through, finally. But good, it's not too late. And now he's going
to a church . . . Pentecostal. He says that there they teach them,
they talk about good and evil, they talk to him in the churches.
He says, "I'm finally healing."

A tragedy that affected not only the Salgueros but the entire nation
was the Vietnam War. In that conflict, deaths and injuries of minority
troops occurred in striking disproportion.[18] During the 1960s,
"Mexican Americans in the Southwest represented 10 to 12 percent of
the population but accounted for almost 20 percent of the casualties"
in Vietnam,[19] a situation that touched Viviana firsthand. Her seventh
son, Guillermo—Memo, for short—served in the conflict, was
wounded, and came home with both physical and emotional scars.

He's not right in the mind, for thinking. He isn't—on account of
Vietnam. And he's not right in his feelings, either—on account
of the same. They wounded him twice over there in Vietnam.
That's why I have his medals. They're the Purple Heart, the
star, and another little medal. But now my daughter-in-law
has them, Roberto's wife. She has a coat from his service in the
army. He didn't want his picture taken with the coat on. He
just put it on a hook, and then she took a picture of it. She has
his little bars. All those, all those benefits he has, but he doesn't
want them. He doesn't want to be indebted to the government.
Who knows?

He isn't well. But he doesn't want to go to a doctor. Memo
isn't right in his mind. And then he's a little deaf. From the
grenades and shooting and everything. He says he didn't have
any hope of getting back to the United States. No. He says it's
very ugly over there. One had to move among the dead, walking among the dead and watching out for himself, also. They
wounded him, but not badly. That's why he has the Purple
Heart, the star, and other medals also. He says he stayed there
shot among the dead, and they came and lifted them to see if
they were dead. He waited until it came again, the airplane that
lifted out all those who were living, and it carried them out.
And that's how it was for him.

They sent us a military policeman to tell us that Memo had
been wounded, but that we didn't have to worry, that he was
well. So then, like a week later, a taxi came to the ranch, carrying a letter—that they send to say if your son died or didn't
die—and the soldier had told us what was in the letter. Jorge
was working, and the boss's wife was out there hanging clothes,
outside. So he arrived and asked the woman if this was the Salgueros' house. She said, "Yes."

He said, "Well, I'm carrying a letter about a dead soldier." It
had scarcely been two days since the soldier had come, that military policeman, to tell us not to worry. Well, right away the boss
went [she starts to cry] to tell Jorge. My daughter Isabel was
with us—all of them are good at reading English and Spanish.

Although Viviana maintained that her husband had no love for
his children, his reaction to this message would seem to indicate
otherwise.

Jorge couldn't open it. So Isabel said to him, "Well, Pa, I'll
open it." And she opened the envelope. [She's crying and I can't
get this clearly.] The letter said the same thing the soldier who
came earlier told us, but the taxi driver said that he had a letter
about a dead soldier. Well, that wasn't true. So then Jorge came
here to Greeley to talk all the way to Vietnam through the Red
Cross. They didn't want to let him, because it was so far away.

"No," they told him. "Well," they said, "We're going to give
you only two words." And yes, he called.

Memo said, "I'm OK," and that was all.

Earlier, from here to Ault, they had taken a dead soldier, a
Mexican. From Platteville, they had brought another. And we
said surely that's the truth from the taxi. So the boss talked to
the office and asked them how they could send this man who
couldn't give a good explanation and who scared the family.
Why? And Jorge said, "No, well, I have to be sure . . . to talk
to him."

Memo only said, "Everything's all right, Pa." [She's teary and
struggling with this.] But he says that he didn't have any hope
of getting back.

When Memo came back, he didn't want me to ask him about anything, about how it was over there or "What did you do?" or "What did you see?" or . . . he didn't want that. Lately, or now from time to time, he talks about it, but not much. He doesn't want to be asked either. Well, God wanted him to come back. He came back.

When he returned, Memo went to live in Chicago, where he found a partner and had two children. Life continued to provide him with challenges, including his partner's struggles with mental and emotional disorders, which led eventually to Memo's becoming the custodial parent and moving back to Colorado. For the first seven years I knew Viviana, he and the children lived with her. His mother worried that although he took on the full responsibility of his children, he didn't buy a home for them and for his own security.

Lieutenant Colonel Dave Grossman cites studies before 1995 concluding that Vietnam left us with more "psychiatric casualties than any other war in American history."[20] Those soldiers returning with post-traumatic stress disorder suffered symptoms from disturbing dreams to difficulty in maintaining significant relationships. Although Viviana expressed concern for her son's love life, her primary interest was his ability to provide a healthy and disciplined environment for his children.

He never married—he met this woman, Elena, in Chicago and had a family of two. She already had a daughter and a son. Memo recognized her like a wife, and the kids grew up beside Memo; they called him "Daddy." Her kids. They were half grown when Memo got with that girl. But, well, it's all in the man. . . . Memo has always gone out, he's been a wanderer. He has to go out. And this girl would worry and worry when he would go out, and in Chicago it's very dangerous. He would go out, and she would worry and worry and worry. She went crazy, from her nerves. They had to put her in the home for the mentally ill. Suddenly her nerves snapped. And she spent a long time very sick in the mental hospital.

But he's very stubborn, like just now, look. He has the opportunity to ask for a government loan to buy a house, but he doesn't want to. He says he doesn't want anything to do with the government. Well, so then when he's old, when God allows him to become an old man, what is he going to do? He'll have to depend on the government as he does now. [I didn't ask her about this comment, but she may have meant that he was receiving disability payments through the Veterans Administration.]

Well, that's how he is. What he doesn't want to do, he doesn't want to do. Jorge would say to him, "You don't have to struggle for a house. Ask for a loan from the government and buy yourself a house. And live separately there, you and your kids, you live there with them. Don't drag them around from house to house."

Look, when he came here from Chicago, he withdrew his retirement funds. They sent him sixty-three thousand dollars. He didn't do anything with it. He didn't even buy a house. He spent it all on running around with women until he lost that one who punctured his tires. Running around to Chicago, to Texas. . . . And well, he didn't stay with anything. He was going to open a bar, or he was going to start a restaurant. Well, neither bar nor restaurant. He spent everything. So . . . there he is now. He didn't have to struggle, but here he ended up living with me. He didn't have to. If he had bought his house when they sent him the money, there were much cheaper houses. Now they're very expensive.

But a person like Memo says, "What do I gain with making money and saving it when I die? Who is going to end up with it?"

I say, "For your children. "You have two children. They can keep the money."

"No," he says. "It's better to blow it." There you have it. When he thinks that way, he's not going to get anywhere. Right? Those thoughts he has, he doesn't do anything, and he's very . . . how do I want to say it? . . . very stubborn. He doesn't care about having anything. One reason is that he himself says he is crazy. [We laugh.] He tells us that he is crazy because he went crazy there in Vietnam, that he's a little deficient in sense, he's a little deficient in the mind.

Beatriz's daughter Pilar was close to Memo and views his postwar experiences somewhat differently than his mother did. When his partner Elena went into the mental facility, he assumed responsibility not only for his biological children but also for the two Elena had when they met. Much of the money he spent went to giving all of the children some experiences he thought they might never have opportunity for again, including a trip to Disneyland. He certainly wasn't as frugal as his mother would have liked, but neither was he indulging only himself. Pilar describes him as a caring and responsible father, but Viviana, who had scratched for every coin, could not help but question the choices he made. By her logic, his injuries had destroyed his mental capacity.

The Salgueros regained their son after his tour of duty, but they had won only a reprieve from death in the family. It was to come even closer to Viviana's heart after her youngest daughter moved to Chicago to work, bringing a tragedy that moved her to deep sadness whenever she spoke of it.

> Constanza had her boyfriend's baby, so Jorge ran her out of the house, and she went to stay with Beatriz [who was living nearby]. The little girl, Manuela, was born while Constanza was living with Beatriz. Her father was here in Platteville, Manuela's father. He is Mexican. His name is Cruz. When Manuela, the little girl, was born, Jorge began to chew Constanza out, and the girls were giving her a hard time also. Well, she told them, "I'm leaving here. I'm going to go to Chicago so none of you can nag at me. So I won't have to listen to you hassling me, 'Why did you do this and why did you do that?'" She went to Chicago.

In Chicago, Constanza found an apartment with her brother Memo, who was already living there. She got a job and eventually married her baby's father. When the marriage went sour in 1973, her husband returned to Colorado and the child's godparents arranged to care for the girl, now four, during the week while Constanza was working. What happened next never became clear to anyone in the family, even the two Salguero sons who went to the court hearing. Viviana was forced to depend on their accounts, various suppositions, and possible gossip to determine the circumstances of her daughter's last few hours.

Constanza married Cruz there in Chicago. My sister-in-law, the wife of Enrique, was caring for Manuela, Constanza's daughter. My brother-in-law and sister-in-law were her godparents. Constanza had a very unnatural character; she was very easily angered. [Constanza era de muy mal naturaleza, muy corajuda.] She got angry and ran Cruz off. And he came back here, and she stayed there.

So then, Constanza had a new boyfriend, who was an Italian. He had a party, that kid, and Constanza went. She had a record player, and she took it to her boyfriend's house. When the party was all over, the others left, and she stayed with her boyfriend. So then she had to go to work, and the man wouldn't let her leave. He locked the door. Then the telephone rang and he went to see who it was. Constanza had already seen her boyfriend's pistol. She went and got the pistol out. When he came back, she was there with the pistol. That's what they say, because no one saw it. So then he tried to take it away from her. They were struggling over the pistol. Then the pistol went off, and the shot hit her.

But that Italian, it might as well be said that he killed her, because he wouldn't let her leave, and then when he shot her, he didn't tell anyone. He had her there, with him there in the house. They say she lasted, like, seven hours, that she didn't die right away. But even considering that, he didn't call the police. Instead of calling the police, he called his lawyer.

The Salgueros had only a small network of family and no connections to influential people in the Chicago area. Distrustful of the system, and even more of the boyfriend's lawyers, Constanza's brothers believed there was little they could do to ensure the court testimony was accurate. The sense that she would never know the complete story only deepened Viviana's frustration.

So when they were looking for Constanza's relatives, because there weren't many in Chicago, they put it on the radio and in the paper and everywhere. Because they didn't know where she was from. So then people began to hear on the radio and the news and in the newspaper about that girl who was lost.

Her relatives finally heard and they went to see. That's what my sister-in-law told me.

When she was found in the boyfriend's house after the shooting, her hair looked as if someone had washed it, a bit. Probably because all of her hair was full of blood where she fell and wallowed in it there. And he didn't call the police. He called his lawyer instead. By the time they found out, the lawyer had fixed up everything—the truth—like it was an accident and everything.

So they took the man to court. But only Diego and Memo went; the others didn't go. Well, they didn't settle anything. Diego told Memo, "We couldn't do anything." He said, "Because he had lawyer uncles. He had brothers in the law. And what were we going to do? Just stand around like this with our arms crossed." And the officials didn't do anything; no, they didn't do anything. He killed her . . . he killed her. There wasn't any investigation or anything. Because only two, Memo and Diego [this makes her sad], what could they do? Nothing. And the Italian was left laughing—about what he did.

It had been scarcely a month since she had come here from Chicago for a visit. And she was driving a new car. But already that car, before that accident happened to her, had been robbed; they stole it. And the police looked for it until they found it. But the robbers had burned it. Brand new, her car, they burned it. Well, no one ever found out who did it.

So someone gave her rides to work, everywhere. Well, that was the case with her. Some say that . . . who knows if she had been mixed up in the Mafia? Memo believes that. Yes, he believes that was it. Because if you get into the Mafia, they don't let you out alive. They kill you. And Constanza was mixed up in the Mafia. . . . Well, that same man, the man who killed her, was mixed up in it. That's why he didn't let her live. So that she wouldn't say anything.

The Salgueros may have been grasping at straws with the Mafia theory in an effort to make sense of their daughter's death, but they had to leave many questions unanswered and deal with the living. By this time, Viviana had raised twelve children and become grandmother to that many again, but she wanted to care for the unfortunate grand-child who was now motherless. To someone for whom family is the strongest bond on earth, there was probably no question about what they should do.

My brother-in-law and his wife brought little Manuela here to Colorado from Chicago—she was four years old. They had cared for her while Constanza was working, while she worked nights. They had her all week—until Friday. On Friday evening Constanza would go for her, and she would have Saturday and Sunday with her. Then on Sunday evening she would take her back again. And when Costanza died, they brought the child back here. My brother-in-law, without seeing a lawyer or a notary public, gave the child to her father. They just came and buried Constanza here in Platteville. When it was all finished, then my brother-in-law went and took the child to Cruz, her father. Because my brother-in-law didn't want anyone to go and give him problems because of the child. So I tried to bring suit against Cruz for the child, because I wanted her. Then the lawyer told me that it was impossible, because they had already given her to him. The lawyer could no longer take her away. It was impossible. He said we couldn't do anything.

And that was the case of Constanza, my girl.

7

Faith as a Bulwark

Conversamos fácilmente con Dios.
[We converse easily with God.]
—*Virgilio Elizondo*[1]

NO MATTER WHAT THE STRUGGLES or crises, Viviana did have one solid refuge that never failed her, and that was her religious faith. Her conversation was punctuated with expressions of gratitude and *si Dios quiere,* if God wills. Though she had no opportunity to attend church during most of her married years, she had grown up in a religiously oriented society, which provided the basis for lifelong belief. She tried her best to live by the Christian values of love and forgiveness, including tolerance for those who believed differently.

In the later years of their marriage, after Jorge began to study the Bible and attend a Pentecostal church, she followed his lead and rejected Catholicism. Their decision was not unusual among US Latinos of the last thirty-five years. Catholicism is still the population's dominant religion, but by 1990, 23 percent of Latinos claimed Protestant or other affiliation.[2] Samora and Simon maintain that the Catholic Church in the United States has not shown the flexibility necessary to incorporate Mexican American popular religion and to provide a foundation for ethnic identity.[3] Since the early Spanish settlements, Mexicans living in what is now the American Southwest have devised a popular form of religion not sanctioned by the church—infant baptism by midwives, home altars and homemade religious figures, local feasts and processions,[4] and brotherhoods that operated in the absence of priests.[5] In the mid-1940s, Catholic leaders began to try to bridge the distance between the hierarchical structure and the membership's desire for a more egalitarian religion, but the Chicano movement of the 1960s and 1970s reinforced the distrust of a church many believed had contributed to Mexican American oppression.[6] Considering the tumultuous history of Catholicism in Mexico, it seems likely that Jorge's rebellion was fostered south of the border as well. Nevertheless, Viviana's conversion indicated some influence of her new country and a change in beliefs from those she held in her native land.

Viviana's faith was deeply personal. When she talked about Jesus, it was with great tenderness, and when she spoke of God, she was obviously soothed. Her experience was not unique. Virgilio Elizondo writes of his mestizo Christianity, "Papacito Dios, Jesús, Maria, y los santos . . . were not dogmas to be believed in, but personal friends to visit, converse with and even argue with. . . . We do not just know about God, but rather we know God personally."[7] Of this personal relationship, María Elena Lucas says, "I feel very close to God so I can get mad at God and nag and talk back when I need to. Sometimes I'll get real frustrated and say, 'Jesus Christ! Give me a break!' I nag, but eventually I give in."[8]

How much autonomy Viviana was exercising by converting is open to speculation. She was obviously influenced by her husband, explaining that he made the initial decision. She could well have been delighted that he was showing any interest in churchgoing, perhaps hoping it would calm his temper. She also indicated that they had attended the new church together, giving her the rare opportunity to get out of the house. She gave no hint that the conversion had been difficult for her personally or that she felt coerced in any way.

Irene Blea has researched reasons why Chicanos have converted to other, particularly fundamentalist, religions, finding two significant causes: contradictions in Catholic theology and the church's heavy use of ceremony and ritual. The dominant role of priests, which creates a distance between believers and their God, disaffects many, as well. In fundamentalist churches, Blea points out, "people are an integral participatory part of the services" and can "ask questions, clap hands to music, cry and pray out loud."[9] The structure is not hierarchical; women testify, lead prayers, and generally take full part in the services.[10] Viviana may have converted because of her husband's preferences, but evangelicalism was a good fit with her own beliefs. Three themes running consistently through her discussions were her gratitude for what God had given her, God's ultimate power, and her own intimate relationship with a loving, caring, and forgiving God.

> I didn't know that there was a church other than the Catholic Church. I didn't even know what a church was. When the children were born, Jorge took them to be baptized in the Catholic Church, and I stayed at home. He didn't go to church regularly, only when he baptized the kids.
>
> One should begin everything one says with God. If you don't trust in God, you are going to do only what you want because you want to. And your work or whatever you do won't come out right. We have to put God first. If you get in your car: "In the name of God." And then God goes with you, taking care of you. And watching out at the stops, who's ahead of you or who's behind you, watching out. When the train is coming, also.
>
> But, well, if any of us don't get—I'm talking about myself—the little bit of help, the little check, you're left in a bad way with your debts. And you don't have anything to pay your bills with. That's why you should give thanks to God [because you do get the little check]. They say it doesn't matter what religion you are, whether it's Pentecostal, or Four-Square, or whatever, or Catholic.
>
> My mother used to say, "The chickens give thanks to God when they drink water [Que las gallinas que dan gracias a Dios cuando toman agua]," because they drink the water and then they raise their little beaks. [She gestures putting her head up to swallow the water—looks at the sky]. My mother said that if the animals give thanks to God, why shouldn't we?

She may have lived in poverty almost her entire life, but gratitude was nonetheless a major part of Viviana's belief system. Partly cultural, the attitude was fostered by her religion as well as by her mother. Blea tells us that Mexican American elderly do not necessarily see themselves as deprived, "because they measure wealth differently" than Anglos, emphasizing the social quality of their lives more than the material aspects.[11] Material aspects do matter, however. Family came and went, some living with her and others visiting frequently, for which she was grateful, but she also had adequate food and clothing. Having known deprivation, she valued each meal.

> There are people who don't give thanks. They are embarrassed. But if it weren't for him, that he went to die on the cross, crucified, we wouldn't be here . . . because when God the Father said, "Who should I send to this world?" Jesus said, "Send me." Then God the Father sent Jesus, and how he suffered! For our most vile sins. You see it during Holy Week. You see it in English, and I see it in Spanish, how they crucified him alive, his feet, how they put one on top of the other, his crown, and then the wound they gave him on his side, and everything. Why? Because he came, he suffered for us. And I don't know why. God the Father sent Jesus to come and save this world.
>
> Whether you're Catholic or you're some other sect, from another religion, you should give thanks at each meal, not just come to the table and eat and eat, not remembering who God is. He's the one who is giving you the food. For your work. Because he lends you the strength to do your work so you can obtain your bread each day. You should give thanks every time you eat. When you are finished, give thanks to God. If two are together, well, the two of them work for the same, for their home, for the food.
>
> But a lot of people don't believe. When Jesus multiplied the fish and the bread, he first gave thanks—before allowing them to eat. It's the same with Sunday. Sunday was made for giving thanks to God. That's why he made seven days in the week, so that the seventh goes for giving thanks. But we don't go. No, we prefer to sleep. We have gotten lazy about getting up. [We laugh.] All week you get up early, and still on Sunday. No, we would rather keep sleeping.

The Salgueros no longer believed in sacraments such as baptism and marriage, regarded by the Catholic Church as means of receiving sanctifying grace. Until the adoption of the Mexican Constitution of 1857, the church had charged exorbitant fees for administering a sacrament; baptism or last rites could cost a peasant as much as five months' income.[12] That practice was abolished when church properties were nationalized in 1861 but was reinstituted after the death of President Juárez in 1872. It was only one of several practices that led the writers of the 1917 constitution to declare the clergy "the most baneful and perverse enemy in our country."[13] During the volatile years of the 1910–1921 Revolution, rebels often acted out their contempt for all aspects of the church, men in particular denouncing it and its rituals.[14]

Women did not drift away from Catholicism as easily as did men.[15] The señora's thoughts on religion often turned to the traditions she no longer believed in, as if she were still working out some of her ideas. Frequently beginning her assertions with "They say," she pointed out that, since she did not read, she had no way of verifying the Bible's actual words. On many points, however, she was adamant.

"Cuando Dios no quiere, los santos no pueden." When God doesn't wish it, the saints can't do it.[16] When used by Mexican Catholics, the phrase means that the saints can advocate for one's case with God, but only if God wishes can they be successful. Having a personal saint is an integral part of Catholicism, but Viviana had her own firmly held opinions on such ideas.

> They didn't baptize Jesus as a little child. He was thirty when John baptized him. And John didn't want to baptize him. But he told him, "I command you to baptize me," and John baptized him. Then a dove appeared. Yes, right? And the children, they baptize them very young; well, they don't know. They don't know who their godparents are or anything. They shouldn't baptize them so young. Some say that baptism has no meaning.
>
> Joseph and Mary weren't married; no, they only lived together. It's not necessary to have a wedding. They say that marriage, confession, and other things, the pope made all of this up . . . and handed it down to the priests. The priests are not fathers. They are priests, and in the Bible, there isn't any such thing as priests. Who knows what is in the Bible? I have forgotten. But they are not fathers. They are priests, they are

officials. The Father is only he who is in heaven, and one's [natural, or earthly] father.

All of those rituals, like marriage, also are not in the Bible. They say the popes have made all that up and passed it on to the priests so that the priests will have more money. Or have more work. And they are raised so popish, the priests, to believe everything the pope says. Before, they didn't talk about the Bible like they do now. Now they read and talk about what is in the Bible, in Spanish.

There are many saints the people created, and they still believe in those saints. But the saints don't do the miracles, God does them. If you read the Bible, the Bible says that in the middle of ignorance, God listens and does miracles. And the people believe that the saints do them. Well, the saints are like a picture. Because it says that the saints have feet, but they don't walk. They have hands but they don't use them, no; they have eyes but they don't see. They have mouths, but they don't speak. They have ears, but they don't hear. Yes, only God. It's he who is hearing your prayers that you ask of him. And God, through your ignorance, he does the miracle, not the saints. Because, look, the sculpted saints are made of plaster. What power can this saint have? Jorge used to say those saints so many people watched cry and talk were bad spirits, that they [the spirits] possessed that figure.

I told Roberto once, "I believed in the saints before, but now I don't worship them." Now, no. Now I believe only in God.

We don't see God. We don't see him like a person sees me. They say only one has seen him, but he saw the shadow. No one has seen him completely. That's why they paint him, but they paint him in order to sell the saints. You have to realize that the saints are just pictures. It depends on one's beliefs.

Even though Jorge became a Protestant in the United States, his decided distaste for the Catholic clergy most likely derived from controversies that had simmered in Mexico for decades. The church's support of the establishment made priests so hated after the 1910 Revolution that the government decreed strict prohibitions against their voting, running religious schools, or wearing clerical robes in public. Patrick Oster relates in addition that many were even "rounded up and forced to marry in order to break their vows of celibacy. Those who refused were executed."[17] It was, in fact, dangerous even to be a priest in those years, illegal to hold church services or administer sacraments. At one point, the government ordered the arrest of all priests and executed many, leading to the Cristero rebellion, a church-vs.-state civil war that lasted for three years.[18] Hatred of the clergy abated significantly in the latter half of the twentieth century as new generations of bishops and priests began to advocate for the people, but it left a legacy difficult to overcome.

One Mexican-born woman in Los Angeles told Earl Shorris, "I don't believe in confessing to a man."[19] She and her husband were nominally Catholic, having been raised in the church, but they didn't relate to priests. Jorge based his scorn for priests on two grounds: stories related to abuse of the confessional and anger over the clergy's claim to sanctity. In keeping with his patriarchal views, the worst term of disparagement he could apply to a priest was the gender-biased epithet "skirt," or *nagualón* in Spanish.

> But look, like the priests, what sins are they going to absolve you of if you go and confess? What sins is he going to absolve you of if he is a man? He is a man the same as your husband, the same as Jorge. What sanctity does he have? He doesn't have sanctity. Nor does the pope have sanctity. God has the sanctity. Jorge said, "Who has given this sanctity to the pope? The people. The people give it to him." There's no other God besides he who came, and he is gone.
>
> Jorge didn't like the priests because they would turn over the person through the confession. A person would go and confess the theft of an animal, for example, and then the owner of the animal would come to the priest. "Well, did so-and-so come?"
> "Yes."
> "What did he tell you?"
> "Well, he said that he was the one who stole it."
> In the night in Mexico, there was a guard of soldiers. Over there they call it a squad. They would come in the middle of the night because the priest would tell them so-and-so was the one. They would come and wake the man, the owner of the

house. They would take him and they would kill him there in the field, there in the open country. He wouldn't come back. Why? Whose fault was this crime? The priest. He turned them in because of the confession. Jorge didn't believe in confession.

He felt the same about marriage, he didn't believe in that either. Because as he began to read the Bible, Joseph and Mary were only united. They never married. That's why he said that nowadays, what the priests are taking, all that is for the pope. Jorge would say, "No, not me." He used to say, "The two times I got married, I haven't said all those sins to the father." That skirt, what is he going to tell us? "Skirt," he would call him because of the tunic [laughing as she speaks] he wears. "What is he going to tell us," he says, "if he is a sinner the same as us? What sin is he going to take away from me? Only God can take it away from me. Yes?" That is what he would argue also.

The same about the communion. He said, "That isn't true either. Because it isn't in the Bible. Communion is our all being united, that we are all in unity. United, all."

To be one, all united. If I don't have anything to eat, you bring me a little lunch. And if you don't have any, I bring you a little lunch. That is being united. In Mexico, they are still doing that. They call it a little bite. "Here, I have a little bite for you." That is communion. Jorge didn't believe in all that other.

The following passage reinforces the complexity of Viviana's relationship with her husband. From her frequent mentioning of what Jorge believed, it was clear that he had influenced her thoughts on religion and that she trusted his judgment on some matters. She also enjoyed his sense of humor and, in this case, appreciated his off-color comment regarding the priest and the hands he used to urinate.

In Mexico, they worshipped the hand of a priest. There, it's the priest standing in the doorway, and everyone who is passing through is greeting him. Jorge would say, "I'm not going to deign to worship that old man's hand." With your and God's pardon [she is addressing me], he would say, "To worship their pissy hands." [De adorarle sus manos meadas.] Well, how are they going to urinate? They have to hold themselves to urinate.

And then still one goes and worships their hands. [She gives a little chuckle.] The Catholics kiss the ring of the pope. All the priests do what the pope tells them. He orders them to do it.

Priests and the pope might be suspect, along with other aspects of Catholicism, but Viviana had no doubts about the story of the crucifixion. The image of Christ as the sacrificial lamb moved her to profound sadness.

In the Catholic church across the street, you can look at the pictures of the past when they crucified him, when they made him carry the cross, when they put the crown of thorns on him . . . they put it all on him, alive. He never complained. Rather, he said to the Father, "Forgive them, Father." He had patience like—the very Bible says it—he had patience like a little lamb, when they take it to the slaughter. The lambs, when they kill them, they don't bleat. They don't cry out. They just moan. The little goats, when they go to kill them, they cry out. And the lamb, no. Only moans. Thus, it is said that Jesus suffered like a little lamb.

And now during Holy Week, they are showing it on television. In Spanish. You can watch it.

Viviana narrated parts of various Bible stories, at times simply because she found them interesting, but more often because they illustrated a point. Some tales she saw as tests of faith, some as illustrations of moral principles for living, and a few as examples of punishment for not heeding God's directives. Her tone became sorrowful when the unbelievers called out to Noah to open the ark and more detached when she described the punishments. The stories fascinated her and seemed to give her respite from the sometimes sad retelling of her own life. She always became animated when talking about or relating them.

It took forty years to make the ark. When it was finished, they announced that this generation was going to die—in water— but the others didn't believe. They said, "Eh, since when are they announcing that the generation is going to die? And when is the water is going to come?" And so on until the day came. When it did, it kept raining for forty days. And the water rose. At the very last minute, Noah came with the ark. Only Noah's family and the animals, a pair of each animal, were the ones who boarded the ark. So when the people wanted to board the ark, they couldn't, because Noah had closed it. There wasn't any way; so they screamed, "Noah, Noah, open to us, open to us."

"No," he said. It's already closed and that's it."

All that is very interesting. For those stories we have to have a lot of memory, to record them. Also in order to be able to talk about them. Jorge had a very good memory. He would read the stories, and then he would talk about them.

César's first wife [a Jehovah's Witness] used to say that everyone is going to disappear; as they say, the earth is going to open. And of all the sects, the religions, only the Jehovah's Witnesses are going to remain, because they are saved. Jehovah's Witnesses don't believe in blood transfusions for the sick, for those who need blood to live again. They don't believe in it; they would rather die. They don't even believe in the day of the rabbit, Easter Sunday. We call it the day of the rabbit. They don't even believe in Christmas. They don't believe in going to fight . . . in war. They don't believe in that either. They don't salute the flag.

They don't go to war to fight. Because they say that they would rather go to jail, to prison, than go to kill a fellow creature. But you know that in the Bible, if you read it, how Abel killed Cain, or Cain killed Abel. They were brothers . . . and one of them killed the other . . . because of envy. So envy comes from as far back as antiquity.

Well, a very little has stayed with me, what Jorge read stays with me. Not all of it, but I remember. Hatred. Discrimination. Everything. It's all written in the Bible. All that happened in antiquity, and what is happening now are acts of the people. They aren't acts of God. Well, a lot of times, yes, they are punishments from God. Punishments from God because there were—how do I want to say it?—cities or like Germany, countries, that don't remember there is a God. And there comes the punishment.

In Viviana's life, punishments had been swift and hard. The Old Testament god of vengeance and capriciousness was not necessarily the one she found comforting, but she didn't question the appropriateness of retribution for bad behavior. Not only did this God punish for transgressions, either directly or through an emissary, but he also might choose to meddle with your health for no apparent reason. In these stories, she focused on the deity's unfettered power.

> I don't know who this story was about. It seems like Moses ... or Aaron ... or I don't know who. All their women, all the maidens, wore rich earrings of gold, necklaces, and everything. Rings, bracelets. The women took off all their jewelry and everything and put it to melt in a big kettle—to boil it down and destroy it. Then they made a calf to worship as if it were God. But when Moses came and found them there celebrating the calf, he got angry. So he destroyed the calf by fire. They shouldn't have done that. Since he arrived, with his power, he destroyed it. They weren't worshipping the saints, only the calf.
>
> That's why I tell you that without [God's] power, nothing is done. If he doesn't want it, nothing happens. Nothing through us unless through him. He heals whatever makes you feel sick. One asks God with all his heart, and when he wishes, immediately he gives you your health. And when he doesn't, there you have it and there you have it [she groans to illustrate not feeling well] until he wishes. That's why one says let his will be done. Not mine but his.

Another story illustrated an important household rule. Having lived through the depression in Mexico, Viviana reminded me of many North Americans who had experienced the economic crisis of the 1930s in the United States. So many came away with strong ideas about conservation and an appreciation for what later seemed a marvel of abundance. Her ability to apply religious stories to daily life was another reason Viviana's faith was so integral to her character. Saint Teresa of Avila wrote in 1588, "God is in the pots and pans,"[20] words Viviana could have lived by.

I say I don't like throwing food away because I heard it in the Bible; it says that food should not be thrown away. The very Bible says it. When the Lord fed the five thousand, he ordered the people to lie down fifty by fifty, while he multiplied the bread. When he had multiplied it, he beseeched the Father. So then he broke the bread, enough bread—the little fish, enough fish meat. It's the legitimate food, fish—fish and the meat of the sheep—it is the principal food. And so then, when he multiplied it all, he had them get up to eat. They all ate until they were full, and there were leftovers on the table. So then he ordered the servants there to gather all of it to put it away, and they gathered up twelve baskets of just scraps. Then at night they again gave them a meal from that same food. That's why we should not throw food away.

Here I fight with the kids because food shouldn't be thrown out. One should make only exactly what you are going to eat. And what is left, save it. But cover it, right? So it doesn't get freezer burn if it is uncovered. It gets the gas from the refrigerator. You can leave it, yesterday's, you can make it again tomorrow. When Jesus multiplied the bread and the little fishes, there were little pieces of bread left. He said, "Pick it up and save it." He didn't say, "Pick it up and throw it away!"

Viviana didn't dwell on the fearsome aspects of the Christian god. She related more fully to his generosity than to his anger, at times using the term *Diosito* as an indicator of affection and intimacy. She also gave him credit for her status as an American citizen and a homeowner.

Some writers see acceptance of God's willingness to cause human suffering as the Catholic Church's encouraging the attitude of *aguantar*,[21] a passive acceptance of one's fate. "Roman Catholic beliefs value acceptance of suffering, destiny, and God's will."[22] Others put the concept of aguantar in a more positive light, seeing the ability to endure as the guarantee of life. Virgilio Elizondo states, "We see it as the greatest strength, which transcends the many destructive forces all around us."[23] Aguantar thus becomes a source of dignity and strength, a way of allowing faith and optimism to carry a person through bad times as well as good. Viviana's faith acknowledged that

God could be the author of adversity, but she maintained on the other hand that humans had their own responsibility for the hardships they created in this world.

> *Diosito* took care of us. And now here we are in the United States. I tell my kids, my daughters-in-law, my friends in the church, like this, I tell them, "No, well, here we are now. Thank God that I have become one of the blue eyes." [We laugh.] I say now thanks to God that he took us out of poverty. [Digo ya gracias a Dios que se nos quito la pobreza.] Why would one say that he is poor? No. It's that God extends his hand and gives us our daily bread so we are nourished.
>
> A lot of times, even though the person has been very good, the Lord makes him suffer. One doesn't know why, only he knows. How many dying people last three days, four days, a week, two weeks, in agony, and they are dying, but they don't die? Only God knows why. Even though the person has been very good. God has to pardon us. "And then," Jorge would say, "one goes there, and God is going to question him. 'What did you do there where you were?' 'Well, no, sir, nothing. I didn't do anything.'" He can change the person, however bad the person is, he can change him. If [the person] approaches him.
>
> Disasters are punishments. Everything, all that you are seeing and everything, they are punishments from God. To see if the people who are still living reform—that they have a strong faith that there is a God who punishes. They say, "God punishes without the stick and the whip." Volcanoes and all that. And floods, yes. Through people themselves, what happened in Oklahoma.[24] God didn't order the destruction of the building and the killing of so many people. People did it. The people did that, not God. [I ask if wars also are another form of punishment.] No, well, when war happens, one nation is defending itself from another. That's why there's war. One nation gets into a fight with another, and neither one wants to leave the other alone, also. They are enemies.

Even though she couldn't quite decide whether God or man was responsible for such disasters as the Timothy McVeigh bombing of the Murrah Federal Building in Oklahoma City, Viviana trusted in God's concern for her. Her children, however, had some worries about her personal safety. By the time of this interview, her son and grandchildren had moved out, and she was living alone in an economically depressed neighborhood, making it difficult to decide exactly what precautions she should take. Her neighborhood—a mix of lower- and lower-middle-class homes—wasn't completely dilapidated. The houses and lots were small, but people kept their places neat—no collections of junk pickups rusting in the yards or old furniture piled on porches. Yards were not manicured, but they were not slovenly, either. One house might need a porch repaired, another new paint, the next some grass in the splotchy yard. She worried about gangs as much as anything, even though the nearby murder of an elderly woman three years before was unrelated to gang activity. Her limited income and mixed messages from her children about possible precautions, some urging more caution and some disparaging her ideas for securing the house, contributed to the quandary. I doubt that her rifle would have been much good to her—she had never mentioned knowing how to shoot it—but the sense of humor with which she brought it up was at least a weapon against defeatism.

> I'm alone here. But I tell my children that I am not alone. God is here with me. He is in the heavens, in the earth, and in every place. Right? God is everywhere. They say to me, "Aren't you afraid being here alone?"
>
> "No," I say. "No. Of what? Of whom am I afraid?"
>
> And the kids tell me, "Mom, don't be telling anyone that you are alone." Why? They say, "Well, because someone is going to come and scare you."
>
> I say, "Well, I have the rifle here." I tell them, "Well, I'll point it at them."

It is sometimes not easy to separate what we should truly fear from exaggerations and urban legends. Viviana worried about a variety of possible eventualities, from escaped prisoners to women with bombs to marauding gangs.

The kids tell me, "There are two prisoners walking around loose—who got out of the prison near there." They are dangerous. And the kids say also that you can't give a ride to anyone, especially a man. And even a woman, don't give her one either. Because you don't know what she's carrying, if she has a bomb or if she will hit you because she's in the backseat or beside you. If that woman is smart, she can hit you and take the car.

[She is not indicating that she drives but giving me advice based on what her children have told her.] That's why they say when you're in the car, close the windows all the way. Close and lock the doors with the key. Don't give a ride to anyone.

During the day, you can leave the windows open [in the house] but not at night, no. I always liked to have the windows closed. Now when Jorge was living, he used to tell me, "Why do you close them?"

"Well, someone is going to come in and beat us up where we are sleeping."

There used to be gangs here, there still are. Gangs of trouble-making kids. And every so often they would go by.

I just shut my doors tight, and the windows. I wanted to put iron bars over them. With those bars, intruders can't get in because the installers screw them on so they can't take them off with a screwdriver. They need to bring a special tool to get them off. But I haven't had the money. I've also been wanting to put the bars on the door. But I can't. I think it would cost me about a hundred and twenty-five dollars, the door. But no, the kids say, "For what? Why put them up? Leave it the way it is."

She didn't think her dog—a mixed-breed resembling a small Newfoundland or Chow, whom she called Rocky—offered much protection. Ultimately, God would act as her shield. The Spanish saying *Dios pondrá las medios,* or "God will provide the means,"[25] captures some of her attitude. My impression is that for Viviana and many Latinos, faith does not seem a matter of choice; it is just part of who they are.

Well, the dog isn't aggressive. He just barks. There are times when he lets people come in. And that's why I want to fix the door and the windows. I have to go see if they will give me credit to make monthly payments. The windows in the kitchen are the same as these. They also just have the screen and the little latch and that's all. Also, thank God, they don't open very easily. But they say, "For robbers, nothing is difficult."

A hymn we sang in church, the song says that holding hands, God and us, we are safe. Holding the hand of God. The only way we're vulnerable is if God should release us from his holy hand. Thank God that up until now I've been very safe. Thanks be to God.   They sent me a letter from the city, asking me if I wanted any help from their employees. I just had to pay twenty dollars a month so the employees would come around here, go around the house, watch it, take care of me. Now and then the police would come around here. But I didn't get the service. The kids didn't let me do it. "Why?" they said. "Why do you want to do it?" There used to be gangs of troublemaking kids here, there still are. And every so often they would go by. But now, they don't. They no longer go by.

I have enough money for food because I have two places where they give me food. And with what is left, yes, I make it, with God's help. God is very great. He takes care of his whole family. He gives you the money to prosper so that you have enough.

Yolanda Nava's mother often encouraged her "to turn my burden over to God whenever I felt overwhelmed by circumstances as an adult. 'You are trying to do it all alone, *mijita*. Let God help you. Don't you know that of ourselves we can do nothing?'"[26] Eschewing the vanity of total self-reliance, Viviana made a good spokesperson for the value of humility, a virtue to which Nava devotes an entire section of her book. "Mystics . . . accurately describe humility as an attitude of serving God . . . a virtue to be developed in opposition to pride."[27]

Diosito extends his hand wherever. To each he gives a little sustenance. He is all-powerful. Without him we couldn't live. As many people say, "No, well, what I have, I have because of myself." No, they have it because God loaned them the strength and the health, their work, so they could work and earn their daily bread. I, with my sweat, yes, but God is the one who does everything. A lot of people indulge in vanity like that. They say, "Well, I made that, because I have the strength, that's why." And no, that's not true. We believe ourselves to be very big, but no. We need to see it the way it is. God says, "Don't glorify yourselves."

But right now people don't want anything to do with God. They're on their own. And they don't heed the word of God. Many don't go to church. On Sundays they don't go. They would rather play ball or go for a walk or go to the parks. One should seek refuge in a church, to confess to God all his needs. So that God will help him. I used to go to church, and now I don't. Nobody takes me.

Viviana's religious outlook might help to answer an interesting question. One of the most intriguing things I learned several years after she died was that she had been a sought-after curandera and partera [midwife], outside as well as within her family, both in Mexico and in the United States. Her granddaughter Pilar told me that Viviana had also spoken to Pilar's high school Spanish class about herbal medicines. She taught her elder daughters about her cures, treated many of her grandchildren, delivered babies, and gave Beatriz her supplies after she could no longer practice. Why she did not share that knowledge of her life in our talks puzzles me even now. Some of the other aspects of her life that she omitted could be explained by embarrassment, priorities, or memory lapse, but in a year and a half of interviews, including one about herbs, she never even hinted that she had been called upon as a healer.

As I pondered this information, I questioned whether she had internalized some of Jorge's criticisms of her intelligence and capabilities, concluding that her healing skills did not compensate for her illiteracy. Or was it possible that she still harbored so much anger against Jorge for his mistreatment of her that she was using our interviews as a way to vent her frustrations, chastising her husband and avoiding her personal strengths? Those answers were not consistent, however, with the persevering Viviana who had birthed, clothed, and nurtured twelve children; walked into a new country nursing a baby; topped beets in the fields; and stood up to an abusive partner. I had to look in another direction.

According to Pilar, the power to heal is believed to be a gift from God. Not just anyone can do it. Viviana's paternal grandfather, an Indian, had been the healer for his tribe and may have passed down some of his skills, but according to the belief, not everyone can develop them. Because that ability is a sacred gift, the curandera does not accept money for her services, nor does she brag about her abilities. She spoke to Pilar's class because she was invited, but I never thought to ask directly if she was a healer. The humility to keep quiet about her healing gift corresponds completely with her religious outlook. Treating all humans as God's children, imparting compassion, and easing pain where she could, she would have been living her beliefs. Considering her opinions about the vanity of claiming credit for what God does, she would most likely have said nothing rather than boast. Even so, I had to conclude that if Jorge's personality was a conundrum, Viviana had her own enigmatic side.

There was nothing enigmatic or ambiguous about her faith, however, or her concern for her children's faith. She was bothered by her son Roberto's agnosticism. Not all of Viviana's children were equally religious, but most were Catholic at least in name. Their particular denomination was not as important to her as their sharing her belief in the Bible as the word of God. She seemed perplexed that anyone could question that belief. Roberto lived in Denver, about an hour's drive away, and frequently came to see her.

> Roberto and his wife are devout Catholics. They don't have pictures there in the living room, but they have them in the rooms where they sleep. There, they have the saints. They are devout Catholics; well, she is. Roberto says he doesn't believe in what the Bible says. He doesn't believe. I don't know why. I don't know what he does believe. He goes to church there in Denver. Once in a while, he goes. Once, he was sitting right here, and he told me he didn't believe in the Bible, in what the Bible said.

She did not comment further to judge or imagine what consequences her son might face, but she indicated that she could not fathom such a lack of belief. How could one sit right here and say such a thing? She didn't have an answer.

Viviana did hold several theories about how the earth would end. Most were based on biblical prophecy, but she also recalled a brief story about Jorge's grandfather, who evidently either read a lot or had a gift for prognostication. He sat the family down and foretold not only the end of the earth but also some of the technological developments of the twentieth century.

> Jorge said that his grandfather would tell him to sit down, and he would talk to them. "Look, one day you're going to see birds that fly in the air, airplanes, birds, and you're going to see the earth cinched—the rails for the train. The earth cinched by the train tracks [sinchadas las tierras con el riel]." That is what happened. And he would say, That was what his grandfather told them. He said also that someday this world is going to end, not the world, but the people are going to come to an end. Because people are not stable. Like, when God sent the rain, that was when the people, everybody who believed, could board the ark, but they didn't believe.

From what Viviana had heard in church, she was willing to predict how the world would end, but she wasn't so sure about what would come after that. Her suggestion to save matches indicates a familiarity with the Book of Revelations, which prophesies a time of darkness and also predicts a fiery end for mankind. The concept of hell was more difficult to grapple with; hers was ultimately a religion of love and forgiveness. What she believed for certain, the guiding principle of her life, was that God has the answers to all questions.

> Mankind is nearing its end, little by little. In the meantime, the people themselves are destroying each other. Also, the rains that fall are sent from God. And then comes the water and carries off the people, drowning them, and everything. Those also are sent from God, because there are a lot of people, a lot of nations that don't praise the Lord.
>
> You should have matches saved because it's going to get dark. This era is going to end in fire. The past era ended in

water. You remember, no? Have you read the Bible? Only the animals, only Noah's family were the ones who were saved. The rest didn't believe, so they drowned. That's the way we are, we don't believe. Right? [She laughs.]

However, this era is going to end in fire; the earth is going to burn. And we're going to burn. We're going to boil together with the earth. The dead are going to come out and move about among the living. Only ash is going to remain. So then God the Father—not Jesus—is going to put new people here. Again. Because he is all-powerful. There is a book one of the disciples wrote. A page is in the Bible—I don't remember if it is a page with red letters—that the Lord set one of his disciples to writing. But I don't know what it could say. I don't know.

They say that hell is the grave. Because yes, there is a hell. There are devils. Well, there is a hell. I don't know. But in the Bible hell exists. Hell is the grave. Who knows? I don't know. Only God knows.

The question of forgiveness came up frequently in our visits, in large part because she was concerned about whether God would pardon her husband for his infidelities and abusive treatment of her. Again, her ambivalence toward the man with whom she had been intimate for more than sixty years became evident. She maintained that she had forgiven him everything, that it was God's job to do the judging.

If you keep reading the Bible, there you will find forgiveness. It's hard to forgive a person. But we have to forgive so that God will forgive us also. God is watching you if you behave badly. If you use bad words, he is listening—. To him we can't tell lies. He sees us from there where he is, he watches us.

Well, anyway, I forgave Jorge because I wasn't bitter. I wouldn't get angry at what he would say to me or because he would beat me—I wasn't bitter. I forgave him for all of it. But one time I said to him, "Yes, look, well, everything you are accusing me of, you are raising false charges, and everything, none of it is true. Let's see, and when you die, you're going to ask my forgiveness, and your tongue is going to dry up."

That's what I told him. I was angry because of everything he was accusing me of, and it wasn't true.

Well, God will have forgiven him, right? Because God is the one who judges, when we die, he is the one who is keeping track, to see what one does here. On the other hand, they say it's not good for you to say that God has forgiven him, that he has him in heaven. Because you don't know. Because here, as the dicho says, "Everything fits in one little jug [Todo cabe en un jarrito]." But with God, no.

I interpreted Viviana's dicho to mean that we make our deeds fit in the jar, but God knows there are some parts we left out. God's perspective is great, while ours is small. She herself often took the broader perspective when talking about her husband. Many of her comments indicated she felt morally superior to him, but she never sounded boastful. Rather, she lamented his failings while trying to understand the disappointments he had encountered in life. One can tell a great deal about the kind of god a person believes in from her own attitude toward others, and Viviana's God, though mysterious and inconsistent, was merciful over all.

Jorge died during the year we were taping our conversations, his death one of the last major transitions Viviana would face on her own life's journey. She spoke only with compassion about his days in the assisted-living home. Although she and some of his children went to see him there, she noted that he did not have many visitors in his last days. Beatriz told him near the end that she wanted him to ask her forgiveness for the way he had treated her. We can't know his motivations, of course, but his angry refusal to honor her request might have indicated acceptance of the credo that a real man lives *sin compromiso,* "without obligations to or dependency" on anyone else,[28] or simply a belief that he had done nothing wrong. George Foster explains that in peasant society, "defense of this valuable self-image may, by the standards of other societies, assume pathological proportions, for it is seen as a basic weapon in the struggle for life."[29] His family knew his character, though, and it is likely that their busy schedules and distance played a part in his relative isolation as well. Four of the children and their families lived in the Greeley area, two in Denver, and the others in Texas, New Mexico, Arizona, and California.

With all of the kids he was very hard, with all of them, he beat all of them. Well, when he was very sick, they didn't come to see him. Some couldn't come every month, because they live far away. Those who were close here didn't come to see him. So he died alone. No one saw him. There in the hospital in Bonnell. He died alone because no one was with him. No children.

One reason she may have been able to come to terms with Jorge's abuses was that she believed she herself would be judged soon. She also had enough distance from those earlier years to wisecrack a bit. Even with God in control, life has its absurdities.

Each of us, you are going to pay for yours, she is going to pay for hers, and I am going to pay for mine. We aren't going to pay all together. We can't say, "Well, Jorge is already dead. He went to God." We still have a Supreme Being who judges us.

I never hated him because of what he did to me. I always had an even temperament toward him, to talk to him, to entreat him. Consider this . . . I didn't love him and I had sixteen pregnancies. [We laugh.] Yes. Well, if I had loved him, I would have had about twenty.

8

Citizenship and Politics

Donde está uno bien, allí está la patria.
[Where I find my well-being, there is my country.]
—*Spanish dicho*

VIVIANA STILL LOVED THE COUNTRY of her birth, indeed maintaining that some aspects of Mexican culture provide a much health-
ier lifestyle than that on this side of the border. She missed the sharing
that goes on in a society with more collectivist values, but she also
recognized flaws in the political systems of both Mexico and the
United States, never doubting that, all things considered, she was
fortunate to have moved to the United States. In this country, she
had been included in an extended family network, birthed children,
changed religious denominations, and sent a son to fight in a contro-
versial war. She was proud that her family had clawed its way out of
poverty, something she did not think would have happened in Mexico. Viviana's nostalgia for the values of community interdependence
and her refusal to forsake the land or language of Mexico emphasize
her Mexican heritage, but her fervent pride in her US citizenship and
pleasure in seeing her family established here confirm her north-of-
the-border identity.

Anzaldúa's theory of *mestizaje* or hybridity was one of the first to
describe the fluid process of identity formation for those living wherever cultures meet and clash.[1] Other writers have built on the concept, explaining, for example, that Latinos in the United States retain
their identification with Mexico or Latin America. Their assimilation

does not lead to rejection of everything Latino.[2] Renato Rosaldo coined the term "cultural citizenship" to express the idea that many Latinos become naturalized citizens but retain a unique sense of who they are—racially, culturally, and linguistically.[3]

Martin Del Campo, a Mexican-born architect who became a US citizen, explains the dilemma of needing to choose one allegiance over another: "It's like saying you love only one parent."[4] Mexican Americans live "in the hyphen,"[5] as Stavans phrases it, but they are no less grounded in their status as US citizens. Suárez-Orozco and Páez offer the terms *binationalism, biculturalism,* and *cultural bifocality* to describe the practice of holding onto familiar cultural practices while acclimating to the new milieu.[6] Refusing to be delineated by one set of allegiances, Viviana proclaimed herself a lover of two nations.

Having spent nearly fifty years in the United States, Viviana had honed her political consciousness here, developing an awareness of both Mexican and US politics. Contrary to the stereotypical passive, uneducated wife who defers to her husband in all matters political, she showed a strong interest in a number of issues. She may well have formed some of her opinions by listening to her husband— she quoted him on many occasions—but she also watched Spanish-language television newscasts and talked with her children. She was aware that the opinions of the electorate and government policies could have a direct effect on her life. Much of her political awareness resulted from the discrimination she and her family had encountered. A collaborative testimonial project established by the Latina Feminist Group concludes that lived experiences are part of what create "resistance to colonialism, imperialism, and racism," among other forms of oppression.[7] Viviana knew firsthand the disrespect often afforded migrant people of color. Her interest in citizenship stemmed partly from the belief that citizens had more recourse against discrimination than noncitizens.

Because she considered citizenship so important, Viviana was dismayed that two of her sons, one of whom lived in California, had never applied for their naturalization papers. She and Beatriz shared their concerns with me regarding California's 1994 passage of Proposition 187, denying undocumented immigrants social services, health care, and public education. Although the proposition was effectively nullified by the courts, the anti-immigrant rhetoric leading up to it created an atmosphere of fear. California senator William Craven had placed all people of Hispanic descent in a "suspect class" by calling for a state regulation requiring all Hispanics "to carry an identification card that would be used to verify legal residence." This was the same senator who, little more than a year earlier, had stated that "migrant workers were on a lower scale of humanity."[8]

Proponents of immigration reform had also announced their agenda to eliminate affirmative action and bilingual education programs and to promote English as the official language.[9] Although her son Mario had resident status, these developments emphasized for Viviana the vulnerability of noncitizens. If the anti-immigration hysteria of the 1990s began to abate somewhat, the terrorist attacks of September 11, 2001, redoubled the xenophobia. The North American Congress on Latin America, an organization devoted to publicizing major trends in Latin America and its relations with the United States, found that since the attacks, "an unprecedented nationwide network of anti-immigration think tanks, policy institutes, and statewide campaigns" has encouraged a resurgence of restrictionist attitudes.[10]

Too unconcerned or neglectful to complete the application process, her sons were not unique; many Latinos do not apply for legitimate status when they become eligible.[11] "Mexican immigrants are reluctant to give up their citizenship. Only 2.4 to 5.0 percent of those eligible choose to become US citizens, as compared with 23 to 33 percent of immigrants from other countries."[12] Gonzales lists several possible reasons for this phenomenon, among them a deep-rooted cynicism toward government.[13] Mexican citizens state such reasons as losing the privilege to buy a home or business in Mexico and strong nationalistic association with their country of origin: "We will always be Mexican."[14]

Some do not feel accepted even if they do become citizens. One Mexican in Greeley who had decided not to pursue naturalization told Esther Schillinger, "Germans, Italians here, get naturalized, are treated like Americans. Mexicans are always treated like Mexicans. That's bad. There's just one sky for everybody."[15] It seemed likely to Viviana, however, that rather than being concerned about acceptance, her sons simply hadn't thought the matter through. Although they had not encountered any major problems, she would have pre-ferred that her offspring enjoy the security of naturalization.

I have two children who didn't get their citizenship, who didn't want to become citizens and still don't. Jorge used to tell them, "It's important that all of you become citizens," he said, "because later you are going to struggle. You'd better get those papers before I die, because I have to sign for you. Later you will have to handle everything as if you had been Mexican nationals." I have two—they are lazy. If they go to Mexico, they can't come back. They can't even vote, either, because they still haven't become citizens. They would have more opportunities, the government would help them out more easily. It's impera-tive to have your citizenship.

I had nine children in Mexico. When we came here, because Jorge was a citizen—he was a citizen of Texas—seven of my kids got their citizenship because of him. And that left two—and me. I had a permanent residency.

The official told Jorge, "What favors you is that you didn't vote in Mexico." He said, "If you had voted, you would have denied the United States. You wouldn't have any rights here in the United States." And that was how he got his papers.

It took me a long time to get my citizenship. I went twice to the class for illiterates, and I didn't learn anything. Noth-ing. [Ya 'tuve dos veces en los analfabetos y no aprendí nada. Nada.] There were only adults in the class. There were some women from Mexico with me. They learned, and they became citizens before I did. And I didn't because I didn't know how to read, and I was afraid to go because they would ask me a lot of questions and I wouldn't know the answers. I have only what stuck in my mind. That's what I learned, because I can't read anything. Only, well, I write my name, that's all.

Viviana had spent most of her life believing that her intelligence was inferior, that she wasn't capable of learning to read or calculate. From her unsuccessful attempts as a primary student in Mexico to the recurrent reminders by her husband, her experience hadn't given her much self-confidence. When she complained about her memory, however, she sounded much the same as any other aging person.

> I have a tape from when I was trying to become a citizen. They gave it to me in English and in Spanish. It has the questions they ask in English, and the questions you have to answer. But nothing stays in my memory. No, I tell the kids that soon I'm going to ask them what my name is, because I forget things. All at once, I take what I have in my hand, and I do something with it, and then afterward, here I am, "Well, where did I leave it?" And there I am looking for it until I find it.
>
> Jorge used to tell me, "No, you are never going to learn, because you have the memory of the crows." He said, "They bury their food and later they don't know where they left it. Afterward, there they are looking to see where they left it. And that's the way you are. You have a memory that doesn't help you." [She laughs.] Yes. But however, thank God that I became a citizen.

Viviana couldn't remember exactly what year she obtained her citizenship papers, but because she went through the process after her son returned from Vietnam, it must have been in the 1970s, when she would have been in her early sixties. Convinced that she couldn't learn anything, she likely experienced great anxiety as she anticipated her interrogation, but with her son's help and an understanding immigration officer, she achieved her goal.

> When Memo came home from Vietnam, he became a citizen. Then I also went. I had already done the applications, but I couldn't go, because who would take me to Denver? The application had expired because nobody took me, and I didn't go until Memo went. Well, I hardly studied the citizenship materials at all. I don't remember the year.
>
> When I got my citizenship, there were different races becoming Americans: Japanese and whites, and Spanish, and blacks, and, well, all races. Quite a few people became citizens, and there were a lot of other people who went to listen. I think they

just came more or less to get an idea, so that when they became citizens, they could learn what they heard there. It was a very big room and completely full. And when they talked to us, with our papers, I was the first. Of all those who were there, they called me first. To give me my papers. A very great gift.

They didn't ask me many questions, because I was an older person, and, well, I don't know how to read. The immigration authority asked me—they speak Spanish well—if I was willing to serve the United States, and I said yes. He asked if I had forgotten Mexico; I said no, because I was born there in Mexico, and I thank God for the United States of America that has given me freedom. [Dijo que si yo olvidaba México; dije que no porque allá había nacido en México y le daba gracias a Dios por los Estados Unidos de América que me había dado la libertad.] That's what I answered. . . . And that was the right answer. He said, "OK."

I said, "Yes," I loved Mexico because I was born there. "And it was my homeland. And after that, the United States of America, because it gave me my citizenship." That was what I told them [she's laughing], and they said that was all right. Then they asked which president had finished his term. Memo was with me, he was talking to me there. They were questioning me in Spanish, and Memo was saying to me, "His name is So-and-so," the name of the man they were asking me about. And then, well, I put my ear to hear what Memo was saying to me. And the one who was investigating me, while he was talking to me, Memo was telling me.

I don't remember the name of the man they were asking me about. I forgot. I don't have a memory that will hold all those words. But already I was more than sixty years old. So I told the immigration official what Memo said. And I didn't have a hard time.

Well, here we are now. Thank God that I have become one of the blue eyes.

After laughing at Viviana's little joke about citizenship conveying membership in the blue-eyed population, we turned serious again. Although aware of the rights and obligations of citizenship, Viviana offered little explanation for why she had never voted. Unlike many post–World War II Mexican immigrants, whom Gonzales character-izes as completely negative toward politics,[16] she did not seem cyni-cal about the US government. Subservience to her husband, her inability to drive, illiteracy, and a sense of inadequacy in the public arena may all have contributed to her situation, but she said only that no one would take her to the polls. Suárez-Orozco and Páez found that as income increases among Latinos, so does political par-ticipation.[17] It is often true that as income and education levels rise, gender equality increases also, another factor Viviana did not have in her favor.

Recognizing that she had not participated fully in the democratic process, Viviana was no less proud of her place as a documented citi-zen. Her attitude was similar to that of a Mexican woman who told Marilyn Davis, "[In] the United States . . . you have your rights. You fight for them and the law supports you."[18] What the immigration authorities told her about her rights also reemphasizes why she felt so strongly about her sons' citizenship status.

I have a book the immigration authorities gave me. It includes all the presidents, and I also have a big paper they gave me. And a letter that they sent me, that told me that, as a citizen, I could get all the benefits from here in the United States. It also says that if there is any discrimination, all I have to do is call, because I have the telephone number, also, on the card. In any case, there are many important stories in the book. Only many times, like, I remember only what sticks in my mind.

I haven't voted here. Not one time, since I became a citizen, I haven't voted because . . . well, they don't take me! I don't even know where the voting is. Well, it's not my fault. They don't take me. The kids, they're the ones who know where the elections are. I don't know when or anything. They don't even tell me, "Well, Mom, you have to go to vote. Let's go, we'll take you, because you need to vote." If they don't take me, well, I don't even know. That's why I haven't voted since I became a citizen. But Jorge, yes, he used to vote.

But now, I have become one of those blue eyes, now I'm an American citizen. I am an American, yes. Yes, yes, yes.

Though an adamant advocate of US citizenship, Viviana experienced nostalgia for family and an idealized memory of the close-knit community she grew up in. She expressed sadness at not seeing her parents before they died, and she also had a longing to return to Mexico before her own death. The physical proximity of the country makes it more accessible than the home countries of many immigrants, often contributing to ambivalence and nostalgia.[19] In discussing the concept of ambiguous loss in Latino immigrant families, Celia Jaes Falicov comments that "after migration it is always possible to fantasize the eventual return or a forthcoming reunion."[20] Patrick Oster quotes from a poem written by a young illegal:

> How beautiful is the United States.
> Illinois, California, and Tennessee.
> But over in my country,
> A piece of the sky belongs to me.[21]

Viviana dreamed wistfully of seeing that sky one more time.

> Beatriz is going to take me to Mexico if God wills. Beatriz and César. They want to go. Because Beatriz, since we came, hasn't been back there. She isn't working, because she's disabled, but she saves, she puts some away, little by little by little. They give her social security; they don't give her much.
>
> Well, I'm praying that I can go to Mexico to see my relatives, that God goes with us to see my family. Who knows if I'll do it or I won't? Because the way is long, and there are very desolate roads, without any people. Well, I don't know . . .

She would not make it back to Mexico before her death, but Viviana was intensely grateful for the comforts she had been able to attain in the latter years of her life, including the medical benefits and the opportunity to own her home. Two years before I met them, the Salgueros had become homeowners, granting the couple a privileged position compared to other foreign-born citizens. Only 38.1 percent of first-generation immigrants of any nationality own their homes,[22] compared to a home ownership rate of 66.2 percent for the population as a whole.[23] Rothenberg puts the rate at 44 percent for

Hispanics and points out that lenders reject minority applicants, even those with high incomes, more frequently than they do whites.[24] The Salgueros were not at the mercy of lenders, but their house came at a high cost, nonetheless. On the farm where Jorge had been working, a truck ran over his feet in 1986, and he received an insurance settlement. As a result of the accident, he never walked unaided again.

> But finally . . . God remembered Jorge. He was overworked. Overworked, and badly treated by life. Because, well, here also he suffered, but not the same as in Mexico.
>
> When the accident happened, he had already saved some social security. He was getting his social security, and he was working. When he didn't put the social security check away, he would put away the one from work. And when they chewed up his legs, well, he got a lawyer. The lawyer didn't get him more than sixteen thousand dollars. The lawyer got two thousand or a thousand, I don't know how much, and he gave Jorge fifteen thousand. And then Jorge had what he had saved. He bought this little place here for ten thousand. The house wasn't in good shape. He tore the inside all down and renovated it. The kids helped him tear it down.
>
> The carpets and the linoleum in the kitchen and the other rooms, I paid for when I got my check that they gave me for my old age. Then everything was cheaper. I paid for everything here, the carpets and the linoleum, all of it. From what I was saving from my checks.

Viviana believed that had she stayed in Mexico, not only would she have been unable to break out of poverty, but she might easily have died as a result of her deprivation. Grateful for her circumstances, she maintained that those who have come to the United States and found a better life should never forget their suffering or that of those who still live in want. She had watched the Mexican economic crisis of the eighties, what Hondagneu-Sotelo called in 1994 "one of the world's most severe, prolonged economic crises,"[25] and had seen how much suffering still existed in her homeland, convinced that government corruption was the primary cause.

She didn't mention Chiapas or Oaxaca specifically, but she was familiar with the grinding poverty that still affects the indigenous peoples of those and other states with large Indian populations. According to Tom Barry, she was correct that government policies in Mexico were leaving the poor without land or food,[26] sending the poverty-stricken primarily to squatter settlements near large cities, where they found only destitution and contamination. Several months before we began taping Viviana's story, the North American Free Trade Agreement (NAFTA) had been ratified, a development that made it impossible for small and subsistence Mexican farmers to compete against agribusiness. Their migration to the cities increased the labor pool and kept wages so low that even those who could find jobs could not feed their families.

> Well, thank God, because if I were in Mexico, I would die of hunger. They don't have enough, as they do here. I would have already died if I were in Mexico, because I was ill there several times, just the same as here. Here, God has lifted me. If one were in Mexico, where would he get money to see the doctor? If you don't have money, life is very hard. And then everything is so expensive. There the children and the grown people go begging for alms. "Give me some charity, some alms." The children go into the restaurants: "Give me a taco." They grab them and throw them out of the restaurant. They don't give them anything, the poor kids in their need. Many are orphans.
>
> There are still states in Mexico in which the people suffer, truly they suffer. There are states where they don't, everything is in abundance. But there are states where it's not. They don't have the comforts to live well. They suffer.
>
> [In Mexico], there aren't programs to help. That's why there are a lot of old people begging for alms, but it's the president's fault. This new president who has just taken office [Vicente Fox] immediately comes and asks for a loan here in the United States. That money, why do they want it? They don't take it to help the people.
>
> Look, here, a man, I don't remember who he is, brought who knows how many millions of dollars to deposit here in the United States. [She is probably thinking of Carlos Salinas de Gortari,

president of Mexico from 1988 to 1994, whose administration siphoned tens of millions of dollars from the Mexican treasury.] Why did he come to deposit it here when there are places they could use it over there, with so many people, so many fields available, so much land open for fields? What is the president good for, then? If the loan he asks for here is to help the people, not for himself, to give to the poor, and he doesn't give it to them, they will continue to live forever in the same poverty. [Si el préstamo que pide aquí es para ayuda de la gente, no para él, para que les dé a los pobres y no les da, siempre siguen en la misma pobreza.]

The presidents there serve six years. So when one goes out of office, he goes out rich, because the dollars, well, he has them hidden away. And when are they going to pay the United States? When? All that money could be given as a pension, like it is here. But he doesn't give anyone anything.

The president from here had first said that he was going to give Mexico a loan of thirty million. Now he says forty, but Congress still hasn't approved it, because they don't want to. When did Mexico ever pay it back? No, I don't agree with loaning this money over there.

I tried to argue that the newly elected President Fox had a reputation for honesty, but she would have no part of it. It was clear that she had been following the news from Mexico and had strong opinions about what needed to be done. The farm crisis and resulting relocation of workers went deeper than her point about lack of water for irrigation, but those developments were a major cause of high unemployment. Not only were agricultural corporations buying farmland from those who could no longer afford to work it, but assembly-intensive US businesses also contributed to the problem. Their factories, or *maquiladoras,* had existed along the US–Mexico border since the 1960s, but after NAFTA relaxed labor and environmental regulations, these plants multiplied. Maquiladoras did little to create the type and quantity of full-time jobs the country needed.[21] Because they could pay women even lower wages than men, they exploited women while failing to decrease unemployment rates for men. Viviana advocated the opening of factories, but she was clearly urging the development of industry jobs with livable wages and benefits.

[In response to my comments about the new president's reputation for honesty] Well . . . to me . . . I don't think so. Because
it goes on the same. The same hunger continues in Mexico, the
same misfortune. The rich people, well, they're rich. They don't
need the government, because they have industries and they
work. The poor people, only in the fields. And right now there
aren't fields for them to work in, because there isn't even water
to irrigate the crops. The only hope they have is that it will rain,
so the plants can get water.

     They should open industries. There are a lot of factories that
even the Japanese have built there in Mexico. The president
doesn't open factories to the Mexicans so they won't come [will
have an alternative to coming] here.

On the other hand, Viviana had some interesting opinions about
begging in Mexico and how some people had made a good life for
themselves by pleading poverty. These people, she explained, had
made it more difficult for those who truly had nothing.

I have a cousin I haven't been in touch with for a long time. She
has an old man, and the old man supports her totally from alms.
He carries his little bag, and he begs for alms . . . so that he can
feed her. They live in Juarez. People give him pennies, money,
to buy soap, to buy butter, or coffee, sugar, and everything. And
they still buy milk for their coffee. Their half liter.

     Many times the women, or the men, ask for alms, but they
also have good houses there in Mexico. That's how they support themselves, begging. The majority of them beg for alms
because they are very poor, but almost a fourth of them have
their good houses, good cars, and furniture. That's how they
live, asking for food. There have been people with good houses
and cars and furniture who have been caught asking for alms,
and that's why [people] just go by and don't give them anything, because there have been people who became very rich
just by begging. And there are others, yes, who have needs
because the children go around naked, only in their underwear—at times no more than a rag instead of even underwear,
without a shirt, without shoes.

Viviana didn't blame people for wanting to come north to find a better life. Tens of thousands of would-be immigrants to the United States never achieve her status as naturalized citizens but are turned away every year. Others are even less fortunate, succumbing to murder, rape, robbery, beatings, and betrayals. The US–Mexican border has been described as "a line of violence and needless cruelty,"[28] and Shorris cites a report released by the Mexican consul in El Paso claiming "over two thousand abuses of human rights in the state of Texas in 1988 alone. All the victims were Mexicans or Mexican Americans."[29] The US government implemented a borderwide crackdown in 1994, called Operation Gatekeeper in California, which sent the death toll spiraling upward.[30]

Those deaths are seldom quick or painless. Luis Urrea's tragic account of twenty-six men, including fourteen who suffered the slow broiling to death of exposure while trying to traverse the Cabeza Prieta wilderness area of southern Arizona in 2001, details the danger of trying to cross the desert on foot. Not only is nature relentless, but Mexican guides, or coyotes, are notoriously untrustworthy. They have abandoned their charges in sealed boxcars, trunks of cars, and cargo trucks, leading to several instances of multiple deaths from asphyxiation and suffocation,[31] no less horrendous, if perhaps faster, than dying in the desert.

Currently, border policies include attempts to seal the border with intermittent National Guard troops and newly constructed walls.[32] In October 2006, the Secure Fence Act was signed by then-president Bush, authorizing the construction of seven hundred miles of physical barriers along the southern border from the Gulf of Mexico to the Pacific. Not one continuous structure, the barriers are concentrated where the highest numbers of illegal crossings have been observed in the past, with the remaining areas monitored by sensors and cameras. Earlier such efforts reduced the flow of immigrants where security was heightened, and increased it in others.[33] The Department of Homeland Security issued a report in 2009, however, concluding that the number of undocumented immigrants dropped from 11.6 million in 2008 to 10.6 million in 2009.

Whether the drop is a result of the physical barriers or the sharp downturn in the US economy is still a matter of debate. Immigration patterns the world over illustrate that people from economically

underdeveloped nations, the majority undocumented and undeterred by barriers, seek escape from poverty by moving to wealthier
countries. According to Daniel Griswold, director of the Cato Institute Center for Trade Policy Studies, at least a third of people living
in the United States illegally did not cross in the dead of night in
some unprotected area but actually entered on legal short-term visas
and quietly overstayed.[34]

If the Mexican economy does not improve and the United States
gradually recovers from the current recession, it is highly likely that
the undocumented will again reach for a better life in the north.
Isaias Lara, who has traveled from El Pedregoso, Michoacan, to
the United States illegally three times, says, "We go because we're
forced to, and we'll keep going, no matter what."[35] Vicki Ruiz has
seen that same determination in the migrant patterns: "Mexicans
will not be deterred from crossing geographic borders."[36] Whenever
Viviana and I discussed the dangers of crossing illegally, it was with
a great deal of sadness and compassion on her part for those making
the journey.

> Here and there some are left dead in the mountains, because
> they die of thirst, or of hunger, trying to get here, and they
> don't make it. Now it's becoming even harder for them, because
> they're placing more immigration officers, so that they can't get
> through to here.
>
> Sometimes they catch them and send them back again.
> Sometimes they make it. And there are some that the ones who
> bring them from Mexico kill on the road. They call those who
> bring them "coyotes." They kill them, and they keep the money.
> Those people never return to Mexico. They are left shot to
> death. [Allí los dejan tirados.] Others die of thirst, [or] an ani-
> mal bites them, and they don't make it; they're left dead on the
> road. Now, those who have come and have been working here
> for a long time are being arrested. They're sending them back to
> Mexico . . . because they don't have papers.

Viviana did not live to see passage of a 2010 Arizona bill that
would give law enforcement the right to stop and arrest, without a
warrant, any person an officer "has probable cause" or a "reasonable

suspicion" to believe might be unlawfully present in the United States. If the suspected person, even a US citizen, is not carrying proof of legal status, he or she may be detained.[37] As Mexican Americans are pointing out, what "probable cause" is more visible than skin color? It is outside the realm of reason to think the law will not lead to racial profiling. I am reminded of Viviana's earlier statement: "I say that discrimination toward the Mexicans is still not over."

On other political issues, however, Viviana's opinions were basically conservative. Richard Rodriguez's autobiography maintains that Latino values "are not liberal,"[38] while current writers describe a political split among Latinos. Liberal grassroots activists may work on issues from support for labor to solidarity with people in Central America and Mexico,[39] but communities that have achieved relative economic prosperity often vote conservatively.[40] Viviana's gratitude for the Social Security benefits she was drawing did not deter her from condemning the abuses of the entitlement system. The misconception that Latino and other immigrants are draining the coffers of state welfare programs is widespread. Waldinger and Lichter quote a US-born woman of Mexican descent in California: "A lot from Mexico . . . come here and think we should support them. . . . They come in with an immigrant status and they get more money than Americans on Social Security."[41] In reality, the woman's conclusion is not supported by evidence that legal immigrants come to the United States in anticipation of collecting public aid. The undocumented, of course, have no papers with which even to apply for assistance. "In fact," Roberto Suro points out, "numerous studies showed that working-age legal immigrants have no greater propensity to end up on cash-transfer social programs than comparable sectors of the native-born population."[42]

By law, undocumented immigrant children may attend K–12 schools, and they are treated in hospital emergency rooms, but Social Security Administration files showed by the end of the 1990s that undocumented workers also pay six to seven billion dollars to the Social Security fund and about one and a half billion dollars in Medicare taxes annually,[43] from which they receive no benefits. "The Urban Institute figures that immigrants in this country contribute about $30 billion more than they use in social services,"[44] and UCLA's North American Integration and Development Center published a twenty-first-century study concluding that undocumented immigrants contribute "at least $300 billion per year to the US gross domestic product."[45] According to an earlier study released by *US News & World Report,* "overall only about four percent of new immigrants receive welfare aid."[46] Jorge blamed women, for the most part, for entitlement abuse, but Viviana had seen evidence that men were exploiting the system also.

Now, as Jorge used to say, we are living the life of the old folks, because the government gives us a retirement benefit. But Jorge said that the government gives only what he earned before.

Who came up with Social Security? Well, Jiltras [her pronunciation is unclear—she may be referring to Herbert Hoover] came up with it, but he didn't make it public. Then Roosevelt was the one who made it public. The other one, Jiltras, had the people, well, dying of hunger, as they say. He would give them only a ration of food. All the time he had them oppressed until Roosevelt came along. Franklin Roosevelt gave them blankets to take to bed, shoes to put on and walk, because they didn't have any of that.

The government helps the people here; yes, it helps because here there is no hunger. They were announcing on television that there is a part of the United States where there is hunger, but I don't believe that. Where there is hunger, it's because those who get welfare, get food stamps, are living with men from Mexico. And the children, they don't give them enough food. They have them, but they don't dress them well because the money is going to the Mexican nationals.

Jorge used to say, "If only I were president, I would order all the help to those women stopped, and I would send them to work." He said, "There is the president, giving so much money so they can sleep warm with those old men from Mexico." The money that they are giving them, they are giving them not for themselves, but for the children.

"When the check comes to them," Jorge used to say, "the government should hire a detective to see how many women are running around with the men, spending the check. Those women should have their children taken away from them." That money is needed. Well, that's the way it is. They give them plenty of stamps, once they have three or four children, up to three hundred dollars or more they give them in food stamps.

Some don't finish their food stamps in a month, but they sell them to someone else. A man used to come here who doesn't come any more. It's been a while since he came. He would give me forty dollars in food stamps for twenty-five in money. That was good, right? He would give me fifteen pesos free just so that he could go drink. I believe that he would steal them from his wife, the food stamps, to sell them.

When I described frequently witnessing patrons in the local post office sending money orders home to families in Mexico, Viviana responded with more concern about those who cheat both the US government and the families left at home. Daniels states that money wired from family members in the United States to those in the Caribbean and Latin America equals "almost a third of the region's foreign direct investment."[47] Estimating remittance amounts is far from an exact science, but President Vicente Fox told reporters that money sent by Mexican workers in the United States reached $12 billion in 2003, becoming Mexico's largest source of foreign income.[48] That index of generosity moved Viviana less than her anger over what she believed wasn't working—a US welfare system that, in her eyes, could too easily be abused.

But many have not sent anything back, and the officials arrest them, and they arrive back in Mexico empty-handed. Well, that's the way it is. Because here they spend it all. They start running around with the women here. They start going to the dances and whatnot. They spend the money, and there in Mexico they leave the poor babies and the wife. The little that they work, and the money from welfare that they get, well, they support themselves with that. And they forget the family there in Mexico.

What might seem most surprising was her negative attitude toward children born in the United States to noncitizen parents. Her socially conservative bent could have resulted from the level of comfort Viviana had found in the United States. Although her income was not large, her house was paid for, and she had access to adequate food and medical care. Still sympathetic to immigrants risking their lives to cross the border, she was nonetheless a fiscal conservative when it came to government spending. On another issue, when one of her unmarried granddaughters became pregnant, she maintained that rather than the government help the girl, the young couple should marry and the teenage boy and his family take financial responsibility. No matter what the issue, domestic concerns or the allocation of large government loans to foreign countries, she was adamant, first, that the government not be cheated, and second, that it use fiscal restraint.

They were saying on the television that the babies who are being born here to the undocumented people, they don't want to give them citizenship here in the United States. A lot of babies are being born here in the United States. They then act as though they are from here, from the United States, even though they are of undocumented parents. When they are old, the government has to support them, right? Yes. And that is exactly what the government doesn't want. In my opinion, it's good [that the government wants to use restraint].[49]

There are many girls, they go to the hospital to have their babies, and who pays? The government. Why don't they require the boys, the boyfriends, to pay? The government is spending a lot of money, and it shouldn't do it. It should require the parents of the children to reconcile for the sake of their children.

The government has a lot of money to help other countries; seventy-five thousand, thirty-five thousand [I think she means million in each case]. That's a lot of money going to other countries. So everything has its, well, there's a phrase they use, "Everything has its cutoff point." Everything has its limit, its culmination. And already, how much money are we sending to other countries? How many soldiers are we sending to other countries? We shouldn't be sending them.

But Jorge used to say that the president does all of that in case there is a war. All nations will help him, here, the president—it doesn't matter which president. That's why the United States gives so many gifts to all the countries. It sends money, it sends clothes to those disasters that are occurring from so many earthquakes or everything else that happens. The president sends help. So that when there's a common [world] war, everyone helps him fight.

Although she couldn't remember exactly how a representative democracy works, Viviana tried to work it out, revealing some gaps in her understanding of the system. She knew what she thought about the relationship between a citizen and her president, however. One of her assertions had overtones of her husband's antipathy toward authority of any kind (remember his strong opinions about the pope), but it also demonstrated her pleasure in the thought that she was as important as any other citizen, including the chief executive. Reared in a peasant background by a father who contributed to the community; tempered by poverty, abuse, and hard work; and challenged by the move to a foreign culture, Viviana had not only come to display an inner sense of dignity and self-worth but had also become incorporated into her new country, whose ideals she felt reflected her valuing of the individual.

The president has someone else to give him orders, right? It's someone else, only I don't know what his name is—and then the Congress also. They give him orders. If Congress doesn't want the president to do something, he won't do it, because Congress doesn't want him to.

I have a tape that says if you are in a church or a meeting and the president comes and there is no chair, because it is the president, you give him the chair. But no, you shouldn't give the president the chair, because you are as much a citizen as the president. [Pero no, usted no debe de darle la silla al presidente, porque usted es tan ciudadano como el presidente.] You shouldn't give him your chair. Let them bring a chair for the president. [She laughs.] Um-hm. Because the president serves the nation. Ultimately, he is responsible for everything, and one should also respect him.

9

Looking Back

La muerte es lo único seguro en esta vida.
[Death is the only guarantee in this life.]
—*Spanish dicho*

MY RELATIONSHIP WITH VIVIANA continued until her death in the year 2000. As she became more frail, she tried to find a grand-child or other relative to live with her in her little house, but none of those arrangements worked out, so both elder daughters opened their homes to her. Mercedes had more resources, and though not always well herself, cared for her mother conscientiously, making sure she ate well, visited the doctor, and was as comfortable as pos-sible. Because Viviana greatly feared living out her years in a nursing home as had Jorge, that was no small gift.

When I visited in her daughter's home, I no longer sat at Viviana's feet, as Mercedes insisted I have a chair. Because Viviana's hearing had deteriorated, it was also more difficult for us to talk. We man-aged, however, to communicate our affection for each other until my final visit, when it was clear she had only a few days to live. She lay in a softly lit bedroom in the front of the house, pale and looking smaller than ever, scarcely able to speak or lift her hand, but beckoning me to come close so she could hear my words. Mercedes had led me into the room and remained while I said my good-byes. Try as I might, I cannot remember what I said to her that day. I left with a sad heart, most importantly because I was losing my friend, but also because I hadn't been able to finish her story in time for her to see it in print.

"Ahora ya mi ataúd se está fabricando por una familia muy buena y en ese deseo ser sepultada."[1] ["Now my coffin has been made by a good family, and in it I wish to be buried."] So wrote Luisa Torres of Guadalupita, New Mexico, in a memoir. Viviana, too, made her preparations for death calmly and matter-of-factly. She seemed comfortable accepting and preparing for it. Even in discussing the fragility she was experiencing as an old woman and her impending death, however, she punctuated her narrative with lighthearted comments and stories. She still had plenty of zest for life, including a spunky sense of humor, and she didn't mind making fun of herself.

> When I went to pick out my casket—I have everything ready for when I die, everything—the one who sells the caskets told me, he said, "Look, if your husband dies first, you have to give him your casket." I said, "No." I said, "I'm not going to give it to him. Let him buy one." [Dije, "No." Dije, "Yo no se lo doy. Que compre él uno."] But they wanted to take my box away from me to give it to him if he were to die first. And I told him, "No. He's cheap." I already have my plot, I have my casket, I have my gravestone. I'm lacking only the cards that they give and the workers who are going to direct the death, the funeral. Where the funeral procession goes, the police, that's all I'm lacking. Thanks to God. I'm really old. I'm already very old. I have everything picked out there in that funeral home by the edge of town.
>
> I've just been thinking about having a will. I don't have much, not much, but it's very necessary to have a little house, for one's going here and there like bouncing balls. [We think she means to keep one from bouncing back and forth, from here to there, homeless.] I haven't made the will. [Here she whispers.] I have it, but they don't know [gesturing toward her son and grandchild in the kitchen]. It doesn't seem like it, but it is necessary. One needs to be prepared. Well, whatever God wants. By now, I'm ready, more ready to leave than to stay.
>
> Yes, I'm an old woman. Let's see what's in the future. Now I can't walk alone. I'm afraid that they'll leave me alone and I'll fall. And if I fall, it'll happen to me as it did to Jorge. I'll go to the hospital, and I won't come out of there. I'm better off here.

I have to eat and chew and chew and chew in order to be able to swallow . . . or to drink water. I can't swallow the water. I can't get the water through my esophagus. When I can no longer swallow water, I'm going to die. [She laughs.] Yeah. There's no cure for that.

Yesterday I went to the dentist, and I went to the eye doctor also. And then we went to the store, to King Soopers. Beatriz asked for a little cart to ride. They are electric. [She giggles.] I said to Beatriz, "I can't drive it."

She says, "Go ahead, let's see if you can drive it."

I was telling people, "Here I come, here I come, here I come," and "Get out of the way, because here I come, here I come, get out of the way." [We laugh because she is saying all of this in Spanish.] I couldn't drive that cart. I was saying, "Hay voy, hay voy." Who was going to understand me? "Hay voy, hay voy."

Beatriz said, "You're going to crush someone there. We'd better leave. We'd better get out of here."

I can barely maneuver those seats that they push. In the wheelchairs, I'm sitting down, and Beatriz pushes me. I carry my basket to put whatever we're buying here in the chair. But in that, no, I couldn't.

Viviana's husband's death, rather than freeing her from a sense of oppression, seems to have made her more conscious of her own impending end. Our talks more frequently included discussions of aging and slipping away. I don't know whether she had osteoporosis, but she and her daughters told me that she had lost both height and weight in recent years. Her frailty had become more evident just in the time I had known her.

People ask me, "How could you have had such a large family when you are so little?" Well, now I'm getting even littler. [We laugh.] "Yes, such a large family you had," they say, "and how little you are." No, I'm getting smaller. Anyway, when we get older, instead of growing up, we grow down. It's impossible to stay young. It would be nice if we could stay young forever, right? But no. The years go by, the days go by, the hours go by, and everything. And a person gets weaker, older. . . .

If there is any compensation for the loss of someone we have come to care for, it may be in knowing that person experienced some joy and fulfillment in her life. Much has been written about the therapeutic benefits of oral history, and I believe the process of telling her story was a beneficial experience for Viviana. I observed her becoming more animated and self-assured the year we were taping than previously. It was clear to me that she looked forward to my visits and sometimes didn't want them to end.

We had set out to document her life, but the process became richer than merely transcribing some stories to paper. As Guy Widdershoven describes it, "By telling a story about our life, we change our life." He explains, "The narrator comes to see [her] experience as a unique and rich event, and [she] comes to understand the story as an edifying articulation of what was going on."[2] The opportunity to recall one's life aloud, to reflect on its conflicts and resolutions, to make sense of it to oneself and to a listener, is an intrinsically valuable experience.[3]

In the early stages of our discussions, I believe Viviana was simply pleased that someone outside the family was validating her story, but as our work progressed, it seemed she became aware that she was sharing hard-won and valuable insights. By putting them into words, she had to recognize some of her wisdom. She still believed her memory was faulty, but she was sure of her opinions on child raising, the value of hard work, and the importance of community. Oral historian Donald Ritchie writes, "Old tellers of tales are not astray in a wilderness of nostalgia. . . . They preserve [their community's] wisdom, settle its disputes, create its entertainment, speak its culture. Without them, local people would have no way to discover themselves."[4] The narration itself is a learning experience, a process of empowerment.

Not just the listener, but the narrator as well, experiences some deeper awareness of her place—in her family, her culture, her world. Both learn more about who they are and what matters to them. No amount of reading on rural Mexican culture or the migrant experience in general could have touched my heart as Viviana did, and the act of telling her story led her to struggle with life's mysteries. In trying to open my eyes, she saw more through her own.

Depth of insight does not always lead to consistency, and Viviana still expressed any number of contradictions. Alternately, she stated that she had always lived in fear of her husband and that she did not fear him, that she loved Jorge and that she had never loved him, that beating is an appropriate way to raise children and that it is not acceptable. She had a wealth of knowledge about preparing foods and clothing, and about healing and midwifery, yet remained convinced that she could not learn. She appreciated the help the government gave Beatriz as a single mother but didn't want that aid extended to young women she considered frauds. I did not challenge her, and she allowed those inconsistencies to go unresolved.

On some issues, however, she did recognize contradictions, in some cases speaking out against injustices. She may have been right that coming to the United States gave her and her children opportunities that they would not have had in Mexico, but there is no question that her family's labor was devalued in both countries. She tempered her pride in her US citizenship with vigilance against the discrimination she knew still existed. Our society has built great wealth for some on the proposition that many others do not matter, do not have compelling stories of their own, and have nothing significant to contribute to our national story. Rosario Castellanos says in a memorial poem, "Do not plunder in the archives, for nothing is recorded,"[5] a lament that could refer to thousands of disregarded peoples.

We have much to learn from the storytellers of any culture, insights that arise out of our collective past and can be beneficial to the future if we choose to heed them. As a nation trying to understand our own history, we are beginning to understand that we have been wearing tinted lenses. We can no longer look only through the filters of privilege: race, gender, and class. Viviana's history is our history. The past includes the myriad experiences of women as well as men, of the underprivileged poor as well as economic and political leaders.

Viviana's narrative emphasizes that we still have much fear and injustice to overcome. The flaws Viviana noticed in both the US and Mexican governments do not seem to be abating. Since her death, a terrorist attack on the United States created an intense xenophobia and led to a draconian state law that encourages racial profiling.[6] The 2006 election in Mexico led to massive demonstrations, charges and countercharges of corruption, and polarizing of the country. Global imperialism, what John Perkins has called the "corporatocracy,"[7] continues its march, failing to ameliorate the suffering of millions of the world's poor. She would not have recognized the term, but she would have related to the pain and hardships still visited on so many.

After we had finished our taping sessions, I asked Viviana if she would like to take an excursion. One of my colleagues was a semiprofessional photographer, and we could take pictures at her house and drive out to the farm where she and Jorge lived after settling in Colorado. Excited by the idea, she worried that she wouldn't be able to find the farm herself, so we decided to invite Roberto and Beatriz to go along.

We drove out to the farm with Roberto directing us and found the two-room tenant house she and the family had lived in, now converted into a tack house. Beyond the horses in the yard stretched the Colorado plain, looking as though it had been smoothed flat by an oversized brickmaker's trowel.

Knocking at the door of the nearby farmhouse, we obtained permission to look into the tenant house. A simple saltbox-style structure with a gabled roof on one section and a shed roof on the other, it was windowless in front. Each room had its own front door, accessible by concrete steps. Viviana and Roberto entered the main room, and I could see light from the windows in the back. The house was wired for electricity, and a chimney in the back suggested a woodburning stove. Viviana looked around briefly and emerged with a delighted smile on her face, having made the three-step climb into what was now a saddle-oil-and-leather-smelling past.

The proprietor of the farm told us that the Swedish American farmer the Salgueros had worked for was no longer living, but his widow lived in the small town about two miles away. The small burg, whose main street was lined with agriculturally related businesses, worn storefronts, a small grocery, and a café, was busy with shoppers and farmers, one of whom directed us to the house we sought, less than a block away from the grocery. We had given no warning and so were pleased when the widow's daughter spoke with her mother, and they allowed all of us to trail into their house for a chat. I don't recall the daughter saying anything about her mother's memory, but it was clear that she did not remember Viviana. Viviana, on the other hand, was obviously thrilled to be reunited with a woman she credited with once saving her life. We were seated in the living room, and she chattered amiably for a few minutes, with Roberto translating, even though the widow just nodded quietly in response. I doubt we were there more than twenty minutes, but those few minutes made tangible much of what Viviana had been sharing with me in our months of conversations.

The past may not have remembered her, at least in that instance, but it was no less real to the woman who had lived it. As we left, Viviana shook hands with her former benefactor, symbolically reaching from one mixed-heritage life to another, and acting from an unquestioned assurance that this meeting was important, that what had transpired in both their lives was significant.

Out of Viviana's struggle came a quiet wisdom. Concha Saucedo, head of the Instituto Familiar de la Raza in San Francisco, says, "The old women are very wise."[8] Not willing to choose between leaving her husband or total subjugation, Viviana decided to live by her own rules, gird her house with flexible steel, and bend rather than break. She chose patience, endurance, and compassion, partly as tools for survival, but overall as the moral standards by which she wanted to live. One of her loveliest insights came out of the unhappiness of her marriage. It may seem like a contradiction, but she believed she knew what a beautiful marriage could be. Sometimes we learn best from what we fail to gain. With a certain wistfulness, she summed up what could have been for her but never was. I asked what had been the happiest day of her life:

> Well, for me it's all been the same. I believe. It's all been the same. As it was with Jorge, it is now that I'm alone with my children. Because, well, I had him, and it was like I didn't have him. He wasn't a loving husband.
>
> Most importantly, life is very beautiful, conducting oneself well—having harmony, communion. Life in a couple is very beautiful. Don't you think? If they treat each other well.

In a later conversation, I asked her what her advice to young people would be today. After a pause, she gave me only these words: "To love one another . . . just to love."

Notes·

Introduction

1. The dialogue in this scene is loosely based on the taping of Viviana's story. She did not create the setting in detail or state exactly what Memo said as they waited, but she did explain that many people who filled the hall were observers, and she narrated the official's questions and her answers. She and her son sought their citizenship shortly after he returned from Vietnam, and it is likely that he was telling her that the president's name was Nixon.

2. Sherna Berger Gluck and Daphne Patai, eds., "Introduction," *Women's Words: The Feminist Practice of Oral History* (New York: Routledge, 1991), 3.

3. Lisa Krissoff Boehm, *Making a Way out of No Way: African American Women and The Second Great Migration* (Jackson: University Press of Mississippi, 2009), x.

4. Sandy Polishuk, *Sticking to the Union: An Oral History of the Life and Times of Julia Ruuttila* (New York: Palgrave Macmillan, 2003), 7.

5. Donald A. Ritchie, in his book *Doing Oral History* (New York: Twayne, 1995, 92), mentions that it is not uncommon for interviewees to "recall only events that cast themselves in a good light."

6. Alessandro Portelli, *The Battle of Valle Giulia: Oral History and the Art of Dialogue* (Madison: University of Wisconsin Press, 1997), 3.

7. Boehm, *Making a Way,* 13.

8. Karen Anderson (*Changing Woman: A History of Racial Ethnic Women in Modern America* [New York: Oxford University Press, 1996], 113) points out that the Bracero program may have actually encouraged illegal immigration. Employers were willing to hire illegal immigrants, and "many workers found that they could secure better wages and conditions outside the legalities of the Bracero system." Manuel G. Gonzales (*Mexicanos: A History of Mexicans in the United States* [Bloomington: Indiana University Press, 1999], 175) states, "It was the contract-labor program itself, as Manuel García y Griego argues, more than any other single factor, which seems to have stimulated the huge wave of *indocumentados.*"

9. Stephen R. Niblo, *Mexico in the 1940s: Modernity, Politics, and Corruption* (Wilmington, DE: Scholarly Resources, 1999), 3.

10. Ibid., 5.

11. Ibid., 23.

12. Shirley Ann Wilson Moore, "'Not in Somebody's Kitchen': African American Women Workers in Richmond, California, and the Impact of World War II," in Elizabeth Jameson and Susan Armitage, eds., *Writing the Range: Race, Class, and Culture in the Women's West* (Norman: University of Oklahoma Press, 1997), 514.

13. Gonzales, *Mexicanos*, 171.

14. Joon Kim, "The Political Economy of the Mexican Farm Labor Program, 1942–64," *Aztlán* 29, no. 2 (Fall 2004): 17. Erasmo Gamboa adds that the Mexican government later included Idaho as a state to which it would not send braceros, also because of flagrant racism and abuses of Mexican workers ("Braceros in the Pacific Northwest, 1942–1947," in Sucheng Chan, Douglas Daniels, Mario García, and Terry Wilson, *Peoples of Color in the American West* [Lexington, MA: D. C. Heath, 1994], 499).

15. Gonzales, *Mexicanos*, 176.

16. Devra Anne Weber, "*Raiz Fuerte*: Oral History and Mexicana Farmworkers," in *Unequal Sisters: A Multicultural Reader in US Women's History*, 3rd ed., ed. Vicki L. Ruiz and Ellen Carol DuBois (New York: Routledge, 2000), 393.

Chapter One

1. Many people in Mexico today do not call the uprisings of the 1910s a revolution, maintaining that they did little to change the political, social, or economic structures of the country. Tom Barry says that contrary to the impression that the Mexican Revolution was an agrarian revolution, as portrayed by some early scholarship and the Rivera murals, it was "essentially a dispute among national elites." Tom Barry, *Zapata's Revenge: Free Trade and the Farm Crisis in Mexico* (Boston: South End Press, 1995), 137. Ronald Takaki (*A Different Mirror: A History of Multicultural America* [Boston: Little, Brown, 1993], 315) calls the conflict a civil war, and Vicki L. Ruiz (*From out of the Shadows: Mexican Women in Twentieth-Century America* [New York: Oxford University Press, 1998], 8) does the same.

2. Julian Samora and Patricia Vandel Simon, *A History of the Mexican-American People* (Notre Dame, IN: University of Notre Dame Press, 1993), 122.

3. Nan Elsasser, Kyle MacKenzie, and Yvonne Tixier y Vigil, *Las Mujeres: Conversations from a Hispanic Community* (New York: Feminist Press, 1980), 23–24.

4. Gloria Anzaldúa, "La Prieta," in *This Bridge Called My Back: Writings by Radical Women of Color*, ed. Cherríe Moraga and Gloria Anzaldúa (New York: Kitchen Table: Women of Color Press, 1983), 201.

5. Ramón A. Gutíerrez, "Community, Patriarchy and Individualism: The Politics of Chicano History and the Dream of Equality," *American Quarterly* 45 (March 1993): 59.

6. Fran Leeper Buss, ed., *Forged under the Sun/Forjada bajo el sol: The Life of Maria Elena Lucas* (Ann Arbor: University of Michigan Press, 1993), 87. Lucas

comments also on p. 279, ". . . we allow our sons to abuse our daughters. This is all over our culture, and we're creating the same situation, reproducing it again."

7. Aída Hurtado, *Voicing Chicana Feminisms: Young Women Speak Out on Sexuality and Identity* (New York: New York University Press, 2003), 75.

8. J. E. Kirkwood, "A Mexican Hacienda: Life on One of the Baronial Estates of Our Southern Neighbor," *National Geographic* 25, no. 5 (1914), 573.

9. Ibid., 571.

10. Boyé Lafayette De Mente, *NTC's Dictionary of Mexican Cultural Code Words: The Complete Guide to Key Words That Express How the Mexicans Think, Communicate, and Behave* (Lincolnwood, IL: National Textbook, 1996), 4.

11. Mark Wasserman, *Everyday Life and Politics in Nineteenth Century Mexico: Men, Women, and War* (Albuquerque: Universit~ ~ ~ ~ 2000), 142.

12. Yolanda Nava, *It's All in the Frijoles* (N~ 2000), 50.

13. Ibid., 50.

14. George M. Foster, "Peasant Society and the I~ ~ ~ ~ ~ ~ ~ ited Good," in *Peasant Society: A Reader,* ed. Jack M. Potter, May N. Diaz, and George M. Foster (Boston: Little, Brown, 1967), 315.

15. Jody Lopez and Gabriel Lopez, with Peggy A. Ford, *White Gold Laborers: The Story of Greeley's Spanish Colony* (Bloomington, IN: Author House, 2007), 80.

Chapter Two

1. Nava, *It's All in the Frijoles,* 190.

2. Earl Shorris, *Latinos: A Biography of the People* (New York: Avon Books, 1992), 105.

3. Ibid.

4. Virgilio Elizondo, "The Sacred in the Latino Experience," in *Americanos: Latino Life in the United States/La Vida Latina en los Estados Unidos,* ed. Edward James Olmos, Lea Ybarra, and Manuel Monterrey (Boston: Little, Brown, 1999), 20.

5. Nava, *It's All in the Frijoles,* 241.

6. A *National Geographic* article from 1914 (Kirkwood, "Mexican Hacienda," 580) shows photos of one such railroad segment. The Mexican workers liked to ride on the railroad so much that at times, "the company's traffic was seriously interfered with by the number of passengers."

7. John Birkinbine, "Our Neighbor, Mexico," *National Geographic* 22, no. 5 (1911), 484.

8. Martha Menchaca, *Recovering History, Constructing Race: The Indian, Black, and White Roots of Mexican Americans* (Austin: University of Texas Press, 2001), 63.

9. Ibid., 51–53.

10. Marilyn P. Davis, *Mexican Voices/American Dreams: An Oral History of Mexican Immigration to the United States* (New York: Henry Holt, 1990), 395–96.

11. Octavio Paz, in *Sor Juana*, calls *mestizos* the "true children" of Mexico and credits them with creating modern Mexico (Davis, *Mexican Voices/American Dreams*, 200–201).

12. Antoinette Sedillo López, ed., *Latina Issues: Fragments of Historia(ella) (Herstory)* (New York: Garland, 1999), 348–49.

13. Anderson, *Changing Woman*, 151.

14. Ibid.

15. Buss, *Forged under the Sun*, 93.

16. Ibid., 117.

17. To make *nixtamal*, the dough for tortillas, "women shucked the corn and soaked the kernels in water with small bits of limestone, which loosened the sheath of the corn, imbued it with calcium, and increased the content of amino acids. . . . Next the women beat the corn in the metate (grinding bowl) for hours. Finally, small pieces of the resulting dough were worked between the hands, tossed and patted and flattened out, until no thicker than a knife blade, after which they were thrown on the steaming hot comal (griddle)." Wasserman's book describes the process as women in the nineteenth century carried it out, but it remained virtually unchanged until the advent of commercially produced tortillas in the mid-twentieth century. Wasserman, *Everyday Life and Politics*, 142.

18. Anderson, *Changing Woman*, 94.

19. Irene I. Blea, *La Chicana and the Intersection of Race, Class, and Gender* (New York: Praeger, 1992), 127. Blea is discussing Chicanos when she says that "boy babies are still preferred," but she makes it clear in her first chapter that the Chicano value system has its roots in Mexican culture.

20. Kirkwood, "Mexican Hacienda," 566.

21. Michelle Fine and Lois Weis, *The Unknown City: Lives of Poor and Working-Class Young Adults* (Boston: Beacon Press, 1998), 186–87.

22. Wasserman, *Everyday Life and Politics*, 182, 187.

23. Kirkwood, "Mexican Hacienda," 573.

24. Wasserman, *Everyday Life and Politics*, 156.

25. Margaret Maud McKellar, *Life on a Mexican Ranche* (Bethlehem, PA: Lehigh University Press, 1994), 226.

26. Birkinbine, "Our Neighbor, Mexico," 495.

27. Niblo, *Mexico in the 1940s*, 10.

28. Birkinbine, "Our Neighbor, Mexico," 497.

29. Suzanne B. Pasztor, *The Spirit of Hildago: The Mexican Revolution in Coahuila* (East Lansing: Michigan State University Press, 2002), 18–19.

30. William Joseph Showalter, "Mexico and Mexicans," *National Geographic* 25, no. 5 (1914), 491.

31. López, *Latina Issues*, 88–89.

32. Ibid., 347n33.

33. Gonzales, *Mexicanos,* 165.

34. Davis, *Mexican Voices/American Dreams,* 233.

35. Blea, *La Chicana and the Intersection,* 151.

36. Earl Shorris (*Latinos,* 220) comments that Mexican-Americans show great respect for and deference to teachers. Viviana's husband could hardly contradict someone with such authority.

37. Nava, *It's All in the Frijoles,* 40.

38. Ibid., 39.

39. Elsasser, MacKenzie, and Tixier y Vigil, *Las Mujeres,* 20.

Chapter Three

1. Takaki, *Different Mirror,* 323.

2. Joon Kim, "Political Economy," 18.

3. Ibid., 17. See also Niblo, *Mexico in the 1940s,* 30. I quote the latter: "Texas was officially prohibited from participating [in the Bracero program] during this period because racism against Mexicans was so extreme in the state."

4. Gonzales, *Mexicanos,*173.

5. Hurtado, *Voicing Chicana Feminisms,* 89.

6. Leo R. Chavez, *Shadowed Lives: Undocumented Immigrants in American Society* (Fort Worth, TX: Harcourt Brace College Publishers, 1992), 4.

7. Compare Earl Shorris's comment (*Latinos,* 129): "On this different axis there are no oceans to cross; often a bus will do to make the trip."

8. Roberto Salguero (pseud.), interview by author, tape recording, Denver, April 12, 1995.

9. Sandra L. Myres, "Victoria's Daughters: English Speaking Women on Nineteenth-Century Frontiers," in *Western Women: Their Land, Their Lives,* ed. Lillian Schlissel, Vicki L. Ruiz, and Janice Monk (Albuquerque: University of New Mexico Press, 1988), 263.

10. Carlos Fuentes, *The Old Gringo,* quoted in Norma E. Cantú and Olga Nájera-Ramírez, eds., *Chicana Traditions: Continuity and Change* (Urbana: University of Illinois Press, 2002), 57.

11. Américo Paredes, "Mexican-American Identity and Culture," in Chan, Daniels, García, and Wilson, *Peoples of Color,* 270.

12. Davis, *Mexican Voices/American Dreams,* 171.

13. Salguero interview, April 12, 1995.

14. Tamar Diana Wilson, "Weak Ties, Strong Ties: Network Principles in Mexican Migration," *Human Organization* 57 (Winter 1998), 394.

15. Devra Anne Weber, "*Raiz Fuerte:* Oral History and Mexicana Farmworkers," in *Unequal Sisters: A Multicultural Reader in US Women's History,* ed. Vicki L. Ruiz and Ellen Carol DuBois, 3rd ed. (New York: Routledge, 2000), 397.

16. Vicki L. Ruiz, *From out of the Shadows: Mexican Women in Twentieth-Century America* (New York: Oxford University Press, 1998), 17.

17. Juan Gonzalez, *Harvest of Empire: A History of Latinos in America* (New York: Viking, 2000), 202-03.

18. Roberto Suro, *Strangers among Us: How Latino Immigration Is Transforming America* (New York: Alfred A. Knopf, 1998), 82.

19. Selden C. Menefee, *Mexican Migratory Workers of South Texas* (Washington, DC: Division of Research, Work Projects Administration, US Gov't., 1941), 32. See also Suro, *Strangers among Us,* 82.

20. Samora and Simon, *History of the Mexican-American People,* 187.

21. Ken Ellingwood, *Hard Line: Life and Death on the U. S.–Mexico Border* (New York: Pantheon Books, 2004), 22.

22. Harry Schwartz, *Seasonal Farm Labor in the United States with Special Reference to Hired Workers in Fruit and Vegetable and Sugar-Beet Production* (New York: Columbia University Press, 1945), 110.

23. According to Viviana's son, it was not Jorge's father but Jorge's stepbrother, the son of his father's new wife, who did not want to be drafted. That would seem more likely, since Jorge's father would probably have been in his forties when the war broke out.

24. Chan, Daniels, García, and Wilson, *Peoples of Color,* 270.

25. Ibid., 273.

26. Glenn Justice, *Valley beneath the Sierra Vieja: A Texas Border Ranch History* (Odessa, TX: Rimrock Press, 2004), 3.

27. Shorris, *Latinos,* 152–53.

28. Evelyn Nakano Glenn, "From Servitude to Service Work: Historical Continuities in the Racial Division of Paid Reproductive Labor," in Ruiz and DuBois, *Unequal Sisters,* 442. Glenn notes that El Paso established its segregated school system in the 1880s, and Gilbert G. Gonzalez writes ("'The Mexican Schools,' 1890s–1930s," in Chan, Daniels, García, and Wilson, *Peoples of Color,* 329) that "as early as 1892, Mexican children were being denied entrance into 'American' schools in Corpus Christi." Based on what Viviana's in-laws had told her, it would seem Mexican-American children were being denied an education much earlier than that.

29. Roger Waldinger and Michael I. Lichter, *How the Other Half Works* (Berkeley, CA: University of California Press, 2003), 11.

30. Pierrette Hondagneu-Sotelo, *Gendered Transitions: Mexican Experiences of Immigration* (Berkeley: University of California Press, 1994), 27.

31. Kim, "Political Economy," 19.

32. Antonia I. Castañeda, "Women of Color and the Rewriting of Western History: The Discourse, Politics, and Decolonization of History," *Pacific Historical Review: American Historical Association* 61 (November 1992), 518.

33. Elizabeth Martínez, *De Colores Means All of Us: Latina Views for a Multi-Colored Century* (Cambridge, MA: South End Press, 1998), 2.

34. De Mente, *NTC's Dictionary,* 32.

35. Schwartz, *Seasonal Farm Labor,* 123.

36. Sarah Deutsch, *No Separate Refuge: Culture, Class, and Gender on an Anglo-Hispanic Frontier in the American Southwest, 1880-1940* (New York: Oxford University Press, 1987), 115.

37. Schwartz, *Seasonal Farm Labor,* 131.

38. Television History: The First 75 Years. www.tvhistory.tv/1945%20QF .htm.

39. Takaki, *Different Mirror,* 323.

40. Lopez and Lopez, *Gold Laborers,* 46.

41. Susan Ferriss and Ricardo Sandoval, *The Fight in the Fields: César Chavez and the Farmworkers Movement* (New York: Harcourt Brace, 1997), 206.

42. Ibid., 207.

43. Buss, *Forged under the Sun,* 76.

44. Shorris, *Latinos,* 247.

45. Richard Griswold del Castillo, "Chicano Families in the Southwest, 1910–1945," in Chan, Daniels, García, and Wilson, *Peoples of Color,* 211.

46. Gonzales, *Mexicanos,* 178–79.

47. Menefee, *Mexican Migratory Workers,* 27.

48. Ibid., 41.

49. Shorris, *Latinos,* 302.

50. Lars Schoultz, *Beneath the United States* (Cambridge: Harvard University Press, 1998), 14.

51. Suro, *Strangers among Us,* 78.

52. Vicki L. Ruiz, "'Star Struck': Acculturation, Adolescence, and the Mexican American Woman, 1920–1950," in *Building with Our Hands: New Directions in Chicana Studies,* ed. Adela De La Torre and Beatríz M. Pesquera (Berkeley: University of California Press, 1993), 121.

53. Deutsch, *No Separate Refuge,* 134; Nava, *It's All in the Frijoles,* 224; "Worlds Apart: Understanding the Two Faces of Weld County," *Greeley (Colorado) Tribune,* December 22, 2002, special section reprint of monthly series, p. 2.

54. Jorge M. Larralde and Richard Griswold del Castillo, "San Diego's Ku Klux Klan 1920–1980," *Journal of San Diego History* 46 (Spring/Summer 2000), 79.

55. Ibid.

56. Suro, *Strangers among Us,* 132.

57. Gonzalez, *Harvest of Empire,* 102.

58. Gilbert G. Gonzalez, "The 'Mexican Schools,' 1890s–1930s," quoted in Chan, Daniels, García, and Wilson, *Peoples of Color,* 329.

59. Ibid.

60. Mario T. García, *Mexican Americans: Leadership, Ideology, and Identity, 1930–1960* (New Haven: Yale University Press, 1989), 256.

61. Griswold del Castillo, 213.

62. Menchaca, *Recovering History, Constructing Race,* 166.

63. Ibid., 12.

64. Alwyn Barr, *Black Texans: A History of African Americans in Texas, 1528–1995*, 2nd ed. (Norman: University of Oklahoma Press, 1996), 17.

65. See Samora and Simon, *History of the Mexican-American People*, 155; Suro, *Strangers among Us*, 78; Gonzalez, *Harvest of Empire*, 103.

66. Takaki, *Different Mirror*, 393.

67. Gonzales, *Mexicanos*, 162.

68. Shorris, *Latinos*, 97. Also, Samora and Simon (*History of the Mexican-American People*, 242–43) tell the heroic stories of several Mexican-American Medal of Honor winners.

69. Gonzales, *Mexicanos*, 164.

70. Takaki, *Different Mirror*, 326.

71. Gonzalez, *Harvest of Empire*, 104.

72. Lopez and Lopez, *Gold Laborers*, 221.

73. Ibid., 215.

74. Takaki, *Different Mirror*, 395.

75. Ibid., 394.

76. Menchaca, *Recovering History, Constructing Race*, 278.

77. Ruiz, *From out of the Shadows*, 40–41.

78. Takaki, *Different Mirror*, 330.

79. Martin Bulmer and John Solomos, eds., "Introduction," *Ethnic and Racial Studies Today* (London: Routledge, 1999), 8.

80. Ibid., 5.

81. Ibid.

82. Menchaca, *Recovering History, Constructing Race*, 11.

83. Martínez, *De Colores*, 2.

84. McKissack, *Chicano Educational Achievement*, 38.

85. Shorris, *Latinos*, 101.

86. The term *Hispanic* didn't excite much response from Viviana at all. Martínez comments (*De Colores*, 2, 17) that the term, imposed by governmental bureaucracy during the Nixon administration and not appropriate in the first place, was easily mocked ("His Panic, Her Panic").

87. Matthew C. Gutmann, Matos Rodriguez, Lynn Stephen, and Patricia Zavella, eds., "Introduction: Understanding the Américas: Insights from Latina/o and Latin American Studies," *Perspectives on Las Américas: A Reader in Culture, History, and Representation* (Malden, MA: Blackwell Publishers, 2003), 3.

88. Suro, *Strangers among Us*, 134.

89. David Mason, "The Continuing Significance of Race? Teaching Ethnic and Racial Studies in Sociology," in Bulmer and Solomos, *Ethnic and Racial Studies Today*, 27.

90. Ruiz, *From out of the Shadows*, xiv.

91. Buss, *Forged under the Sun*, 35n.

92. Sondra Hale ("Feminist Method, Process and Self-Criticism: Interviewing Sudanese Women," in Gluck and Patai, *Women's Words*, 131) maintains that feminist research should include empowerment and validation of its subjects.

Chapter Four

1. Buss, *Forged under the Sun,* 279.
2. Anderson, *Changing Woman,* 119.
3. Ibid., 120.
4. De Mente, *NTC's Dictionary,* 173.
5. Anderson, *Changing Woman,* 132.
6. Ramón Saldívar, *The Borderlands of Culture: Américo Paredes and the Transnational Imaginary* (Durham, NC: Duke University Press, 2006), 307.
7. Isabel Valle, *Fields of Toil: A Migrant Family's Journey* (Pullman: Washington State University Press, 1994), 81.
8. Stuart Chase's *Mexico: A Study of the Americas* (New York: Literary Guild, 1931) is a book not to be missed, not only for its discussion of the "machineless" society but also for its engaging illustrations by Diego Rivera.
9. Ibid., 208.
10. Martínez, *De Colores,* 183.
11. Lea Ybarra, "The Family," in Olmos, Ybarra, and Monterrey, *Americanos: Latino Life,* 84.
12. Linda Gordon, "Family Violence, Feminism, and Social Control," in Ruiz and DuBois, *Unequal Sisters* (1990 ed.), 147.
13. Michael Maccoby, "Love and Authority: A Study of Mexican Villagers," in Potter, *Peasant Society,* 342.
14. Octavio Paz, *The Labyrinth of Solitude and Other Writings* (New York: Grove Press, 1985), 81.
15. One of the central findings of Hondagneu-Sotelo's work (*Gendered Transitions,* 1994) on gender and migration is that family structures have evolved as Mexican immigrants have adapted to US culture, resulting in more gender equality and less compliance on the part of children.
16. Magdalena Mora and Adelaida R. Del Castillo, eds., *Mexican Women in the United States: Struggles Past and Present,* Occasional Paper no. 2 (Los Angeles: Chicano Studies Research Center Publications, University of California, 1980), 33; Gloria Anzaldúa, *Borderlands:/La Frontera: The New Mestiza* (San Francisco: Spinsters/Aunt Lute, 1987), 83.
17. Hondagneu-Sotelo, *Gendered Transitions,* 188.
18. Buss, *Forged under the Sun,* 13.
19. Melody Graulich, "Violence against Women: Power Dynamics in Literature of the Western Family," in *The Women's West,* ed. Susan Armitage and Elizabeth Jameson (Norman: University of Oklahoma Press, 1987, Based on papers from the 1983 Women's West Conference in Sun Valley, Idaho), 113.
20. Buss, *Forged under the Sun,* 25.
21. Ibid.
22. Ibid., 94.
23. Maxine Baca Zinn, "Gender and Ethnic Identity among Chicanos," *Frontiers* 5, no. 2 (1980), 20.

24. Ibid.

25. Ibid.

26. Rosa Linda Fregoso, *MeXicana Encounters: The Making of Social Identities on the Borderlands* (Berkeley: University of California Press, 2003), 34.

27. Reyes Ramos, "Discovering the Production of Mexican American Family Structure," *De Colores Journal* 6 (1982), 129–30.

28. Beatriz Salguero [pseud.], interviewed by author, tape recording, Greeley, Colorado, February 4, 1995.

29. "A number of social scientists who have examined Mexican American culture have stressed the importance of respect." Norma Williams, *The Mexican American Family: Tradition and Change* (Dix Hills, NY: General Hall, 1990), 25.

30. Nava, *It's All in the Frijoles,* 43.

31. Juan Carlos Heredia, "I Asked My Grandfather What *Macho* Meant," in Olmos, Ybarra, and Fuentes, *Americanos: Latino Life,* 97.

32. Gloria Anzaldúa, quoted in Anderson, *Changing Woman,* 145.

33. Elsasser, MacKenzie, and Tixier y Vigil, *Las Mujeres,* 23; Nava, 188.

34. Nava, *It's All in the Frijoles,* 188.

35. Ibid., 257.

36. Oscar Lewis, *The Children of Sánchez* (New York: Random House, 1961), 482. (Although the Lewis study is dated, I believe the attitude expressed by that particular interviewee sheds light on the issue of child rearing.)

37. As translated by Elsasser, MacKenzie, and Tixier y Vigil, *Las Mujeres,* 22.

38. National Women's Health Resource Center, "Violence against Women," www.healthywomen.org/condition/violence-against-women.

39. Buss, *Forged under the Sun,* 285.

40. Anderson (*Changing Woman,* 119–20) lists these limitations for rural Mexican-American women as factors that precluded radical revisions in gender roles or authority patterns.

41. Bernice Rincon, "La Chicana: 'Her Role in The Past and Her Search For a New Role in the Future,'" *Regeneracion* 1 (1971), 15–16.

42. De Mente, *NTC's Dictionary,* 32.

43. Alan Riding, *Distant Neighbors: A Portrait of the Mexicans* (New York: Vintage Books, 1989), 8.

44. Ruiz, *From out of the Shadows,* 132.

45. Kathleen Barry, cited in Jennifer L. Dunn, "'Victims' and 'Survivors': Emerging Vocabularies of Motive for 'Battered Women Who Stay,'" *Sociological Inquiry* 75 (February 2005), 13.

46. National Women's Health Resource Center, "Violence against Women: Overview."

47. Buss, *Forged under the Sun,* 127.

48. Ibid., 27.

49. Graulich, "Violence against Women," 115.

50. Buss, *Forged under the Sun,* 44n.

51. De Mente, *NTC's Dictionary,* 179.

52. Myralyn F. Allgood, ed., *Another Way to Be: Selected Works of Rosario Castellanos* (Athens: University of Georgia Press, 1990), xxxi.

53. Barbara Smith and Beverly Smith, "Across the Kitchen Table: A Sister to Sister Dialogue," in Moraga and Anzaldúa, 115–16.

54. Riding, *Distant Neighbors,* 232. See also De Mente (*NTC's Dictionary,* 38), who states, "From the early 1600s to the middle of the twentieth century it was the official policy of most of the powerful Catholic bishops of Mexico that Indians and poor mixed-bloods should not be educated, and should not be encouraged or helped to improve their condition. (Until the civil war of 1910–1921 the Catholic Church controlled all education in Mexico.)"

55. Kirkwood, "Mexican Hacienda," 573.

Chapter Five

1. David Hayes-Bautista, "Latino Contributions/Contribuciones Latinas," in *Americanos: Latino Life,* 40.

2. R. W. Roskelley, "Beet Labor Problems in Colorado," *Proceedings of the Western Farm Economics Association, Thirteenth Annual Meeting* (Pullman: State College of Washington, and Moscow: University of Idaho, 1940), 67; Schwartz, *Seasonal Farm Labor,* 126–29.

3. Davis, *Mexican Voices/American Dreams,* 339.

4. Hondagneu-Sotelo, *Gendered Transitions,* 21.

5. Anderson, *Changing Woman,* 126–27.

6. Ernesto Galarza, Herman Gallegos, and Julian Samora, *Mexican-Americans in the Southwest* (Santa Barbara, CA: McNally and Loftin, 1969), 21.

7. Alfredo Mirandé and Evangelina Enríquez, *La Chicana* (Chicago: University of Chicago Press, 1981), 107.

8. Ibid.

9. Buss, *Forged under the Sun,* 278.

10. Potter, *Peasant Society,* 297.

11. Raquel Bessudo, a Mexican-born Jewish girl of European parents who arrived in Mexico just before the Second World War, says of the Mexican peasant, "Here the poor are even more open-hearted than others. They will always have a piece of *tortilla* and some *frijoles* and, of course, the *mole* will never be missing if the reason is to greet you and make a feast for you as the most important person in the world." Nava, *It's All in the Frijoles,* 281–82.

12. Davis, *Mexican Voices/American Dreams,* 41.

13. Michael Parfit, "Mexico City: Pushing the Limits," *National Geographic* 190 (August 1996), 27.

14. Castañeda, "Women of Color," 522–23.

15. Davis, *Mexican Voices/American Dreams,* 334–36, 340.

16. See Navar's discussion of why she left Mexico to come to the United States. Davis, *Mexican Voices/American Dreams,* 340.

17. Ruiz, *From out of the Shadows,* xv.

18. Buss, *Forged under the Sun,* 3. See also Takaki, *Different Mirror,* 327–28.

19. Chan, Daniels, García, and Wilson, *Peoples of Color,* 330.

20. V. Carl Allsup, "Hernandez V. Driscoll CISD," *Handbook of Texas Online,* http://www.tshaonline.org/handbook/online/articles/jrh02.

21. "MALDEF Settles Historic Desegregation Case: Texas Desegregation Case Filed in 1970 on Behalf of Children and Parents from Uvalde Public Schools," http://www.maldef.org/news/releases/texas_deseg_091608.

22. Greeley Committee, Earle U. Rugg, Chair. *Final Report, 1946-1949, on Intergroup Relations* (Greeley, CO: Colorado State College of Education, 1949), 71.

23. Deutsch, *No Separate Refuge,* 139–40.

24. Greeley Committee, 68, 120.

25. García, *Mexican Americans,* 252–67.

26. Lopez and Lopez, *Gold Laborers,* 148.

27. Greeley Committee, 119–20.

28. She is referring to Susan Smith, whose story dominated the media, Spanish-speaking and English-speaking alike, in October of 1994. Smith pushed her car into a lake near Union, South Carolina, with her two young children restrained inside.

29. De Mente, *NTC's Dictionary,* 285.

30. Ilan Stavans, *The Hispanic Condition: Reflections on Culture and Identity in America* (New York: Harper Collins, 1995), 121.

31. Patrick Oster, *The Mexicans: A Personal Portrait of a People* (New York: William Morrow and Company, 1989), 244.

32. Deutsch, *No Separate Refuge,* 59.

33. Marc Simmons, *Witchcraft in the Southwest: Spanish and Indian Supernaturalism on the Rio Grande* (Lincoln: University of Nebraska Press, 1974), 7.

34. Elsasser, MacKenzie, and Tixier y Vigil, *Las Mujeres,* 20–21.

35. Simmons, *Witchcraft in the Southwest,* 165–66.

36. Ibid., 163.

37. De Mente, *NTC's Dictionary,* 173.

38. Buss, *Forged under the Sun,* 283.

39. Nasario García, *Brujerías: Stories of Witchcraft and the Supernatural in the American Southwest and Beyond* (Lubbock: Texas Tech University Press, 2007), 294.

40. Emma Pérez, "Decolonizing Chicana History," *Women's Review of Books* 17 (February 2000), 107.

41. José E. Limón, "La Llorona, The Third Legend of Greater Mexico: Cultural Symbols, Women, and the Political Unconscious," in *Between Borders: Essays on Mexicana/Chicana History,* ed. Adelaida R. Del Castillo (Encino, CA: Floricanto Press, 1990), 411.

42. Elsasser, MacKenzie, and Tixier y Vigil, *Las Mujeres,* 23n.

43. Mirandé and Enríquez, *La Chicana,* 31.

44. María Herrera-Sobek, "Danger! Children at Play: Patriarchal Ideology and the Construction of Gender in Spanish-Language Hispanic/Chicano Children's Songs and Games," in Cantú and Nájera-Ramírez, 96.

45. "Worship of the 'Indian' Virgin of Guadalupe provides a powerful unifying thread among most Indian groups." Riding, *Distant Neighbors,* 215.

46. Stavans, *Hispanic Condition,* 107.

47. Carrol Norquest, *Rio Grande Wetbacks: Mexican Migrant Workers* (Albuquerque: University of New Mexico Press, 1972), 42.

48. Nasario García, *Brujerías,* 252–53.

49. Ibid., 252–57.

Chapter Six

1. Nava, *It's All in the Frijoles,* 204.

2. Ybarra, "Family," 84.

3. Limón, "La Llorona," 423.

4. Chan, Daniels, García, and Wilson, *Peoples of Color,* 263.

5. Graulich, "Violence against Women," 113.

6. Gutíerrez, "Community, Patriarchy and Individualism," 58.

7. Stavans, *Hispanic Condition,* 93.

8. Fernando Peñalosa, "Mexican Family Roles," *Journal of Marriage and the Family* (November 1968), 687. Mudita Rastogi and Karen S. Wampler ("Adult Daughters' Perceptions of the Mother–Daughter Relationship: A Cross-Cultural Comparison," *Family Relations* 48 [July 1999], 333) also point out "the enduring significance of the mother–daughter intergenerational bond" in the European, Asian, and Mexican American cultures.

9. Denise M. Oleske and Jerome J. Hahn, "Work-Related Injuries of the Hand: Data from an Occupational Injury/Illness Surveillance System," *Journal of Community Health* 17 (August 1992), 205. In 1992, the journal reported that hand and finger injuries made up 30 percent of all nonfatal occupational injuries. Nearly 20 percent resulted "from a crushing motion," and hands "being caught in machines or struck by metal items or hand tools accounted for 36.2 percent of the injuries."

10. "Hispanics Have High Injury, Low Health Coverage Rates." *Employee Benefit News.* By Kelley M. Blassingame (January 2004), 31, 41. In *Business Source Premier,* http://o-search.ebscohost.com.source.unco.edu/login.aspx?direct=true&db=buh&AN=11988806&site=ehost-live.

11. National Women's Health Resource Center, "Violence Against Women: Facts to Know," www.healthywomen.org/condition/violence-against-women.

12. Smith and Smith, "Across the Kitchen Table," in Moraga and Anzaldúa, *This Bridge Called My Back,* 116.

13. Shorris, *Latinos,* 224.

14. Paula S. Rothenberg, *Race, Class, and Gender in the United States: An Integrated Study*, 5th ed. (New York: Worth, 2001), 98.

15. Blea, *La Chicana and the Intersection*, 153.

16. Shorris, *Latinos*, 46.

17. Waldinger and Lichter, *How the Other Half Works*, 160–64.

18. Shorris, *Latinos*, 320.

19. Ruiz, *From out of the Shadows*, 114–15.

20. Dave Grossman, *On Killing: The Psychological Cost of Learning to Kill in War and Society* (Boston: Little, Brown, 1995), 277.

Chapter Seven

1. Elizondo, "Sacred in the Latino Experience," 20.

2. Peggy Levitt, "Two Nations under God? Latino Religious Life in the United States," in *Latinos: Remaking America*, ed. Marcelo M. Suárez-Orozco and Mariela M. Páez (Berkeley: University of California Press, 2002), 153.

3. Samora and Simon, *History of the Mexican-American People*, 232.

4. Anthony M. Stevens-Arroyo and Anna María Díaz-Stevens, "Religious Faith and Institutions in the Forging of Latino Identities," *Handbook of Hispanic Cultures in the United States: Sociology*, ed. Félix Padilla (Houston, TX: Arte Público Press and Instituto de Cooperación Iberoamericana, 1994), p. 265, 270.

5. Moisés Sandoval, *On the Move: A History of the Hispanic Church in the United States* (Maryknoll, NY: Orbis Books, 2006), 22.

6. Matt Meier and Feliciano Rivera, *Mexican Americans/American Mexicans* (New York: Hill and Wang, 1993), 227.

7. Elizondo, "Sacred in the Latino Experience," 20.

8. Buss, *Forged under the Sun*, 295.

9. Blea, *La Chicana and the Intersection*, 141.

10. Ibid., 141.

11. Ibid., 84.

12. De Mente, *NTC's Dictionary*, 149.

13. Ibid., 150.

14. Ibid., 290.

15. Shorris (*Latinos*, 374) and De Mente (*NTC's Dictionary*, 152) both point out that priests find many more devoted women than men among their flocks. De Mente comments on the irony of this situation, considering the church has held women to a high standard of Christian morality while allowing men to do pretty much as they pleased. That result may not be so ironic as it seems. When one is held to a higher standard, she may actually be more invested in an institution. Perhaps it is men to whom the church has offered a disservice.

16. Eric R. Wolf, "Closed Corporate Peasant Communities in Mesoamerica and Central Java," in Potter, *Peasant Society*, 230.

17. Oster, *Mexicans*, 203.

18. Ibid., 204.

19. Shorris, *Latinos*, 374.

20. Nava, *It's All in the Frijoles*, 126.

21. De Mente, *NTC's Dictionary*, 152; Shorris, *Latinos*, 377.

22. Celia Jaes Falicov, "Ambiguous Loss: Risk and Resilience in Latino Immigrant Families," in Suárez-Orozco and Páez, *Latinos*, 281.

23. Elizondo, "Sacred in the Latino Experience," 23.

24. Timothy McVeigh bombed the Alfred P. Murrah Federal Building in Oklahoma City, on April 19, 1995, killing 168 people.

25. Charles Aranda, *Dichos: Proverbs and Sayings from the Spanish* (Santa Fe: Sunstone Press, 1977), 9.

26. Nava, *It's All in the Frijoles*, 111.

27. Ibid., 170.

28. Foster, "Peasant Society and the Image of Limited Good," 313.

29. Ibid.

Chapter Eight

1. Gutmann, Rodriguez, Stephen, and Zavella, *Perspectives on Las Américas*, 10.

2. Hayes-Bautista, "Latino Contributions/Contribuciones Latinas," 40.

3. William V. Flores and Rina Benmayor, eds., *Latino Cultural Citizenship: Claiming Identity, Space, and Rights* (Boston: Beacon Press, 1997), 1.

4. Davis, *Mexican Voices/American Dreams*, 414.

5. Stavans, *Hispanic Condition*, 9.

6. Falicov, "Ambiguous Loss," 277.

7. Gutmann, Rodriguez, Stephen, and Zavella, *Perspectives on Las Américas*, 12.

8. Ibid., 419.

9. Ibid.

10. Tom Barry, "Anti-Immigrant Backlash on the 'Home Front,'" *NACLA Report on the Americas* 38 (May/June 2005), 34–35.

11. Lisa J. Montoya, "Gender and Citizenship in Latino Political Participation," in Suárez-Orozco and Páez, *Latinos*, 411.

12. Davis, *Mexican Voices/American Dreams*, 411.

13. Gonzales, *Mexicanos*, 186–87.

14. Davis, *Mexican Voices/American Dreams*, 238, 243.

15. Lopez and Lopez, *Gold Laborers*, 220.

16. Gonzales (*Mexicanos*, 186) cites the corruption of the Mexican government and the exclusion of peasants from the political process in Mexico as just two of the reasons immigrants choose not to participate in the political process in the United States. See also Manuel Gamio on the attitude of the mine worker, cited in Chan, Daniels, García, and Wilson (*Peoples of Color*, 129), who say it

doesn't do any good for poor people to get mixed up in politics. "Let those who have offices, who get something out of it, get into it. But he who has to work hard, let him live from his work alone."

17. Montoya, "Gender and Citizenship," 415.

18. Davis, *Mexican Voices/American Dreams*, 239.

19. Falicov, "Ambiguous Loss," 274. See also Davis's oral history *Mexican Voices/American Dreams* in which several interviewees who came to the United States to work expressed their preference for living in Mexico (153, 175, 194, 210, 236). Many others, however, found just as many reasons to make the United States their new home, illustrating the ambivalence of Mexican immigrants.

20. Falicov, "Ambiguous Loss," 274.

21. Oster, *Mexicans*, 65.

22. Leif Jensen, "The Demographic Diversity of Immigrants and Their Children," in *Ethnicities: Children of Immigrants in America,* ed. Rubén G. Rumbaut and Alejandro Portes (Berkeley: University of California Press, 2001), 30.

23. "Record Proportion of Americans Now Own Their Homes," *National Center for Policy Analysis,* May 23, 2001, www.ncpa.org/sub/dpd/index.php?Article_ID=8272.

24. Rothenberg, *Race, Class, and Gender,* 271.

25. Hondagneu-Sotelo, *Gendered Transitions,* 31.

26. Barry, *Zapata's Revenge,* 183.

27. Ibid., 195.

28. Shorris, *Latinos,* 259.

29. Ibid., 265.

30. Ellingwood, *Hard Line,* 4–5.

31. In the summer of 1987 (Oster, *Mexicans,* 63–67), eighteen illegal immigrants died of asphyxiation in an overheated and hermetically sealed boxcar in Sierra Blanca, Texas. Just a day later, a second group was found near death in a boxcar close by, and a third group, all unconscious, was discovered near San Clemente, California, in a sealed truck. More recently (Simon Romero and David Barboza, "Trapped in Heat in Texas Truck, 18 People Die," *New York Times,* May 15, 2003, late ed.–final, sec. A, nat. desk, 1), eighteen people died in the trailer of an eighteen-wheeler near Victoria, Texas. About a hundred people had been packed into the trailer, which was detached from the cab and abandoned. While the vehicle was a refrigeration truck, the cooling unit was apparently not turned on, and the interior soon turned into an oven. As temperatures reached over ninety degrees Fahrenheit outside—and well over one hundred in the trailer itself—people tried to bore or punch holes into the door in a desperate attempt to let in fresh air. Among the survivors was a girl who turned fifteen the day after her rescue, but not so lucky were a fourteen-year-old boy and his father. In some instances (Luis Alberto Urrea, *The Devil's Highway: A True Story* [New York: Back Bay Books/Little, Brown, 2004], 70), unfortunate migrants are locked in the trunk of a car or actually strapped to the engine blocks. "In the trade, these riders are known as 'coffin loads.'"

32. For David Maung's photo of the National Guard at work on a border wall, see the Associated Press story: Olga R. Rodriguez, "Crossing the Border," *(Portland) Oregonian*, June 13, 2006, sec. A, p. 4.

33. Sylvia Moreno, "'Catch and Remove' More Effective than 'Catch and Release,'" *Sunday Oregonian*, June 18, 2006, sec. A, p. 7 (LA Times-Washington Post Service).

34. Daniel Griswold, *Departing Congress Approves 700-Mile "Wall to Nowhere,"* Cato.org, October 30, 2006. This article also appeared as "Guest Opinion: Without Immigration Reform Border Fence Will Be 'Fence to Nowhere,'" *Tucson Citizen,* November 9, 2006, opinion sec.

35. Esmeralda Bermudez, "Where the Future Is a Long Way Off," *Sunday Oregonian,* May 28, 2006, sec. A, p. 12.

36. Ruiz, cited in Emma Perez, "Decolonizing Chicana History," *Women's Review of Books* 17 (February 2000), 2.

37. Arizona State Senate, Forty-ninth Legislature, Second Regular Session, Amended Fact Sheet for S.B. 1070. www.azleg.gov/legtext/49leg/2r/summary/s.1070pshs_caucus-floor.doc.htm.

38. Shorris, *Latinos,* 426.

39. Martínez, *De Colores,* 201.

40. Gonzalez, *Harvest of Empire,* 188.

41. Waldinger and Lichter, *How the Other Half Works,* 163–64.

42. Suro, *Strangers among Us,* 290.

43. Eduardo Porter, "Illegal Immigrants Are Bolstering Social Security with Billions," *New York Times,* April 5, 2005, bus. sec.

44. Jose-Antonio Orosco, "An Opportunity to Think about Justice: The Immigration Protests," *Oregonian,* May 3, 2006, ed. sec., C 07.

45. Urrea, *Devil's Highway: A True Story,* 217.

46. Jorge Ramos, *The Other Face of America: Chronicles of the Immigrants Shaping Our Future* (New York: HarperCollins, 2002), 65.

47. Roger Daniels, *Guarding the Golden Door: American Immigration Policy and Immigrants since 1882* (New York: Hill and Wang, 2004), 188.

48. Bermudez, A13.

49. Viviana is actually supporting a tenet that later became part of the 1996 Republican platform, a call for a constitutional amendment "declaring that children born in the United States of parents who are not legally present in the United States or who are not long-term residents are not automatically citizens." Daniels, *Guarding the Golden Door,* 245.

Chapter Nine

1. "*Palabras de una Viejita: Habla Luisa Torres de Guadalupita, New Mexico/* The Words of an Old One: Luisa Torres writes of her life in Guadalupita, New Mexico," collected and transcribed by Gioi Brandi, *El Palacio* 84 (Fall 1978), 18.

2. Guy A. M. Widdershoven, "The Story of Life: Hermeneutic Perspectives on the Relationship between Narrative and Life History," *The Narrative Study of Lives,* vol. 1, ed. Ruthellen Josselson and Amia Lieblich (Newbury Park, CA: Sage, 1993), 13.

3. Daphne Patai, "U.S. Academics and Third World Women: Is Ethical Research Possible?" in Gluck and Patai, *Women's Words,* 142.

4. Ritchie, *Doing Oral History,* 196.

5. Allgood, *Another Way to Be,* 35.

6. At this writing, the Arizona law has been declared unconstitutional in federal court, but Georgia and Alabama have passed similar bills.

7. John Perkins, *Confessions of an Economic Hit Man* (San Francisco: Berrett-Koehler, 2004), xii.

8. Shorris, *Latinos,* 109.

Bibliography

Allgood, Muralyn F., ed. and trans. *Another Way to Be: Selected Works of Rosario Castellanos*. Athens: University of Georgia Press, 1990.

Anderson, Karen. *Changing Woman: A History of Racial Ethnic Women in Modern America*. New York: Oxford University Press, 1996.

Anzaldúa, Gloria. *Borderlands: La Frontera: The New Mestiza*. San Francisco: Spinsters/Aunt Lute, 1987.

———. "La Prieta." In Moraga and Anzaldúa, *This Bridge Called My Back*, 198–209.

Aranda, Charles. *Dichos: Proverbs and Sayings from the Spanish*. Santa Fe: Sunstone Press, 1977.

Armitage, Susan. "Women and the New Western History." *Organization of American Historians Magazine of History* 9 (Fall 1994): 22–27.

Armitage, Susan, and Elizabeth Jameson, eds. *The Women's West*. Norman: University of Oklahoma Press, 1987. Based on papers from the 1983 Women's West Conference in Sun Valley, Idaho.

Barr, Alwyn. *Black Texans: A History of African Americans in Texas, 1528-1995*. 2nd ed. Norman: University of Oklahoma Press, 1996.

Barry, Kathleen. *Female Sexual Slavery: From Prostitution to Marriage, the Landmark Study of All the Ways Women Are Sexually Enslaved*. New York: Avon Books, 1979.

Barry, Tom. "Anti-Immigrant Backlash on the 'Home Front.'" *NACLA Report on the Americas* 38 (May/June 2005): 28–41.

———. *Zapata's Revenge: Free Trade and the Farm Crisis in Mexico*. Boston: South End Press, 1995.

Behar, Ruth. *Translated Woman: Crossing the Border with Esperanza's Story*. Boston: Beacon Press, 1993.

Birkinbine, John. "Our Neighbor, Mexico." *National Geographic* 22, no. 5 (1911): 475–508.

Blassingame, Kelley M. "Hispanics Have High Injury, Low Health Coverage Rates." *Employee Benefit News* (January 2004), 31, 41. In *Business Source Premier*, http://o-search.ebscohost.com.source.unco.edu/login.aspx?direct=true&db=buh&AN=11988806&site=ehost-live).

Blea, Irene I. *La Chicana and the Intersection of Race, Class, and Gender*. New York: Praeger, 1992.

Boehm, Lisa Krissoff. *Making a Way out of No Way: African American Women and The Second Great Migration*. Jackson: University Press of Mississippi, 2009.

Bowen, Kurt. *Evangelism and Apostasy: The Evolution and Impact of Evangelicals in Modern Mexico*. Montreal: McGill-Queen's University Press, 1996.

Bulmer, Martin, and John Solomos, eds. *Ethnic and Racial Studies Today*. London: Routledge, 1999.

Buss, Fran Leeper, ed. *Forged under the Sun: The Life of María Elena Lucas*. Ann Arbor: University of Michigan Press, 1993.

Cantú, Norma E., and Olga Nájera-Ramírez. *Chicana Traditions: Continuity and Change*. Urbana: University of Illinois Press, 2002.

Castañeda, Antonia I. "Women of Color and the Rewriting of Western History: The Discourse, Politics, and Decolonization of History." *Pacific Historical Review: American Historical Association* 61 (November 1992): 501–33.

Chan, Sucheng, Douglas H. Daniels, Mario T. García, and Terry P. Wilson, eds. *Peoples of Color in the American West*. Lexington, MA: D. C. Heath, 1994.

Chase, Stuart. *Mexico: A Study of the Americas*. New York: Literary Guild, 1931.

Chavez, Leo R. *Shadowed Lives: Undocumented Immigrants in American Society*. Fort Worth, TX: Harcourt Brace College Publishers, 1992.

Coulson, N. Edward. "Why Are Hispanic- and Asian-American Homeownership Rates So Low? Immigration and Other Factors." *Journal of Urban Economics* 45 (March 1999): 209–27.

Daniels, Roger. *Guarding the Golden Door: American Immigration Policy and Immigrants since 1882*. New York: Hill and Wang, 2004.

Davis, Marilyn P. *Mexican Voices/American Dreams: An Oral History of Mexican Immigration to the United States*. New York: Henry Holt, 1990.

De la Torre, Adela, and Beatríz M. Pesquera, eds. *Building with Our Hands: New Directions in Chicana Studies*. Berkeley: University of California Press, 1993.

Del Castillo, Adelaida R., ed. *Between Borders: Essays on Mexicana/Chicana History*. La Mujer Latina Series. Encino, CA: Floricanto Press, 1990.

De Mente, Boyé Lafayette. *NTC's Dictionary of Mexican Cultural Code Words: The Complete Guide to Key Words That Express How the Mexicans Think, Communicate, and Behave*. Lincolnwood, IL: National Textbook, 1996.

Deutsch, Sarah. *No Separate Refuge: Culture, Class, and Gender on an Anglo-Hispanic Frontier in the American Southwest, 1880–1940*. New York: Oxford University Press, 1987.

The Dictionary of Chicano Spanish: The Most Practical Guide to Chicano Spanish. Robert A. Galván, ed. Lincolnwood, IL: National Textbook, 1995.

Dolan, Jay, and Gilberto M. Hinojosa. *Mexican Americans and the Catholic Church, 1900–1965*. Notre Dame, IN: University of Notre Dame Press, 1994.

Donato, Rubén. *Mexicans and Hispanos in Colorado Schools and Communities, 1920–1960*. Albany: State University of New York Press, 2007.

Dunn, Jennifer L. "'Victims' and 'Survivors': Emerging Vocabularies of Motive for 'Battered Women Who Stay.'" *Sociological Inquiry* 75 (February 2005): 1–30.

Elizondo, Virgilio P. *The Future Is Mestizo: Life Where Cultures Meet*. Oak Park, IL: Meyer-Stone Books, 1988.

——. "The Sacred in the Latino Experience." In *Americanos: Latino Life in the United States/La Vida Latina en los Estados Unidos,* ed. Edward James Olmos, Lea Ybarra, and Manuel Monterrey. Boston: Little, Brown, 1999, 20–23.

Ellingwood, Ken. *Hard Line: Life and Death on the U.S.–Mexico Border*. New York: Pantheon Books, 2004.

Elsasser, Nan, Kyle MacKenzie, and Yvonne Tixier y Vigil. *Las Mujeres: Conversations from a Hispanic Community*. New York: Feminist Press, 1980.

Falicov, Celia Jaes. "Ambiguous Loss: Risk and Resilience in Latino Immigrant Families," in Suárez-Orozco and Páez, *Latinos*, 274–88.

Ferriss, Susan, and Ricardo Sandoval. *The Fight in the Fields: César Chavez and the Farmworkers Movement*. New York: Harcourt Brace, 1997.

Fine, Michelle, and Lois Weis. *The Unknown City: Lives of Poor and Working-Class Young Adults*. Boston: Beacon Press, 1998.

Flores, William V., and Rina Benmayor, eds. *Latino Cultural Citizenship: Claiming Identity, Space, and Rights*. Boston: Beacon Press, 1997.

Foster, George M. "Peasant Society and the Image of Limited Good." In Potter, Diaz, and Foster, eds., *Peasant Society* (Boston: Little, Brown, 1967), 300-23.

Fregoso, Rosa Linda. *MeXicana Encounters: The Making of Social Identities on the Borderlands*. Berkeley: University of California Press, 2003.

Galarza, Ernesto, Herman Gallegos, and Julian Samora. *Mexican-Americans in the Southwest*. Santa Barbara, CA: McNally and Loftin, 1969.

Gamboa, Erasmo. "Braceros in the Pacific Northwest, 1942-1947." In Chan, Daniels, García, and Wilson, *Peoples of Color*, 496–504.

García, Mario T. *Mexican Americans: Leadership, Ideology, and Identity, 1930–1960*. New Haven: Yale University Press, 1989.

García, Nasario. *Brujerías: Stories of Witchcraft and the Supernatural in the American Southwest and Beyond*. Lubbock: Texas Tech University Press, 2007.

Glenn, Evelyn Nakano. "From Servitude to Service Work: Historical Continuities in the Racial Division of Paid Reproductive Labor." In Ruiz and DuBois, *Unequal Sisters* (3rd ed.), 436–65.

Gluck, Sherna Berger, and Daphne Patai, eds. *Women's Words: The Feminist Practice of Oral History*. New York: Routledge, 1991.

Gonzales, Manuel G. *Mexicanos: A History of Mexicans in the United States*. Bloomington: Indiana University Press, 1999.

Gonzalez, Gilbert G. "The 'Mexican Schools,' 1890s–1930s." In Chan, Daniels, García, and Wilson, *Peoples of Color,* 328–35.

Gonzalez, Juan. *Harvest of Empire: A History of Latinos in America*. New York: Viking, 2000.

Gordon, Linda. "Family Violence, Feminism, and Social Control." In Ruiz and DuBois *Unequal Sisters* (1990 ed.), 141–56.

Graulich, Melody. "Violence against Women: Power Dynamics in Literature of the Western Family." In Armitage and Jameson, *Women's West*, 111–25.

Greeley Committee, Earle U. Rugg, Chair. *Final Report, 1946–1949, on Intergroup Relations*. Greeley: Colorado State College of Education, 1949.

Griswold del Castillo, Richard. "Chicano Families in the Southwest, 1910–1945." In Chan, Daniels, García, and Wilson, *Peoples of Color*, 208–13.

———. *North to Aztlan: A History of Mexican Americans in the United States*. Immigrant Heritage of America Series. New York: Twayne, 1996.

Grossman, Dave. *On Killing: The Psychological Cost of Learning to Kill in War and Society*. Boston: Little, Brown, 1995.

Gutiérrez, David G. *Between Two Worlds: Mexican Immigrants in the United States*. Jaguar Books on Latin America. Wilmington, DE: Scholarly Resources, 1996.

Gutiérrez, Ramón A. "Community, Patriarchy and Individualism: The Politics of Chicano History and the Dream of Equality." *American Quarterly* 45 (March 1993): 44–72.

Gutmann, Matthew C., Felix V. Matos Rodriguez, Lynn Stephen, and Patricia Zavella, eds. *Perspectives on Las Americas: A Reader in Culture, History, and Representation*. Malden, MA: Blackwell, 2003.

Hayes-Bautista, David. "Latino Contributions/Contribuciones Latinas." In Olmas, Ybarra, and Fuentes, *Americanos: Latino Life*, 40.

Herrera-Sobek, María. "Danger! Children at Play: Patriarchal Ideology and the Construction of Gender in Spanish-Language Hispanic/Chicano Children's Songs and Games." In Cantú and Nájera-Ramírez, *Chicana Traditions*, 81–99.

Hondagneu-Sotelo, Pierrette. *Gendered Transitions: Mexican Experiences of Immigration*. Berkeley: University of California Press, 1994.

Hurtado, Aída. *Voicing Chicana Feminisms: Young Women Speak Out on Sexuality and Identity*. New York: New York University Press, 2003.

Jameson, Elizabeth, and Susan Armitage, eds. *Writing the Range: Race, Class, and Culture in the Women's West*. Norman: University of Oklahoma Press, 1997.

Jensen, Leif. "The Demographic Diversity of Immigrants and Their Children." In Rumbaut and Portes, *Ethnicities*, 21–56.

Justice, Glenn. *Valley beneath the Sierra Vieja: A Texas Border Ranch History*. Odessa, TX: Rimrock Press, 2004.

Kim, Joon. "The Political Economy of the Mexican Farm Labor Program, 1942–64." *Aztlán* 29 (Fall 2004): 13–53.

Kirkwood, J. E. "A Mexican Hacienda: Life on one of the Baronial Estates of Our Southern Neighbor." *National Geographic* 25, no. 5 (1914): 563–84.

Larralde, Jorge M., and Richard Griswold del Castillo. "San Diego's Ku Klux Klan 1920–1980." *Journal of San Diego History* 46 (Spring/Summer 2000): 68–88.

Levitt, Peggy. "Two Nations under God? Latino Religious Life in the United States." In Suárez-Orozco and Páez, *Latinos: Remaking America* (Berkeley: University of California Press, 2002), 150–64.

Lewis, Oscar. *The Children of Sánchez: Autobiography of a Mexican Family*. New York: Random House, 1961.

Limón, José E. "La Llorona, The Third Legend of Greater Mexico: Cultural Symbols, Women, and the Political Unconscious." In Del Castillo, *Between Borders*, 399–432.

López, Antoinette Sedillo, ed. *Latina Issues: Fragments of Historia(ella) (Herstory)*. New York: Garland, 1999.

Lopez, Jody, and Gabriel Lopez, with Peggy A. Ford. *White Gold Laborers: The Story of Greeley's Spanish Colony*. Bloomington, IN: Author House, 2007.

Maccoby, Michael. "Love and Authority: A Study of Mexican Villagers." In Potter, *Peasant Society*, 336–45.

Martínez, Elizabeth. *De Colores Means All of Us: Latina Views for a Multi-Colored Century*. Cambridge, MA: South End Press, 1998.

Mason, David. "The Continuing Significance of Race? Teaching Ethnic and Racial Studies in Sociology." In Bulmer and Solomos, *Ethnic and Racial Studies Today*, 13–28.

McKellar, Margaret Maud. *Life on a Mexican Ranche*. Lehigh University Press, 1994.

McKissack, Elena Aragón de. *Chicano Educational Achievement: Comparing Escuela Tlatelolco, a Chicanocentric School, and a Public High School*. New York: Garland, 1999.

Meier, Matt, and Feliciano Rivera. *Mexican Americans/American Mexicans*. New York: Hill and Wang, 1993.

Menchaca, Martha. *Recovering History, Constructing Race: The Indian, Black, and White Roots of Mexican Americans*. Austin: University of Texas Press, 2001.

Menefee, Selden C. *Mexican Migratory Workers of South Texas*. Washington, DC: Division of Research, Work Projects Administration, U.S. Gov't., 1941.

Mirandé, Alfredo, and Evangelina Enríquez. *La Chicana: The Mexican-American Woman*. Chicago: University of Chicago Press, 1979.

Montoya, Lisa J. "Gender and Citizenship in Latino Political Participation." In Suárez-Orozco and Páez, *Latinos*, 410–29.

Moore, Shirley Ann Wilson. "'Not in Somebody's Kitchen': African American Women Workers in Richmond, California, and the Impact of World War II." In Jameson and Armitage, *Writing the Range*, 513–16.

Mora, Magdalena, and Adelaida R. Del Castillo, eds. *Mexican Women in the United States: Struggles Past and Present*. Occasional Paper no. 2. Los Angeles: Chicano Studies Research Center Publications, University of California, 1980.

Moraga, Cherríe, and Gloria Anzaldúa, eds. *This Bridge Called My Back: Writings by Radical Women of Color*. New York: Kitchen Table: Women of Color Press, 1983.

Myres, Sandra L. "Victoria's Daughters: English Speaking Women on Nineteenth-Century Frontiers." In *Western Women: Their Land, Their Lives*, ed. Lillian Schlissel, Vicki L. Ruiz, and Janice Monk, 261–81. Albuquerque: University of New Mexico Press, 1988.

Nava, Yolanda. *It's All in the Frijoles*. New York: Simon and Schuster, 2000.

Niblo, Stephen R. *Mexico in the 1940s: Modernity, Politics, and Corruption*. Wilmington, DE: Scholarly Resources, 1999.

Norquest, Carrol. *Rio Grande Wetbacks: Mexican Migrant Workers*. Albuquerque: University of New Mexico Press, 1972.

Oleske, Denise M., and Jerome J. Hahn. "Work-Related Injuries of the Hand: Data from an Occupational Injury/Illness Surveillance System." *Journal of Community Health* 17 (August 1992): 205–19.

Olmos, Edward James, Lea Ybarra, and Manuel Monterrey. *Americanos: Latino Life in the United States/La Vida Latina en los Estados Unidos*. Boston: Little, Brown, 1999.

Oster, Patrick. *The Mexicans: A Personal Portrait of a People*. New York: William Morrow, 1989.

"*Palabras de una Viejita: Habla Luisa Torres de Guadalupita, New Mexico*/The Words of an Old One: Luisa Torres writes of her life in Guadalupita, New Mexico." Collected and transcribed by Gioi Brandi. *El Palacio* 84 (Fall 1978): 8–18.

Paredes, Américo. "Mexican-American Identity and Culture." In Chan, Daniels, García, and Wilson, *Peoples of Color*, 263–73.

Parfit, Michael. "Mexico City: Pushing the Limits." *National Geographic* 190 (August 1996): 24–43.

Pasztor, Suzanne B. *The Spirit of Hildago: The Mexican Revolution in Coahuila*. East Lansing: Michigan State University Press, 2002.

Patai, Daphne. "U.S. Academics and Third World Women: Is Ethical Research Possible?" in Gluck and Patai, *Women's Words*, 137–53.

Paz, Octavio. *The Labyrinth of Solitude and Other Writings*. New York: Grove Press, 1985.

Peñalosa, Fernando. "Mexican Family Roles." *Journal of Marriage and the Family* 30 (November 1968): 680–89.

Perez, Emma. "Decolonizing Chicana History." *Women's Review of Books* 17 (February 2000): 13–14.

Perkins, John. *Confessions of an Economic Hit Man*. San Francisco: Berrett-Koehler, 2004.

Polishuk, Sandy. *Sticking to the Union: An Oral History of the Life and Times of Julia Ruuttila*. New York: Palgrave Macmillan, 2003.

Portelli, Alessandro. *The Battle of Valle Giulia: Oral History and the Art of Dialogue*. Madison: University of Wisconsin Press, 1997.

Potter, Jack M., May N. Diaz, and George M. Foster, eds. *Peasant Society: A Reader*. Boston: Little, Brown, 1967.

Ramos, Jorge. *The Other Face of America: Chronicles of the Immigrants Shaping Our Future*. New York: HarperCollins, 2002.

Ramos, Reyes. "Discovering the Production of Mexican American Family Structure." *De Colores Journal* 6 (1982): 120–34.

Rastogi, Mudita, and Karen S. Wampler. "Adult Daughters' Perceptions of the Mother–Daughter Relationship: A Cross-Cultural Comparison." *Family Relations* 48 (July 1999): 327–36.

Riding, Alan. *Distant Neighbors: A Portrait of the Mexicans*. New York: Vintage Books, 1989.

Rincón, Bernice. "La Chicana: Her Role in the Past and Her Search for a New Role in the Future." *Regeneration* 1 (1971): 15–18.

Ritchie, Donald A. *Doing Oral History*. New York: Twayne, 1995.

Rodriguez, Roberto. *Justice: A Question of Race*. Tempe, AZ: Bilingual Press, 1997.

Roskelley, R. W. "Beet Labor Problems in Colorado." In *Proceedings of the Western Farm Economics Association*. Pullman: State College of Washington and Moscow: University of Idaho, 1940.

Roskelley, R. W., and Catherine R. Clark. *When Different Cultures Meet: An Analysis and Interpretation of Some Problems Arising When People of Spanish and North European Cultures Attempt to Live Together*. Denver: Rocky Mountain Council on Inter-American Affairs, 1949.

Roskelley, R. W., and Michel Pijoan. *Nutrition and Certain Related Factors of Spanish-Americans in Northern Colorado*. Denver: Rocky Mountain Council on Inter-American Affairs and Western Policy Committee, 1943.

Rothenberg, Paula S. *Race, Class, and Gender in the United States: An Integrated Study*, 5th ed. New York: Worth, 2001.

Ruiz, Vicki L. *From out of the Shadows: Mexican Women in Twentieth-Century America*. New York: Oxford University Press, 1998.

———. "'Star Struck': Acculturation, Adolescence, and the Mexican American Woman, 1920–1950." In de la Torre and Pesquera, *Building with Our Hands*, 109–24.

Ruiz, Vicki L., and Ellen Carol DuBois, eds. *Unequal Sisters: A Multicultural Reader in U.S. Women's History*. 1st ed. New York: Routledge, 1990.

———. *Unequal Sisters: A Multicultural Reader in U.S. Women's History*. 3rd ed. New York: Routledge, 2000.

Ruiz, Vicki L., and Virginia E. Sanchez Korrals, eds. *Latinas in the United States: A Historical Encyclopedia*. Brooklyn: Brooklyn College of the City of New York Press, 2003.

Rumbaut, Rubén G., and Alejandro Portes, eds. *Ethnicities: Children of Immigrants in America*. Berkeley: University of California Press, 2001.

Saldívar, Ramón. *The Borderlands of Culture: Américo Paredes and the Transnational Imaginary*. Durham, NC: Duke University Press, 2006.

Samora, Julian, and Patricia Vandel Simon. *A History of the Mexican-American People*. Notre Dame, IN: University of Notre Dame Press, 1993.

Sandoval, Moisés. *On the Move: A History of the Hispanic Church in the United States*. Maryknoll, NY: Orbis Books, 2006.

Schlissel, Lillian, Vicki L. Ruiz, and Janice Monk, eds. *Western Women: Their Land, Their Lives*. Albuquerque: University of New Mexico Press, 1988.

Schoultz, Lars. *Beneath the United States*. Cambridge: Harvard University Press, 1998.

Schwartz, Harry. *Seasonal Farm Labor in the United States with Special Reference to Hired Workers in Fruit and Vegetable and Sugar-Beet Production*. New York: Columbia University Press, 1945.

Shorris, Earl. *Latinos: A Biography of the People*. New York: Avon Books, 1992.

Showalter, William Joseph. "Mexico and Mexicans." *National Geographic* 25, no. 5 (1914): 471–93.

Simmons, Marc. *Witchcraft in the Southwest: Spanish and Indian Supernaturalism on the Rio Grande*. Lincoln: University of Nebraska Press, 1974.

Smith, Barbara, and Beverly Smith. "Across the Kitchen Table: A Sister-to-Sister Dialogue." In Moraga and Anzaldúa, *This Bridge Called My Back*, 113–27.

Stavans, Ilan. *The Hispanic Condition: Reflections on Culture and Identity in America*. New York: Harper Collins, 1995.

Stevens-Arroyo, Anthony M., and Anna María Díaz-Stevens. "Religious Faith and Institutions in the Forging of Latino Identities." In *Handbook of Hispanic Cultures in the United States: Sociology*, ed. Félix Padilla. Houston: Arte Público Press and Instituto de Cooperación Iberoamericana, 1994, 257–75.

Suárez-Orozco, Marcelo M., and Mariela M. Páez. *Latinos: Remaking America*. Berkeley: University of California Press, 2002.

Suro, Roberto. *Strangers among Us: How Latino Immigration Is Transforming America*. New York: Alfred A. Knopf, 1998.

Takaki, Ronald. *A Different Mirror: A History of Multicultural America*. Boston: Little, Brown, 1993.

Trujillo, Charley, ed. *Soldados: Chicanos in Vietnam*. San Jose, CA: Chusma House, 1990.

Urrea, Luis Alberto. *The Devil's Highway: A True Story*. New York: Back Bay Books/Little, Brown, 2004.

Valle, Isabel. *Fields of Toil: A Migrant Family's Journey*. Pullman: Washington State University Press, 1994.

Waldinger, Roger, and Michael I. Lichter. *How the Other Half Works: Immigration and the Social Organization of Labor*. Berkeley: University of California Press, 2003.

Wasserman, Mark. *Everyday Life and Politics in Nineteenth Century Mexico: Men, Women, and War*. Albuquerque: University of New Mexico Press, 2000.

Weber, Devra Anne. "*Raiz Fuerte*: Oral History and Mexicana Farmworkers." In Ruiz and DuBois, *Unequal Sisters* (2000), 393–402.

Widdershoven, Guy A. M. "The Story of Life: Hermeneutic Perspectives on the Relationship between Narrative and Life History." In *The Narrative Study of Lives*, vol. 1., ed. Ruthellen Josselson and Amia Lieblich. Newbury Park, CA: Sage, 1993, 1–20.

Williams, Norma. *The Mexican American Family: Tradition and Change*. Dix Hills, NY: General Hall, 1990.

Wilson, Tamar Diana. "Weak Ties, Strong Ties: Network Principles in Mexican Migration." *Human Organization* 57 (Winter 1998): 394–403.

Wolf, Eric R. "Closed Corporate Peasant Communities in Mesoamerica and Central Java," in Potter, *Peasant Society,* 230–45.

Zinn, Maxine Baca. "Gender and Ethnic Identity among Chicanos." *Frontiers* 5, no. 2 (1980): 18–24.

About the Author

JOYCE LACKIE is Professor Emeritus of English from the University of Northern Colorado. While earning her PhD in English Education at the University of Alabama in the 1970s, she took a Spanish-language workshop, which led to a fascination with Latin America and immigration issues especially. She has since attended Spanish-language schools in Morelia and Oaxaca, Mexico; Cuzco, Peru; and Santiago, Chile.

Pursuing her interest in the language, she began to visit elderly Spanish-speaking residents in Greeley, Colorado, in 1988 and discovered oral history as a means of drawing attention to women's stories. Her interests also include globalization and women's roles in the changing world economies, and microlending as a step toward eradicating poverty. She is currently researching volunteer opportunities with microlending projects in Spanish-speaking countries, hoping to combine her interest in the language with improving economic conditions for women and their families.

Before retiring in 1997, Professor Lackie wrote short reviews of young adult books for the *Journal of the Assembly on Literature for Adolescents,* a subsidiary of the National Council of Teachers of English. She also gave numerous presentations on learning styles and young adult literature at national and regional English and Language Arts conferences. After retiring, she has been freer to indulge her other interests as well, including hiking, singing as half a duet called the Spring Chickens, enjoying independent and foreign films, attending theater, and of course, traveling. She and her husband, John Hendricks, live in Portland, Oregon.